CAREERING AND RE-CAREERING

FOR THE 1990's

THE COMPLETE GUIDE TO PLANNING YOUR FUTURE

Ronald L. Krannich, PhD.

IMPACT PUBLICATIONS
MANASSAS, VIRGINIA

CAREERING AND RE-CAREERING FOR THE 1990s: The Complete Guide to Planning Your Future

Library of Congress Cataloging-in-Publication Data

Krannich, Ronald L.
   Careering and re-careering for the 1990's.

   Bibliography: p.
   Includes index.
   1. Vocational guidance — United States. 2. Career
development — United States. 3. Career changes — United
States. I. Title.
HF5382.5.U5K69   1989   650.1'4   88-13523
ISBN 0-942710-10-X
ISBN 0-942710-09-6 (pbk.)

Cover designed by Orion Studios, 1608 20th St., NW, Washington, DC 20009

Typesetting by Marlene Hassell, Route 2, Copper Hill, VA 24079, 703/929-4344

For information on distribution or quantity discount rates, call 703/361-7300 or write to: Sales Department, IMPACT PUBLICATIONS, 10655 Big Oak Circle, Manassas, VA 22111-3040. Distributed to the trade by National Book Network, 4720 Boston Way, Suite A, Lanham, MD 20706, 301/459-8696.

ACKNOWLEDGEMENTS

This book could not have been completed without the assistance of Caryl Rae Krannich. She encouraged me to take on the subject, provided invaluable suggestions, wrote most of the section on interviewing, and spent numerous hours editing the manuscript. Her sense of form, style, and quality are found throughout the book. My frequent reference to "we" in the text indicates our joint effort and ongoing partnership.

Marlene Hassell typeset the manuscript with a rare and wonderful combination of speed, accuracy, judgment, and humor. In the end, we all got through it without experiencing burnout or having to re-career in the process.

TABLE OF CONTENTS

PART I:
PREPARE FOR TURBULENCE
AND NEW OPPORTUNITIES

CHAPTER THREE
Identify the Jobs of Tomorrow 40

CHAPTER FOUR
Acquire the Necessary Skills
Through Education and Training 63

CHAPTER FIVE
Understand Processes For Success 82

PART II:
DEVELOP POWERFUL
CAREERING AND RE-CAREERING SKILLS

PART III:
CREATE YOUR OWN OPPORTUNITIES THROUGH ADVANCEMENT, RELOCATION, AND ENTREPRENEURSHIP

INTRODUCTION

The future is something we all would like to better know and control. Most people prefer to plan their future rather than wait to see what tomorrow will bring. But how do you better plan for tomorrow when much of life seems to be beyond one's control?

KNOW WHERE YOU ARE GOING

The future may not be predictable but it is something you can shape for yourself. You must first know where you are at present and then develop a clear vision of where you want to go. But most important of all, you should develop *and* implement a plan of action for making your vision come true. Without an analysis of your present, a vision of the future, and a plan of action, your future will most likely be a repeat performance of your past patterns of behavior.

TAKE CHARGE OF YOUR FUTURE

This book is about taking better charge of your future in one of the most important areas of your life — your career. Few people actually plan their lives. Instead, they appear to be on the receiving end of life. They are at best great "getters": they *get* an education, they *get* married, they *get* a house, they *get* a job, they *get* taxed, and they *get* buried. They may do some planning before life is thrown at them, but few people consciously shape their future through deliberate action.

A career is something you can shape if you plan properly. However, the popular notion that all you need to do is get a good education that will lead to a good job and career has been eroded in a society that has undergone rapid change in education, training, occupations, and the workplace. The "one job, one career, one work life" phenomenon has all but ended for many occupations. The "15 jobs, 5 careers, and many work lives" phenomenon is now upon us in a new careering and re-careering era. In this era the future becomes synonymous with change. Individuals are well advised to *plan for change*.

EXAMINE THE EVIDENCE

The 1980s was a turbulent decade for American workers. Millions of workers experienced unemployment brought on by larger structural changes taking place in both the international and domestic economies. Rapid technological changes made their skills increasingly obsolete for the jobs of today and tomorrow. While many of the unemployed expected to return to work once the economy improved, many would not because their skills were no longer appropriate for the job market. Unfortunately, they were not likely to acquire the necessary skills, because they failed to take initiative, and neither the public nor private sectors were preparing them for new jobs. In the meantime, high unemployment existed in the midst of major labor shortages.

We are in the midst of a profoundly revolutionary period which will require individuals to career and re-career several times during their work lives. Knowing job search skills alone will be insufficient to function effectively in the job markets of the 1990s. Such skills must accompany concrete work-content skills. To be successful, individuals must continuously acquire new skills in order to adjust to job market realities.

USE A NEW APPROACH

So why write another career planning and job search book? Because there is a need for an approach to employment that also focuses on the future. Previous approaches have not prepared individuals well for the coming changes in American society. Educational institutions, for example, primarily exist to provide employment for educators rather than to train individuals for jobs and careers. Government mainly provides training programs for the hardcore unemployed — the ones least likely to be trainable or benefit from training. Business continues to maximize short-run profits, restructures through mergers rather than innovation, and views training as a luxury or perk to be given primarily to supervisors and managers. And many career counselors still preach a job search doctrine most appropriate for the 60s and 70s: "Anyone can find a job if they only know how to find a job." They train people in developing and using *job search skills* regardless of whether they have marketable *job performance skills*.

This book was written to fill the need for an expanded perspective on jobs and careers for the 90s. For the problem of jobs, careers, and employment is not being addressed with the larger future in mind. Many so-called experts tend to "stand where they sit" as well as "major in their own problems". Educators, for example, believe people need to come to them and their institutions for training when, in fact, educational institutions are more often the problem than the solution, and educators continue to face important employment problems themselves. Politicians and bureaucrats tend to think in narrow policy terms: create another government program which they hope "this time" will produce results. Today they propose a "jobs training program" for the hardcore unemployed and a few displaced workers. Tomorrow they will probably suggest another "tax credit incentive program"for the middle and upper classes. And career counselors and futurists are unprepared to provide practical guidance to unemployed workers in the depressed economies of West Virginia, Michigan, Alabama, and Mississippi.

The perspective developed in this book synthesizes the skills training and job search approaches within the framework of a society undergoing major social, economic, and political restructuring. It begins with placing full responsibility for employment and training squarely on the shoulders of the *individual*. No one owes anyone a job or a career, and few people have valid excuses for not acquiring the education and training necessary to function effectively in the job market. Therefore, you must be responsible for your own employment fate. You shape your own future by the decisions you made yesterday and today as well as by those you will make tomorrow. The book is designed to prepare you for turbulent times by giving you the necessary knowledge to *make informed choices about your future.*

ORGANIZE YOUR THINKING

This book should become a flexible guide to your future which you can use over and over again. The 16 chapters that follow move from description and explanation to prediction and prescription. Since each chapter is related to the others, the sections and chapters are best read in sequence. However, you may wish to read them in a different order, or go directly to only a few chapters that are of greatest interest to you.

If, for example, you are interested in moving to another community, go directly to Chapter Fourteen for information on how to relocate. If you are scheduled for a job interview in a few days, examine Chapter Eleven on how to conduct an effective interview. And if you are curious about the future, read Chapter Two on 25 coming changes. We purposefully designed the book to be a flexible and usable guide for readers with different interests and needs. Each part, as well as most chapters, can stand alone in addressing important issues of concern to millions of individuals.

Part.I sets the stage for subsequent how-to chapters by analyzing industries and occupations, explaining the educational and job markets, and predicting future changes in occupations and employment. Taken together, these chapters develop a vision of what the future may bring for careering and re-careering. If read in sequence, this section will help you better understand the how-to strategies and tactics in Parts II and III. But if descriptions, explanations, analyses, and predictions are not of interest to you, feel free to skip this section altogether.

If you are mainly interested in prescriptions for finding a job, then go directly to Chapter Five. This chapter provides an important introduction for the seven how-to chapters in Part II. These practical chapters focus on each step in conducting an effective job search, from developing a job objective to writing resumes and conducting interviews.

Part III addresses important careering and re-careering opportunities you can create for yourself, from advancing on the job to relocating to another community or starting your own business. Many readers may find this section to be the most useful since it includes important career and lifestyle issues not normally addressed in other career planning and job search books.

The three appendices at the end of the book include examples of effective resumes and letters as well as a bibliography of useful resources for further reading.

CAREER AND RE-CAREER FOR THE FUTURE

The processes we call careering and re-careering recognize the need to prepare for an uncertain future by *linking work skills to job search skills and relocation issues*. Careering and re-careering prepare individuals for dealing with the turbulent job markets of today and tomorrow. The chapters that follow outline how you can career and re-career in the decades ahead. Most important, they show you how to turn turbulence into new, and hopefully, exciting opportunities in the world of work!

PART I

PREPARE FOR TURBULENCE AND NEW OPPORTUNITIES

Chapter One

PROJECT AND PLAN YOUR FUTURE

Think about your future. You may have come a long way, but you still have many years ahead. What do you want to do with those years — before you retire? Let's begin by looking at the future and your goals.

What exactly are your goals? What, for example, do you want to do with your life over the next 5, 10, or 20 years? Are your goals realistic given your skills, motivation, patterns of behavior, and image of the future? What types of jobs and careers will you choose? Will these choices be the right ones for you? How will they affect your lifestyle? How much control do you want over your life? What are you willing to risk in the 1990s?

The beginnings and ends of decades are times for reflection, assessment, and redirection. The 1980s were turbulent years for jobs, careers, and lifestyles. The best laid plans were subjected to unprecedented changes as millions of Americans entered the job market for the first time, experienced unemployment, or changed jobs and careers several times. Life in the 1980s was a struggle for meaningful lifestyles in the face of a turbulent economic world where jobs and careers were as unpredictable as the economy.

PREPARE FOR LIFE IN A
BOOM AND BUST ECONOMY

The 1980s began with serious economic problems and ended with few promises of improved future performance. These were the

1

best and worst of times, depending on where and how you lived. Unemployment soared to nearly 11% in 1982 — the worst since the Great Depression. Yet it fell to less than 6% in 1988, the lowest in 15 years.

Economic problems in the 1980s baffled the best of minds as the economy underwent major restructuring, millions of individuals experienced unemployment, and the education and political systems remained inert. Inflation and high unemployment during the first half of the 1980s was blamed on a variety of evils, including excessive public spending, the Vietnam War, Wall Street, irresponsible labor unions and corporations, the rich and the poor, liberals, conservatives, Democrats, Republicans, FDR, and the Japanese. Huge deficit spending and major trade imbalances during the 1980s were blamed on similar culprits as trade protectionist sentiments misdiagnosed the long-term nature of America's economic and employment problems. The key problem was *productivity* — or the lack thereof — rather than the need to artificially limit competition in world markets in order to protect jobs at home.

Although some thinking about employment began to change, most continued to be based upon outmoded theories and short-term approaches to stimulating the economy, creating jobs, and finding employment. A relatively uninnovative educational system, lagging a decade behind the times, remained mired in irrelevant debates about educational theories and approaches. It failed to provide individuals with the skills necessary for functioning in the emerging economy of the 1990s. The unemployment insurance system continued to provide short-term income support rather than to invest in the long-term employment future of the unemployed by providing support for relocation, retraining, and job search. The tax code provided few incentives for employers and workers to seek retraining, and pension plans discouraged relocation. The public policy failures of America's checkerboard political system in the 1980s were enormous, and they would most likely continue to plague the economy and employment picture throughout the 1990s.

Despite a great deal of tough public talk, leadership in the 1980s failed to develop effective education and training programs to produce long-term employment results. In the meantime, educators continued to manage an education system of questionable quality and reconfirmed what they do best — debate educational theories and approaches in meaningless jargon. At the same time, politicians continued to articulate and develop high visibility policies for the poor but with few program successes. Somehow America's relatively nondirected, fragmented, and decentralized economic and political systems were supposed to resolve the education, employment, and economic problems of the country. The results were otherwise: they wasted human capital rather than invest it for the future.

The end of the 1980s began to close with a booming economy experiencing unprecedented levels of employment. The economy had generated the largest number of new jobs ever in the history of the United States. Indeed, nearly 3 million new jobs were created each year. But accompanying this temporary flight into prosperity was the cumulative yearly litany of millions of unemployed, thousands of business failures, an incredible national deficit, and major international dislocations — all threatening to restructure the American economic and employment pictures in the decade ahead in the direction of the early 1980s, or even worse.

For many Americans, the 1990s would be best approached as another turbulent and unpredictable roller coaster decade punctuated by boom and bust cycles and a repeat performance of public policy failures in the areas of education and employment. Both employment and unemployment will most likely reach new highs and lows in the 1990s — fluctuating between a low of 5 percent and a high of 12 percent. Millions of Americans will enter the job market for the first time; millions of others will experience unemployment; and millions more will change jobs and careers. Assuming continuing inertia in the public sector, individuals will face an uncertain job and career future requiring greater initiative to regularly acquire new skills, change jobs and careers, develop greater financial security, and relocate to growing communities.

If Americans learned anything about economics and employment in the 1980s it was this:

> We live in a highly complex society with an unpredictable and risky market place where even the best kept plans go awry due to numerous changes beyond one's control. Since economic and employment futures are unpredictable, one is well advised to develop flexible job and career strategies for dealing with uncertainty.

At the very least these strategies must address the issues of skills, lifestyles, opportunities, and risk-taking at the most significant level in society — the individual. In other words, you are on your own in a sea of change, so you had better take initiative in shaping and securing your own economic and employment future. No one else will do it for you.

UNDERSTAND EMPLOYMENT
DYNAMICS IN A DUAL SOCIETY

Employment in the United States is closely tied to an economic restructuring process taking place at the international, national, and local levels. During the past two decades the United States rapidly moved from a primarily industrial and technological society to one based on high technology, energy, and services. It also moved from a credit nation to a debtor nation — fueling the international economy with its high level of spending but positioning itself for even more vulnerable economic times.

The signs of an economy and job market undergoing major restructuring is especially apparent when examining the paradoxical unemployment/labor shortage problem: high unemployment persists at the same time major labor shortages exist. As millions of Americans become unemployed, millions of jobs also go unfilled at the two extreme ends of the job market: those requiring high level skills and those requiring low level skills. Many unemployed individuals lack the necessary skills to function in a newly emerging post-industrial, high-tech society; refuse to take low-paying service jobs; or do not know how to find a job appropriate for their level of skills and experience. Like the dual societies of Third World countries — one rural/agricultural and another urban/industrial — America is quickly becoming a dual society of a different type.

The emerging dual society in America consists of two sectors. The first and most traditional sector is located mainly in the older urban centers of the Northeast and North Central regions. Known as America's "rust belt" and based largely on manufacturing and related service industries, this sector was characterized by stagnation, decline, and high levels of unemployment and underemployment in the early 1980s. A disproportionate number of poor, unskilled, and displaced people live in these aging communities which also have serious problems with deteriorating infrastructure, excessive welfare burdens, and high costs of living. The state of Michigan led this sector in 1983 with a depressing 18 percent unemployment rate. Ohio, Illinois, West Virginia, Indiana, and Pennsylvania were not far behind.

The latter half of the 1980s witnessed a resurgent economy as some of the highest unemployment rates since the Great Depression were replaced by some of the lowest rates recorded in decades. Michigan's 18% unemployment rate, for example, fell below 8%; Illinois and Ohio managed to achieve 7.2% and 6.3% unemployment rates. And Massachusetts — once a troubled state with high unemployment — took the honors with one of the lowest unemployment rates in the country – 2.9%. But these unemployment figures were only low in comparison to historical highs. With 6 million Americans unemployed and unproductive each day, the actual numbers of unemployed remained high. The goal of full employment remained elusive.

While unemployment in Michigan, Illinois, Ohio, West Virginia, and Pennsylvania decreased during the later half of the 1980s, many communities in these states will remain vulnerable in the boom and bust economy of the 1990s. Economic recovery in these states will take time given continuing plant closures and the high cost of doing new business in these areas.

The second sector points us toward a more promising yet unpredictable future. Located mainly in younger suburban areas and in the rapidly growing cities of the West and Southwest as well as in a few cities in the East, this sector is based on high-tech, communication, and service industries requiring a highly educated and skilled workforce. In contrast to the first sector, this one is characterized by dynamic growth and relatively high employment and is populated by a disproportionate number of well educated, skilled, and affluent people. Growth in these communities is mainly constrained by shortages of highly skilled workers and the overall boom and bust nature of the economy. Communities heavily dependent on the energy and computer industries, such as Houston, Denver, and the Silicon Valley of California, witnessed both high employment and high unemployment in the 1980s as their local economies went bust due to major downturns in the energy and computer industries. Other more economically diversified communities, such as metropolitan Boston, Washington, DC, Atlanta, and Los Angeles, led the way with strong economic and employment performance throughout the 1980s. These communities will most likely lead the way in the economy of the 1990s as more and more individuals relocate from the first sector into the second sector of America's dual society.

Similar to the 1980s, the most serious economic and employment problems in the 1990s will be disproportionately felt by the unskilled poor in America. Lacking effective retraining programs and mechanisms for relocation and job search, the majority of these individuals will continue to live in and burden first sector communities. Their plight is further evidence of the inability or unwillingness of the political system to deal seriously with the pressing issues of productivity and income generation. Time-honored welfare and income support programs, scattered with a few train-the-poor initiatives, remain classic American subsidy approaches to the unemployed and poor. Such approaches have produced few cases of success.

America is a skills-based society where individuals market their skills in exchange for money and position. Without the proper skills to function in such a society — or the means to acquire the necessary training, relocation, and job search assistance — many Americans will remain permanently displaced or take jobs which generate little income nor promote long-term skills development. The emerging high-tech and service economy of the 1990s will require individuals with marketable skills who are willing to retrain and relocate when necessary.

FACE INCREASED STRUCTURAL UNEMPLOYMENT

Much of America's unemployment problem is structural in nature. The economy has entered into a major period of *structural unemployment*. While the normal pattern of unemployment is *cyclical* — people lose their jobs because of temporary business downturns and then are rehired when business rebounds — structural unemployment has permanent features. Moreover, this type of unemployment has far reaching consequences for the economy, workers, and employment strategies in the 1990s.

Structural unemployment is caused when industries and skills become obsolete due to technological advances. In the past, street sweepers, buggy-whip makers, tailors, and shoemakers became victims of such unemployment. More recently, aerospace scientists and engineers, auto workers, tire makers, steel workers, farm laborers, and slide-rule makers have experienced structural unemployment. Like their buggy-whip maker and shoemaker counterparts of yesterday, the recent victims must acquire new skills and change careers in order to join the ranks of the gainfully employed.

Unfortunately, few people are prepared or willing to deal with the changing structure of employment in America. Many unemployed auto and textile workers, for example, still believe their condition is due to cyclical unemployment, with "unfair" Japanese, Taiwanese, Korean, Hong Kong, and Mexican competition being the major culprits. They expect to be rehired when the business cycle improves — hopefully brought about through protectionist trade policies. While union leaders have begun to recognize the significance of structural unemployment by negotiating for more job security, give-backs, and retraining programs for their members, management introduces the latest industrial robot technology in a continuing effort to improve the productivity and competitiveness of the American auto industry. During the 1980s the major American automakers spent billions of dollars to modernize their production lines with robot technology. The end result of such modernization would be to permanently displace workers. Such workers must acquire new skills and find new jobs and careers if they are to survive and prosper in the job markets of tomorrow.

Following a pattern developing in the 1980s, the 1990s will be a decade of accelerated structural unemployment. The dual issues of ***productivity and competitiveness*** are forcing corporate America to apply the latest cost-saving technology to the work place. Protectionist labor unions are correct in their analysis of the problem: increases in productivity displace high-cost labor which, in turn, erode union membership. But at the same time, more than 1.5 million new jobs are created each year to absorb many of the structurally unemployed.

The major issue for the 1990s began in the 1980s: how to retrain and relocate an increasing number of structurally unemployed in a relatively unplanned and unpredictable economy. Assuming continuing public policy failures to deal with economic and employment problems in the decade ahead, individuals must develop their own strategies for navigating their careers in the boom and bust economy of the 1990s.

TAKE YOUR OWN INITIATIVE

Some experts estimate that somewhere between 50 and 75 percent of American factory workers will be displaced by robots by the end of this century! Peter Drucker confirms such estimates by projecting that 10 to 15 million manufacturing jobs will disappear during the 1980s and 1990s. Contrary to popular perception of an American manufacturing sector in decline, manufacturing is further strengthening itself through the application of new technology which inevitably displaces factory workers. Beginning in the 1950s and further accelerating today, the real source for new jobs is found in the rapidly growing service sector, especially in retail sales, food service, and health care.

But few people, especially displaced workers facing structural unemployment, are taking the initiative to provide or acquire the necessary skills training and retraining — and for good reasons. The tax, unemployment insurance, and pension systems were designed for a different era where structural unemployment was not a major issue. Such systems have yet to come in line with the employment realities of a profoundly different society in the 1980s and 1990s which is based upon high-technology and service industries and which experiences a high level of structural unemployment.

The tax, unemployment insurance, and pension systems provide few incentives for retraining, relocation, and job search. Few employers, for example, are given *tax incentives* to retrain or outplace displaced workers. The *unemployment insurance system* is designed to give temporary income support for individuals facing cyclical unemployment. It does little to encourage the structurally unemployed to seek retraining, develop job search skills, or relocate. And the limited portability of most *pension systems* discourages individuals from changing jobs and relocating.

As structural unemployment becomes more pervasive in the 1990s, the problem of what to do with millions of unemployed workers with obsolete skills may become a national crisis. Some analysts believe a major national training and retraining program, which goes far beyond the limited scope of the Jobs Training Partnership Act (JTPA), is desperately needed. Others see this as naive and nearly impossible to implement given the highly decentralized and fragmented nature of policy-making and implementation in America.

What will displaced workers do — many of whom are highly skilled in older technologies? What actions can be taken now, and by whom, to make a positive transition to the job market of the high-tech and service society?

We believe the answers to these questions primarily lie with the *individual* rather than with government or corporations. Indeed, one of our major purposes in writing this book is to see that you *become self-reliant and effective* in dealing with the job markets of today and tomorrow. While government and the private sector may provide incentives and opportunities as well as a few limited-scale programs, *the individual ultimately must be responsible for his or her own employment fate*. We assume that both government and the private sector will be slow in responding to the obvious retraining, relocation, and job search needs of individuals and society. In the meantime, a serious national employment and economic development crisis is brewing, and many people are being hurt by public and private sector inaction. Individuals, therefore, must take their own initiative to acquire the necessary skills for success in the job markets of today and tomorrow.

PREDICT AND PREPARE
FOR AN UNCERTAIN FUTURE

We see six major developments in the 1990s which will have important implications on the employment futures of most Americans. These include:

PREDICTION 1: Boom and bust economic cycles will continue throughout the 1990s as the economy experiences a combination of good times and bad times which, in turn, create a great deal of uncertainty for planning individual careers and life styles.

IMPLICATION: You need to acquire the necessary work-content and job search skills for quickly changing jobs and careers. Also, be prepared to relocate to more prosperous communities as well as develop greater financial security to bridge the bust-boom cycles.

PREDICTION 2: Millions of jobs will be created and eliminated throughout the 1990s. New jobs will be created at the rate of 1 to 2 million each year. At the same time, nearly 1 million new jobs will be eliminated each year. In the midst of these changes nearly 20 million Americans will experience some form of unemployment each year; between 6 and 12 million Americans will be unemployed each day.

IMPLICATION: While you have a high probability of experiencing some form of unemployment during the 1990s, new opportunities for careering and re-careering will abound for those who know the "what", "where", and "how" of finding jobs and changing careers.

PREDICTION 3: The rapidly expanding service sector will create the largest number of new jobs. These will be disproportionately found at the two extreme ends of the job market — high paying jobs requiring high-level skills and low paying jobs requiring few specialized skills.

IMPLICATION: You should focus on acquiring specialized education and skills for the high-end of the job market. Many of your skills also should be sufficiently general and marketable so you can easily make job and career transitions without becoming a victim of structural unemployment and bust economic cycles.

PREDICTION 4:   **Structural unemployment will accelerate due to a combination of business failures in the boom-bust economy and continuing productivity improvements in both the manufacturing and service sectors as new technology and improved decision-making and management systems are introduced to the workplace.**

IMPLICATION: You need to acquire the necessary skills to adjust to the coming changes in the workplace and job market. Careering and re-careering should become your central focus in deciding which skills to acquire.

PREDICTION 5:   **Thousands of stagnant communities will generate few jobs to provide sufficient careering and re-careering opportunities. "Rust belt" and "welfare-subsidy" communities, as well as those lacking a diversified service economy, will provide few job opportunities in the decade ahead.**

IMPLICATION: Individuals in stagnant communities must find ways to create their own employment or relocate to those communities offering long-term careering and re-careering opportunities. The most likely candidates will be growing metropolitan areas with diversified local economies.

PREDICTION 6:   **Public policy failures to resolve education, training, and unemployment problems as well as initiate effective job generation, relocation, and job search approaches for promoting a more employable society will continue throughout the 1990s.**

IMPLICATION: Given the highly decentralized and fragmented governmental and policy systems in America, politicians and public policy relevant to promoting full employment will remain relatively inert. Since most politicians will continue to be preoccupied with form and style rather than with substance and results in dealing with pressing economic and employment issues, individuals must take their own initiative in acquiring skills, finding jobs, changing careers, and relocating.

These predictions form a set of assumptions upon which we propose strategies for managing your career(s) throughout the 1990s. Our careering and re-careering approaches are especially relevant to a job market undergoing the types of turbulent changes we foresee for the 1990s.

Whether our predictions turn out to be 30, 70, or 100 percent accurate is beside the point. What is important is that you be aware, anticipate, and prepare for change. In so doing, you will be ready to seize new opportunities regardless of whatever direction the economy and employment takes in the 1990s.

The changes taking place in the workplace have important implications for individuals in the decade ahead. As more and more jobs become obsolete and new opportunities arise in the high-tech and service economy, workers must be better prepared to function in today's evolving job market. At the very least, they must learn how to *career and re-career for the 1990s*.

CAREER AND RE-CAREER
FOR TODAY AND TOMORROW

The nature of work and the process of finding employment have changed dramatically during the past few decades. For those who lived through the Great Depression, a job — indeed, any job — was something you were lucky to have. A good job — one you enjoyed and earned a good living from — was something only a few people were lucky enough to have.

As white-collar employment expanded in the 1950s and 1960s, a new philosophy of work evolved. Work was to be enjoyed and based upon one's strongest skills. Individuals also were advised to change jobs and careers when they were no longer happy with their work.

Pioneered in the career planning methods of Bernard Haldane in the 1950s and 1960s and popularized in Richard Bolles' self-directed *What Color Is Your Parachute?* in the 1970s and 1980s, *job search* was placed on center stage as a skill that could be learned and applied with considerable success. Reflecting the do-your-own-thing philosophy of the 1960s and primarily emphasizing the importance of *self-assessment and self-reliance*, individuals were strongly advised to identify what they do well — their strengths — and enjoy doing. Based on this knowledge, they were further advised to take initiative in seeking employment outside the deceptive formal job market of classified ads and employment agencies by engaging in *informational interviews*, that is, asking people for information and advice about jobs and employment. The key principles for successful job search were the familiar sales approaches of *prospecting and networking* — methods for developing job contacts and acquiring job information, advice, and referrals. Changing careers primarily involved a strategy of identifying and communicating *transferable skills* to employers rather than acquiring new job-related skills.

The process identified by Haldane, Bolles, and other career counselors for finding employment is what Adele Scheele calls "successful careering". It requires the use of certain marketing skills and strategies for selling yourself. According to Scheele (*Skills for Success*), these skills are (1) self-presentation, (2) positioning, and (3) connecting. Other writers refer to these skills as (1) role playing, (2) risk taking, and (3) networking — key skills, principles, or strategies applicable to most sales and marketing situations.

The job search skills promoted during the past three decades are based on a business-sales analogy. According to many career counselors, finding a job is like selling — you sell yourself in exchange for status, position, and money. The emphases here are on the *process* of selling and the *form* of self presentation — not the *substance* of work-content skills. Seldom, if ever, do these career counselors address the equally critical issues of *job generation* and *relocation* nor advise individuals to acquire new *work-content skills* which are more responsive to the changing job market. Doing so requires more comprehensive approaches as well as a major investment of time and effort which may seem beyond the immediate employment needs of many individuals.

As more and more jobs require technical skills, and as the job market becomes restructured in response to the emerging high-tech and service economy, the career planning approaches of the past three decades need to be reoriented in light of new realities for the 1990s. Emphasizing process and form to the exclusion of such critical issues as job generation, relocation, and work-content skills, these approaches are at best incomplete in today's job market. Few individuals, for example, who network to market such soft functional skills as reading, writing, and interpersonal communication will be successful in finding employment with a promising future. As many displaced homemakers and liberal arts students learned in the 1980s, such strategies have limitations in a job market requiring specific technical skills. Lacking appropriate work-content skills, these individuals may become the displaced, underemployed, and discontented workers of tomorrow.

The dual issues of job generation and relocation are critical in planning one's career future. We should never forget that people work *in* or *from* specific communities from which they rent or own property and develop life styles. If, for example, you live in an economically stagnant community that generates few job opportunities for someone with your interests and skills, using job search skills to find a great job in such a community would be frustrating, if not useless. Your options and approaches in such a situation come down to four:

1. **Find a local job that may not fit well** with your particular mix of interests and skills in the hope that more appropriate opportunities will open for you in the future as this community generates more job and career options.

2. **Commute to a job in another community** within your region that offers opportunities appropriate for your interests and skills.

3. **Start a business that is not dependent on local economic cycles** — one that is broadly based with a diversified regional, national, or international clientele.

4. **Relocate to a growing community** that appears to be capable of generating many new jobs in the future. Such communities offer an ideal setting where job generation, relocation, and job search come together in providing individuals with numerous opportunities for careering and re-careering in the future.

The processes we call "careering" and "re-careering" address present and future job realities. Re-careering goes beyond the standard "careering" skills popularized during the past three decades, which were based upon an understanding of a job market in an industrial economy. As the job market becomes restructured in the direction of high technology and services, a new approach to job hunting, responsive to new economic realities, is required for the 1990s.

We anticipate a very different job market in the future. The major dynamic for restructuring the job market is the emergence of a high-tech and service society requiring highly specialized and skilled workers who are prepared to make job and career changes. These workers must not be overly specialized or too narrow in their perception of the future demand for their present skills. Instead, tomorrow's workers must be *flexible* in learning new skills, for their specialized jobs may become obsolete with the continuing advancement and adaptation of technology to the workplace. Furthermore, tomorrow's workers must be *adaptive* to new jobs and careers. Overall, *success in tomorrow's job market will require a new breed of worker who anticipates, prepares, and eagerly adapts to change*. Such individuals prepare for career transitions by acquiring new skills and actively seeking new work environments through the use of effective job search strategies and relocating to new communities and work settings.

Careering is the process of preparing to enter the job market with marketable skills to land the job you want. *Re-careering* is the process of repeatedly acquiring marketable skills and changing careers in response to the turbulent job market of the high-tech society. The standard careering process of the past three decades, therefore, must be modified with four new re-careering emphases:

1. Acquiring new marketable skills through retraining on a regular basis.

2. Changing careers several times during a lifetime based on a combination of job search skills, new work-content skills, and relocation.

3. Using more efficient communication networks for finding employment.

4. Relocating to communities experiencing promising long-term job growth.

APPROACH THE SUBJECT DIFFERENTLY

This book departs from much of the standard career planning and job search literature of the past three decades. Many such books are extremely useful yet redundant and static — largely focused on individual self-assessment within a never-changing job search process perhaps most relevant for the 1960s and 1970s. Preoccupied with one or two techniques, few such books relate one technique to another or look beyond the individual in attempting to develop strategies for finding employment.

We offer a different approach for the 1990s. We place the job search processes of careering and re-careering within a more comprehensive employment framework than previously examined. In so doing, we outline job search strategies appropriate for new realities in the job market for the 1990s. The result is a new synthesis and approach for career planning that (1) links the individual and job search strategies to larger employment issues and processes in society, and (2) focuses on managing an uncertain future. We feel such an approach will better prepare individuals for finding employment and changing careers in the years ahead than the much narrower focus on individual self-assessment within the job search process.

The following chapters address the problems of jobs and careers in the turbulent 1990s as well as outline the necessary skills and strategies for finding employment in the challenging job markets of today and tomorrow. Written for every working individual in the decade ahead, the book gives practical advice on how to prepare for new jobs and careers as well as how to make career changes. Individual chapters outline ways to identify and acquire marketable skills, state goals, write resumes and letters, prospect, network, interview, negotiate salaries, and advance and change careers. Special chapters address the challenges of career advancement, relocation, starting a business, and achieving results.

ACHIEVE RESULTS

Our goals in writing this book are concrete, specific, and oriented toward action and results. You should acquire certain careering and re-careering skills which will result in positive changes in your future. Upon completing this book you should be able to:

- Understand the changing nature of jobs and careers in the decade ahead and how they relate to your future.

- Identify desirable jobs and careers you may wish to pursue.

- Assess your goals in relation to your values and the demands of the job market.

- Identify your present skills as well as the skills you can best transfer to other jobs and careers.

- Specify your need for skills training as well as know how to acquire the necessary training.

- Communicate your goals, skills, and qualifications to employers.

- Conduct research on alternative jobs, careers, organizations, and communities.

- Write different types of effective resumes and job search letters.

- Prospect for job leads and contacts.

- Network for job information, advice, and referrals.

- Conduct informational and job interviews.

- Negotiate salaries and the terms of employment.

- Advance your career.

- Relocate to other communities.

- Start your own business.

- Implement your career goals.

In the end, our goal is to lead you to *action* which will have a positive impact on your future.

Chapter Two

PREPARE FOR CAREER CHALLENGES OF THE 1990s

Whether we realize it or not, we have some image of the future that influences important decisions in our lives. Assuming you are like most people, you would not, for example, purchase a new home, relocate to another community, or change careers unless you first projected what the future might hold for you over the next five to ten years.

People orient themselves to the future in different ways. Some people always view the future pessimistically. They find numerous reasons for doing what they always do — not taking risky actions. Others fantasize about the future and "hope" a prosperous future will come to them without having to take action. And others set goals and work toward achieving an image of a positive future.

Finding employment and charting careers in the job markets of today and tomorrow require strategies based on an understanding of new realities as well as a different image of the future. But few people know how to plan for uncertainty. Many, instead, deny new realities and thus continue to operate on old assumptions. Their adjustment to change is at best difficult.

TURN TURBULENCE INTO NEW OPPORTUNITIES

How do you anticipate the future and plan accordingly? During relatively stable times, planning proceeds along a relatively predict-

17

able path: assume the future will be very similar to the past and present. Therefore, a good plan is one that is based on an analysis of history — you follow the lessons of the past in charting your future.

But during turbulent times planning based on an analysis of history becomes a problem. Peter Drucker's (*Managing in Turbulent Times*) observations on planning for turbulent times are especially relevant for the 1990s. Traditional planning:

> assumes a high degree of continuity. Planning starts out, as a rule, with the trends of yesterday and projects them into the future — using a different "mix" perhaps, but with very much the same elements and the same configuration. This is no longer going to work. The most probable assumption in a period of turbulence is the unique event which changes the configuration — and unique events cannot, by definition, be "planned." But they can often be foreseen. This requires strategies for tomorrow, strategies that anticipate where the greatest changes are likely to occur and what they are likely to be, strategies that enable a business — or a hospital, a school, a university — to take advantage of new realities and to convert turbulence into opportunity.

Turbulent times can be dangerous times for people who fail to anticipate and adjust to new changes. Assuming continuity, or a return to a previous time, they engage in wishful thinking. Many of these people are today's victims of structural unemployment. For others, who take action based upon an understanding of coming realities, turbulent times can offer new and exciting opportunities. These people anticipate where the greatest changes will take place and accordingly adapt to change as they advance with the new jobs and careers of tomorrow.

The economic transformation of American society has far reaching social and political implications which you should be aware of in planning your future. The projected changes are discussed at length in several books by Toffler (*The Third Wave*), Naisbett (*Mega-trends*), Ferguson (*The Aquarian Conspiracy*), and Cetron (*Jobs of the Future*). Our major concern is not in predicting the future with any degree of precision. Rather, we are concerned with formulating an image of the future and outlining the implications of turbulent times for jobs, careers, and you.

The question we need to address is this: *What future should you prepare for in the world of work?* Based on an understanding of new trends in the workplace and anticipating the impact of unique events on the economy, we believe you can develop strategies for converting turbulence into new opportunities.

Two powerful currents — one demographic and another technical — are converging at present in the workplace and affecting the future of work in America. These changes, in turn, are precipitating the emergence of 25 new trends for careering and re-careering in the 1990s.

FACE NEW DEMOGRAPHICS

The paradox of major labor shortages in the midst of high unemployment is partly due to the impact of demographic changes on today's labor market. For the American population is undergoing fundamental changes at the same time the economy shifts from an industrial to a high-tech and service base.

The major demographic changes characterizing today's labor force are found at the entry level: fewer young people are filling entry-level jobs while more females, minorities, and immigrants are entering the job market.

The major implication of these demographic changes for the high-tech and service society during the next decade will be continuing labor shortages for entry-level jobs. However, the paradox of high unemployment may continue if millions of displaced workers are not retrained for new jobs.

Forces

Two major demographic changes took place in the post-World War II period to help shape the present labor force. The first change was the baby-boom. As birth rates increased nearly 50 percent between 1947 and 1949, a new labor force was created for the latter part of the twentieth century. American industry in the 1960s and 1970s absorbed some of this new labor force, but the rapidly growing service sector absorbed most of it. The U.S. economy, especially the service and high-tech sectors, was able to provide employment for 10 million new workers between 1963 and 1980 — a remarkable achievement for such a short time span. Between 1983 and 1988 the economy generated 16 million new jobs — the most remarkable performance in the history of the labor market.

The second major demographic change has been the rapid increase of women, minorities, and immigrants entering the labor force. This demographic current continues. For example, in 1980 over 50 percent of women worked outside the home. By 1990 more than 60 percent of women will be in the labor force.

By the year 2000 the baby-boom generation will reach middle age. The number of traditional 16 to 21 year olds entering the labor market will fall dramatically. About 80 percent of all new labor force entrees will be women, minorities, and immigrants. These groups will be less educated and skilled than the new job entrees of previous decades. For example, despite the $300 billion spent each year on education in the United States, basic literacy and skill levels remain alarming for industries that must dip deeper into the entry-level labor pool. In a recent assessment of literacy among 21- to 25-year-olds, the Education Department found these alarming statistics:

- Only 60 percent of whites, 40 percent of Hispanics, 25 percent of blacks can find specific information in a news article or almanac.

- Only 25 percent of whites, 7 percent of Hispanics, and 3 percent of blacks can understand a bus schedule.

Furthermore, 63 percent of white and 14 percent of black high school graduates have only attained a "basic" skill level required by the armed forces for training.

The implications of these trends will be costly for industries in the coming decade. Given rising skill requirements for entry-level jobs, coupled with the low skill levels of job applicants, many industries will experience severe labor shortages. They will most likely respond to this problem by cutting back on services and production and/or investing more resources on educating and training what is basically an entry-level labor force ill-prepared for the jobs of today and tomorrow.

Implications

Declining birth rates between the 1960s and 1980s, with America now approaching a zero-population growth rate, have important implications for the future labor market. Assuming the American economy will continue to expand, stimulated by the high-tech and service industries, major labor shortages, especially for individuals with proper work skills, are likely to occur during the 1990s. The continuing entry of women, minorities, and immigrants into the labor force as well as the expansion of automation in the workplace will not significantly offset this labor deficiency.

Since birth rates declined in the 1960s and 1970s and immigration laws were changed in 1986, there are fewer young people and immigrants available for entry-level and low wage positions. In ad-

dition, women, who used to take part-time, low paying sales positions, are fast leaving this labor scene for better paying full-time
positions. Teenagers, who make up a disproportionate share of the
labor forces of fast-food restaurants, are scarcer because there are
fewer teenagers in the population as a whole than during the previous
30 years.

Adjustments in the changing labor force have already begun.
Fast-food restaurants employ older workers and introduce more
self-service menus. Department stores recruit lower quality sales
clerks — generally individuals who are less educated, skilled, stable,
and responsible; training demands increase accordingly. Many small
businesses, especially the "Mom and Pop" stores with fewer than
five employees, experience difficulty recruiting and retaining the
traditional young, low-salaried entry-level workers. Instead, many
businesses cut back services and production as well as look toward
the elderly, particularly retired individuals, for new recruits.

The changing population structure also has important implications for the quality of the labor force. While the private sector
spends approximately $50 billion each year on training, much of this
expenditure goes to training inexperienced entry-level personnel.
Given the growing shortage of this traditional labor pool, high-tech
industries will be forced to recruit and then *retrain* displaced workers. This will require a new emphasis on training — as well as a greater
expenditure on retraining.

Other population dynamics have additional implications for the
work force of tomorrow. Minorities, especially blacks and Hispanics,
will enter the labor force at a faster rate because of their higher birth
rates. As a result, minorities will disproportionately occupy entry-
level positions. Furthermore, there will be greater pressure from
minorities for advancement up the ranks, even though the upper
ranks have become glutted with middle age managers and executives
who were rapidly promoted when they were young people during the
1960s and 1970s.

With the entry of more women into the labor force and the con-
comitant emergence of the two-career family, individuals have
greater freedom of choice to change jobs or careers, take part-time
positions, retire, or drop out of the labor force altogether. Job-
hopping may increase accordingly. In addition, employee benefit
programs, many of which are still based on the model of the traditional male head of household supporting a family, will change in
response to the two-career family with one, two, or no children.

Careering and re-careering are directly related to these changing
demographics. As the work force ages, life expectancy lengthens,
the social security system becomes modified, and labor shortages

abound, fewer people will enter traditional retirement in their 60s or retire at all. An individual's worklife may well become one's total adult life. Re-careering will become a standard way of functioning within tomorrow's labor markets. Thus, it will not be unusual for individuals to change careers in their 40s, 50s, and 60s. Mid-life crises may well disappear as more individuals experience *re-careering transitions*.

Responses

Population changes also will create a more heterogeneous work force. Along with increased minority representation in entry-level positions, more and more immigrants may come to the United States — both legally and illegally — to meet the expanding labor needs. Despite the 1986 changes in immigration laws to document illegal immigrants and stem the tide of illegal immigration into the United States — political efforts totally at odds with America's growing labor needs — each year nearly 600,000 immigrants enter the U.S. legally each year and another 600,000 immigrants, mainly from Mexico and the Caribbean, probably enter the U.S. illegally. Most of these people take low-paying, manual, and service jobs which non-minorities avoid. Hispanic-Americans, who now number about 18 million, are expected to constitute one-fifth of the population, or 50 million out of 250 million, in the year 2000.

Assuming continuing low birth rates among middle class white Americans which, in turn, may contribute to labor shortages in the future, the government may be forced into a major policy reversal: relax enforcement of the 1986 immigration laws as well as open the doors to immigrants in order to alleviate the coming labor shortages. If and when this happens, training and retraining programs will become a more urgent need for the future of the high-tech and service society.

Peter Drucker, however, outlines another scenario which is by far one of the most interesting organizational forms for coping with the coming labor shortages in developed countries and the explosive expansion of working-age people in the developing countries. Under a *production sharing system*, developing countries with surplus labor would be responsible for labor-intensive aspects of production. Developed countries, such as the United States, would provide the needed capital, technology, and managerial skills for operating transnational companies. Such an arrangement would fully employ the surplus educated and skilled people in the developed countries without experiencing the social, economic, and political dislocation attendant with large scale migration.

Production sharing forms of organization are already in place for various industries in the United States, Japan, Singapore, Hong Kong, Malaysia, Taiwan, Korea, and Brazil — the so-called First and Second World countries. As Drucker sees this system,

> Production sharing is the best hope — perhaps the only hope — for most of the developing countries to survive without catastrophe the explosive expansion of working-age people in search of a job. . . for the standard of living of the developed world can also be maintained only if it succeeds in mobilizing the labor resources of the developing world. It has the technical resources, the entrepreneurial resources, the managerial resources — and the markets. But it lacks, and will increasingly lack, the labor resources to do the traditional stages of production.

Whether or not production sharing becomes a predominate organizational form, the changing population dynamics over the next two decades provide further evidence of the need for major skills training and retraining of the American labor force. Population dynamics undoubtedly will be a major force affecting the turbulent employment environment.

EXPERIENCE THE IMPACT OF NEW TECHNOLOGIES

The second major current transforming the American workplace is technical in nature. The electronics revolution began in 1948 in Western Electric Company's Allentown, Pennsylvania manufacturing plant. There, the transistor was produced, and it began an electronics revolution which has continued to evolve into even more revolutionary forms since the invention and application of the microprocessor in the 1970s. The end of this revolution is nowhere in sight. Many experts believe we are just at the initial stages of a profound transformation which will sweep across our society during the next two decades.

Evidence of a coming transformation began in the 1950s as white-collar workers began to outnumber blue-collar workers. The electronics revolution, when applied, initiated an information and communication revolution. In 1950, for example, approximately 17 percent of the population worked in information-related jobs. Today this proportion has increased to over 50 percent. During the 1970s, when nearly 19 million new jobs were created, only 16 percent were in the manufacturing and goods-producing sector.

As John Naisbett (*Megatrends*) and other futurists have noted, during the 1980s we began to move full-force into the second stage of technological development — the **application of technology to old industrial tasks**. Recognizing the urgent need to increase productivity in order to become more competitive on international markets, manufacturing industries have made major efforts to retool their plants with the latest labor-saving technologies and have thereby displaced workers skilled in the technologies of previous decades.

Movement into the third stage of technological development — *innovation*, making new discoveries with second stage technologies — should proceed throughout the 1990s. By the year 2000 many American manufacturing and service industries will be completely transformed by second and third stage technological developments. Entry into the labor market in the year 2000 will require a much higher level of educaton and skills than in the 1980s. Those who will be in the best position to advance into the best jobs for the year 2000 will be those who seriously focus on careering and re-careering issues by:

- acquiring new work-content skills through regular training and retraining

- developing effective job search skills

- relocating when necessary

The impact of the high-tech revolution is *structural* in nature. As computers, fiber optics, robotics, and genetic engineering generate new businesses and integrate into everyday life, the economy and workplace will be fundamentally altered. For example, fiber optics, which makes copper wire obsolete, will further revolutionize communication. Genetic engineering will create major changes in agriculture and medicine. The main-frame computer, which was developed for practical use in 1945, in the form of today's micro computer is now a common tool in many workplaces. With the continuing impact of fiber optics and new generation micro-processing chips — not to mention some still unknown technological breakthroughs — computers with vastly expanded capabilities will become common tools in the home over the next decade.

The micro-processor has dramatically altered the workplace, from robots replacing assembly line workers to word processors replacing traditional typists. Office automation has transformed many secretaries into area managers, who are now in charge of coordinating work flows and managing equipment. Factory workers either become displaced or are retrained to deal with the new technology. Unfortunately, many displaced workers, who have not been retrained, have become permanently displaced or have moved into lower paying, high turnover, unskilled service jobs — the negative unemployment and under-employment consequences of structural changes.

Many futurists predict an even more radical transformation of the workplace — the emergence of the electronic cottage. Computers and word processors will create a decentralized workplace where individuals can work from their homes on assignments received and processed via computer terminals. The electronic cottage, in turn, will alter family relationships, especially child rearing practices, and the structure of the traditional central business district. Many workers no longer will need to commute to the office, face traffic jams, and experience the accompanying office stress. Such changes, however, do not bode well for owners of downtown office buildings, parking lots, and businesses frequented by the noontime employee-shopper. The communication revolution may be the final death blow for those cities hoping to revitalize their downtown areas.

These technological changes, coupled with the demographic currents, are transforming the nature of jobs. Yesterday's and today's workers are increasingly being displaced into an environment which is ill-equipped to help them gain advantages in tomorrow's high-tech society. Instead, a new class of individuals, skilled in the technology of previous decades, may become permanently displaced in the turbulent job market of tomorrow.

PREPARE FOR 25 COMING CHANGES

Several additional trends are evident, and they will affect both the work force and the workplace in years ahead. These trends are mainly stimulated by the larger demographic and technological changes taking place within society. We see 25 changes emerging in the areas of job creation, youth, elderly, minorities, women, immigrants, part-time employment, service jobs, education and training, unions and labor-management relations, urban-rural shifts, regionalism, small businesses and entrepreneurship, and advancement opportunities. Together these changes point to both dangers and new opportunities.

CHANGE 1: **Shortage of competent workers, with basic literacy and learning skills, creates serious problems in developing an economy with an adequate work force for the jobs of the 90s.**

Given the double-wammy of over 20 million functionally illiterate adults — or 1/6 of the potential labor force unable to read, write, or perform simple computations — and the availability of fewer easily trainable young entry-level workers, a large portion of the workforce is destined to remain at the lowest end of the job market despite the fact that over 15 million new jobs will be created in the 1990s. Most of these adults will remain permanently unemployed or underemployed while major labor shortages exist. As skill requirements rise rapidly for both entering and advancing within the workforce, the nation's economic development will slow due to the lack of skilled workers. Both public and private sector worker literacy, basic education, and training programs will continue to expand, but their contribution to improving the overall skill levels of the workforce is minimal. The American economy and workforce begin showing classic signs of Second and Third World economies — potential economic performance outstrips the availability of a skilled workforce.

CHANGE 2:   **A renewed and strong U.S. manufacturing sector will create few new jobs; service industries will be responsible for most job growth throughout the 1990s.**

Despite popular notions of the "decline" of American manufacturing industries, these industries are following the model of American agriculture — increased productivity accompanied by the increased displacement of workers. American manufacturing industry is becoming one of the strongest economic sectors in terms of production output but the weakest sector in terms of its contribution to job growth and job creation. At the same time, American manufacturing is moving in the direction of Drucker's "production sharing system" by exporting the remaining high-cost, labor intensive aspects of the industries. As large manufacturing companies rebound in the 1990s by becoming productive with smaller and more highly skilled workforces, most new manufacturing jobs will develop among small manufacturing "job shops" employing fewer than 50 workers. The service industries, especially those in finance, retail, food, and health care, will continue to expand their workforces during the first half of the 1990s. The second half of the 1990s will witness major "productivity" and "management" improvement movements among service industries that developed among large manufacturing industries in the 1980s — a push for greater productivity because of (1) major labor shortages and (2) the adaptation of new technology to increasingly inefficient, high-cost, labor intensive service industries, especially in the retail and health care industries.

CHANGE 3: **Unemployment remains high, fluctuating between a low of 5 percent and a high of 12 percent.**

These fluctuations are attributed to a combination of boom and bust cycles in the economy as well as the persistence of structural unemployment exacerbated by millions of functionally illiterate adults on the periphery of the economy.

CHANGE 4: **Government efforts to stimulate employment growth continues to be concentrated at the periphery of the job market.**

Most government programs aimed at generating jobs and resolving unemployment problems will be aimed at the poor and unskilled. These groups also are the least likely to relocate, use job search skills, develop standard work habits, or be trained in skills for tomorrow's job market. Given the mixed results from such programs and political pressures to experiment with some form of government-sponsored work-fare programs, the government finally develops programs to directly employ the poor and unskilled on government programs as well as contract-out this class of unemployed to government contractors who will provide them with education and training along with work experience.

CHANGE 5:   **The U.S. deficit declines and trade becomes more balanced as the U.S. regains a more competitive international trade and debt position due to improved productivity of U.S. manufacturing industries and the devaluation of the U.S. dollar.**

International and domestic issues become closely tied to employment issues. Emphasis shifts to issues of unemployment, productivity, population growth, consumption, and regional conflicts in Third and Fourth World countries that threaten the stability of international markets and thus long-term employment growth in the U.S.

CHANGE 6:   **A series of domestic and international crises — shocks and "unique events", some that already occurred in the 1980s — emerge in the 1990s to create new boom and bust cycles contributing to high rates of unemployment.**

The most likely sources for the international crises will be problems developing among poor Third and Fourth World nations: energy and precious metals shortages due to a depletion of current stocks and regional military conflicts; the collapse of financial markets due to default on international debts; and dislocation of lucrative resource and consumption markets due to continued wars in the Middle East, South Africa, and South Asia. The most likely domestic crises will center on energy, water, and the environment. An energy crisis will once again revitalize the economies of Texas, Colorado, and Alaska. A new crisis — major water shortages — in the rapidly developing Southwest, will slow employment growth in the booming economies of Southern California and Arizona. Environmental issues, such as acid rain and water pollution, will emerge as important international and domestic crises.

CHANGE 7: **New jobs will be created at the rate of 1 to 2 million each year, with some boom years resulting in the creation of more than 3 million jobs each year.**

The good news is that employment will increase in most occupations throughout the 1990s. Economic expansion in the service sector, coupled with the low productivity and low cost of labor in many parts of the service sector, contributes over 90 percent of all new jobs. Large scale manufacturing experiences labor declines while small scale manufacturing "job shops" contribute most of the minimal job growth in the manufacturing sector. The labor declines will be offset by increases in related service jobs, especially in manufacturing sales and marketing.

CHANGE 8: **A major shortage of skilled craftsmen will create numerous production and service problems throughout the 1990s.**

During the 1980s the number of apprenticeship programs declined significantly; fewer individuals received training in blue-collar occupations; and interest among the young in blue-collar trades declined markedly. The impact of these changes will be felt throughout the 1990s as production and service industries requiring critically skilled craftsmen experience major labor shortages. Expect to personally encounter the effects of these labor shortages — long waiting periods for servicing your automobile and for repairing your home and major appliances as well as very expensive charges for such services.

CHANGE 9:   As the baby-boomers reach middle age and as
                the birth-rate continues at a near zero-popula-
                tion growth rate, fewer young people will be
                available for entry-level positions during the
                1990s.

                Businesses will either recruit and train more of
                the hard-core unemployed, unskilled, and the
                elderly, and/or they will automate. As a result,
                more stopgap job opportunities will be avail-
                able for individuals losing their jobs or wishing
                to change jobs or careers.

CHANGE 10:   More job and career choices will be available
                for the elderly.

                As the workforce increasingly ages, the trend
                toward early retirement from the workforce
                will decrease. Many people will never retire,
                preferring instead part-time or self-employment
                in their later years. Others will retire from one
                job and then re-career after age 60. Fewer
                social security benefits and higher costs of
                retirement will further transform retirement
                practices and systems throughout the 1990s.
                Expect to see more elderly working in the Mc-
                Donald's and 7-Eleven stores of tomorrow.

CHANGE 11:   More blacks and Hispanics, due to their dis-
                proportionately high birth rates, low education
                and skill levels, poor economic status, and im-
                migration, will enter the job market.

                A large proportion of minorities will occupy
                the less skilled entry-level, service positions
                where they will exhibit marked language, class,
                and cultural differences. Upwardly mobile
                minorities may find advancement opportuni-
                ties blocked because of the glut of relatively
                young supervisors, managers, and executives
                already in most organizations.

CHANGE 12:   Women will continue to enter the labor mar-
                ket, accounting for over 60 percent female

participation during the 1990s.

The entry of women into the workforce during the 1990s will be due less to the changing role of women than to the economic necessity of women to work in order to survive in an expensive consumer-oriented society. Women will account for two-thirds of the growth in all occupations. They will continue to expand into non-traditional jobs, especially production and management positions. Both men and women in a growing number of two-career families will have the flexibility to change jobs and careers frequently.

CHANGE 13: **More immigrants will enter the U.S. — both legally and illegally — to meet labor shortages at all levels.**

Despite major efforts of the INS to stem the flow of illegal immigrants, labor market demands will require more immigrants to occupy low-paying, entry-level service jobs in the 1990s. The brain drain of highly skilled scientific and technical workers from developing countries to the U.S. will accelerate. Unskilled immigrants will move into service positions vacated by upwardly mobile Americans.

CHANGE 14: **Part-time and temporary employment opportunities will increase.**

With the increase in two-career families, the emergence of electronic cottages, and the smaller number of retirees, part-time and temporary employment will become a more normal pattern of employment for millions of Americans. More women, who wish to enter the job market but not as full-time employees, will seek new part-time employment opportunities. Temporary employment services will experience a boom in business as more and more companies attempt to lower personnel costs as well as achieve greater flexibility in personnel by hiring larger numbers of temporary employees.

CHANGE 15: **White-collar employment will continue to expand in the fast growing service sector.**

Dramatic growth in clerical and service jobs will take place in response to new information technology. The classification of workers into blue- and white-collar occupations as well as into manufacturing and service jobs will become meaningless in a service economy dominated by white-collar workers.

CHANGE 16: **The need for a smarter work force with specific technical skills will continue to impact on the traditional American educational system with a demand for greater job market relevance in educational curriculum.**

Four-year colleges and universities will continue to face stable to declining enrollments as well as the flight of quality faculty to more challenging and lucrative jobs outside education. Declining enrollments will be due to the inability of these institutions to adjust to the educational and training skill requirements of the high-tech society as well as to the demographics of fewer numbers in the traditional 17-21 year-old student age population. The flight of quality faculty will be replaced by less qualified and inexpensive part-time faculty. Most community colleges, as well as specialized private vocational-technical institutions, will adapt to the changing demographics and labor market needs and flourish with programs most responsive to community employment needs. As declining enrollments, budgetary crises, and flight of quality faculty accelerates, many of the traditional four-year colleges and universities will attempt to shut down or limit the educational scope of community colleges in heated state political struggles for survival of traditional education programs. More and more emphasis will be placed on providing efficient short-term, intensive skills training programs than on providing traditional degree programs — especially in the liberal arts. Re-careering will become a major emphasis in educational programs; a new emphasis will be placed on both specialization and flexibility in career preparation.

CHANGE 17: **Union membership will continue to decline as more blue-collar manufacturing jobs disappear and interest in unions wanes among both blue- and white-collar employees.**

As unions attempt to survive and adjust to the new society, labor-management relations will go through a turbulent period of conflict, co-optation, and cooperation. Given declining union membership and the threat to lay-off employees unless unions agree to give-back arrangements, unions will increasingly find themselves on the defensive, with little choice other than to agree to management demands for greater worker productivity. In the long-run, labor-management relations will shift from the traditional adversarial relationship to one of greater cooperation and participation of labor and management in the decision-making process. Profit sharing, employee ownership, and quality circles will become prominent features of labor-management relations which will contribute to the continuing decline, and eventual disappearance, of traditional unions in many industries. New organizational forms, such as private law firms specializing in the representation of employees' interests and the negotiation of employment contracts, will replace the traditional unions.

CHANGE 18: **The population will continue to move into suburban and semi-rural communities as the new high-tech industries and services move in this direction.**

The large, older central cities, especially in the Northeast and North Central regions, will continue to decline as well as bear disproportionate welfare and tax burdens due to their declining industrial base and deteriorating infrastructure. Cutbacks in their city government programs will require the retraining of public employees for private sector jobs. Urban populations will continue to move into suburban and semi-rural communities. Developing their own economic base, these communities will provide employment for the majority of local residents rather than serve as bedroom communities from which workers commute to the central city. With few exceptions, and despite noble attempts to "revitalize" downtown areas with new office, shopping, and entertainment complexes, most large central cities will continue to decline as their upwardly mobile residential populations move to the suburbs where most of the good jobs, housing, and education is found.

CHANGE 19: **The population, as well as wealth and economic activity, will continue to shift into the West, Southwest, and Florida at the expense of the Northeast and North Central regions.**

By the year 2000 the South and West will have about 60 percent of the population. These areas will also be the home for the Nation's youngest population. Florida, Georgia, Texas, California, and Arizona will be the growth states of the 1990s; construction and local government in these states will experience major employment increases. Michigan, Ohio, Illinois, Indiana, and Pennsylvania will be in for continuing difficult times due to their declining industrial base, excessive welfare burdens, older population, and aging infrastructure. However, these same states may experience a strong recovery — based on the Massachusetts model of the 1980s — due to important linkages developing between their exceptionally well developed higher educational institutions and high-tech industries which depend on such institutions.

The growth regions also will experience turbulence as they see-saw between shortages of skilled labor, surpluses of unskilled labor, and urban growth problems. A "unique event", such as a devastating earthquake in Southern California or major water shortages in California and Arizona could result in a sudden reversal of rapid economic and employment growth in the Southwest region.

The problems of the declining regions are relatively predictable: they will become an economic drain on the Nation's scarce resources; tax dollars from the growth areas will be increasingly transferred for nonproductive support payments. A new regionalism, characterized by numerous regional political conflicts, will likely arise centered around questions concerning the inequitable distribution of public costs and benefits.

CHANGE 20: **The number of small businesses will continue to increase as new opportunities for entrepreneurs arise in response to the high-tech and service revolutions and as more individuals find new opportunities to experiment with re-careering.**

Over 700,000 new businesses will be started each year during the 1990s. These businesses will generate 90 percent of all new jobs created each year. The number of business failures will increase accordingly, especially during the bust cycles of the boom-bust economy. Increases in self-employment and small businesses will not provide great numbers of new opportunities for career advancement. The small promotion hierarchies of these businesses will help accelerate increased job-hopping and re-careering. This new entrepreneurship is likely to breed greater innovation, competition, and productivity.

CHANGE 21:   **As large companies continue to cutback, major job growth will take place among small companies and millions of new start-up businesses.**

The best employment opportunities in terms of challenges, salaries, and advancement opportunities will be found among growing companies employing fewer than 2,500 employees but more than 100 employees. The large Fortune 1000 companies will continue to cut back personnel as they attempt to survive intensive competition by becoming more productive through the application of new technology to the workplace and through the introduction of more efficient management systems. Cutbacks will further lower the morale of remaining employees who will seek new careering and re-careering opportunities.

CHANGE 22:   **Opportunities for career advancement will be increasingly limited within most organizations.**

Organizations will have difficulty providing career advancement for employees due to (1) the growth of small businesses with short advancement hierarchies, (2) the postponement of retirement, (3) the continuing focus on nonhierarchical forms of organization, and (4) the already glutted managerial ranks. In the future, many of today's managers will have to re-career into nonmanagerial positions. Job satisfaction will become less oriented toward advancement up the organizational ladder and more toward such organizational perks as club memberships, sabbaticals, vacations, retraining opportunities, flexible working hours, and family services.

CHANGE 23:   **Job satisfaction will become a major problem as many organizations will experience difficulty in retaining highly qualified personnel.**

Greater competition, fewer promotions, frustrated expectations, greater discontent, and job-hopping will arise in executive ranks due to limited advancement opportunities. Managerial and executive turnover will increase accordingly. The problem will be especially pronounced for many women and minorities who have traditional aspirations to advance to the top but will be blocked by the glut of managers and executives from the baby-boom generation. Many of these frustrated individuals will initiate affirmative action cases to open the closed upper ranks as well as become entrepreneurs by starting their own businesses in competition with their former employers.

CHANGE 24: **Many employers will resort to new and unorthodox hiring practices and improved working conditions in order to recruit and retain critical personnel.**

In an increasingly tight job market for skilled workers, employers will use new and more effective ways of finding and keeping personnel: job fair weekends; headhunters and executive search firms; temporary employment services; raids of competition's personnel; bonuses to present employees for finding needed personnel; entry-level bonuses for new recruits; attractive profit-sharing packages for long-term commitments; vacation and travel packages; relocation and housing services; flex-time and job-sharing; home-based work; and day care services.

CHANGE 25: **Job-hopping will increase as more and more individuals learn about the joys of re-careering.**

As more job and career opportunities become available for the skilled and savvy worker, as pension systems become more portable, and as job search and relocation techniques become more widely known, more and more individuals will change jobs and careers in the 1990s. The typical employee will work in one job and organization for four years and then

move on to a similar job in another organization. Within 12 years this individual will have
acquired new interests and skills and thus decide to change to a new career. Similar four
and 12-year cycles of job and career changes
will be repeated by the same individual. Job-
hopping will become an accepted and necessary way of getting ahead in the job and career
markets of tomorrow.

BE REALISTIC

While many individuals look toward the future with unques-
tioned optimism, there are good reasons to be cautious and less than
enthusiastic. The 1990s may be the worst of times for many people.
Take several examples which indicate a need to be cautiously optimistic. Factory workers who remain unemployed after five years
will have received an industrial death sentence of continuing unemployment, underemployment, or socio-economic decline. Many poor,
unskilled minorities, with high birth rates, are destined to remain at
the bottom of society; their children may fare no better. Large
cities in the Northeast and North Central regions, and even small
communities in these and other regions, will have difficult adjustment, if not survival, problems. And we should not forget that America has not solved its energy and environmental problems.

The best of times are when *you* are gainfully employed, enjoy
your work, and look to *your* future with optimism. In the turbulent
society, people experience both the best and worst of times at the
same time. Those who are unprepared for the growing uncertainty
and instability of the turbulent society may get hurt.

We lack a healthy sense of reality in facing change. Indeed, the
future is seldom what we think it is. Only recently have we begun to
take a second look at the high-tech and service revolutions and raised
some sobering questions about their impact on work and the workplace. We have not fully explored *unanticipated consequences* of
new structural changes and individuals and society.

The 25 changes we forecast will create dislocations for individuals, groups, organizations, communities, and regions. These dislocations will require some form of public-private intervention. For
example, the question of renewable energy resources has not been
adequately dealt with in relation to the high-tech revolution. Many
of the key metals for fueling the high-tech economy are located in
politically unstable regions of Africa as well as in the Soviet Union.

Such resources must be secured or substitutions found in order for the revolution to proceed according to optimistic predictions. Capital formation, investment, and world markets must also be secure and stable. New management systems must evolve in response to the changes. In other words, these key factors are *variables* or "if's", and not the constants underlying most predictions of the future. As such, they are unpredictable.

The clearer picture of unanticipated consequences of the technological changes are already evident on the changing assembly lines, in the automated offices, and in the electronic cottages of today. While automation often creates more jobs as it displaces workers — usually at higher skill levels — the jobs may be psychologically and financially less rewarding. Supervising robots eight hours a day can be tedious and boring work with few on-the-job rewards. The same is true for the much touted "office of the future". Interacting at a work station with a computer terminal and screen eight hours a day is work that many may find tedious, tiring, and boring; and job burnout may be accelerated.

The electronic cottage has similar unanticipated consequences. Many people may miss the daily interaction with fellow workers — the gossip, the politics, the strokes. Instead of being rewarding, work at home can become druggery. It also may be low paying work, a 21st century version of the sweat shop.

The optimists often neglect the fact that the *nature of work itself* provides rewards. Many people intrinsically enjoy the particular job they perform. Furthermore, many rewards are tied to the *human dimension of work* — the interaction with others. Thus, the high-tech and service society will have to deal with serious management and motivational problems arising from the changing nature of work and the workplace.

Many workers may need to re-career in order to overcome the boredom and burnout accompanying many of the new jobs or work situations of tomorrow. And even if the high-tech and service society does not emerge in the form outlined by us and other forecasters, the need to re-career will become necessary given the job and career uncertainty of a turbulent society.

Chapter Three

IDENTIFY THE JOBS OF TOMORROW

"*Where* are the jobs, and *how* do I get one?" These are the first questions most people ask when seeking employment. But one other equally important question should precede these traditional questions:

"*What* are the jobs of tomorrow?"

For the nature of jobs is changing rapidly in response to (1) technological innovations, (2) the development and application of new technology to the workplace, and (3) the demand for a greater variety of consumer services. Today's job seeker needs answers to the "what", "where", and "how" of jobs for the 1990s and beyond.

Many jobs in the year 2000 will look very different from those in the 1980s. Indeed, if we project present trends into the future and believe what futurists tell us about emerging new careers, the 21st century will offer unprecedented and exciting careering and re-careering opportunities.

But such changes and opportunities have costs. The change in jobs and occupations will be so rapid that skills learned today may become obsolete in another five to ten years. Therefore, knowing what the jobs are becomes a prerequisite to knowing how to prepare for them, find them, and change them in the future.

BEWARE OF CHANGING
OCCUPATIONAL PROFILES

A few words of caution are in order on how you should and should not use the information in this chapter. If you wish to identify a growing career field to plan your own career, do so only *after* you have identified your interests, skills, and abilities — the subjects of Chapter Six. You need to determine if you have the proper skills or the aptitude and interests to acquire the necessary skills. The next step is to acquire the training before conducting a job search. Only then should you seriously consider pursuing what appears to be a growing field.

At the same time you should be aware that the statistics and projections on growing industrial and occupational fields may be inaccurate. First, they are based on traditional models and economic studies conducted by the U.S. Department of Labor, Bureau of Labor Statistics. Unlike fortune tellers and soothsayers who communicate in another world and many futurists who engage in "informed flights of fancy" and "brainstorming", the Bureau conducts "empirical studies" which assume a steady rate of economic growth throughout the 1990s — similar to the 1950s. Such occupational projections are nothing more than "best guesses" based upon a traditional planning model which assumes continual, linear growth. This planning model does not deal well with the reality of cyclical changes, as evidenced by its failures during the turbulent 1980s when boom and bust cycles, coupled with the emergence of unique events and crises, invalidated many of the Bureau's employment and occupational forecasts. For example, The Department of Labor projected a high unemployment rate of 7.6 percent for 1982; but in 1982 unemployment actually stood at 10.8 percent. In addition, the deepening recession and the government program cuts brought on by a series of international crises, domestic economic failures, and ideological changes were unanticipated developments which resulted in the actual decline in public employment for the first time since World War II. Thus, in 1982 there were 316,000 fewer public employees than in the year before! The turbulent 1990s may well provide us with more unique economic scenarios which produce similar unpredictable outcomes.

Second, during a period of turbulent change, occupational profiles may become quickly outdated. Training requirements change, and thus individuals encounter greater uncertainty in career choices. For example, based on trend analyses, many people believe that promising careers lie ahead for computer programmers. This may be true *if* thousands of newly trained individuals do not glut the job market with computer programming skills. Moreover, it may be true *if* computer technology remains stagnant and the coming generation of self-programmed computers does not make computer programmers — like their keypunch counterparts in the 1960s and 1970s — obsolete. If either, let alone both, of these "if's" occur, many computer programming jobs may disappear, and many newly trained computer programmers may become displaced workers in need of re-careering.

A similar situation arises for students pursuing the much glamorized MBA and law degrees. Today, as more MBA's graduate and glut the job market with questionable skills, the glitter surrounding this degree has diminished, and the MBA may fast become an obsolete degree as employers turn to degree fields that emphasize greater communication and analytical skills. A similar situation appears relevant to the law field. While the demand for lawyers increased substantially in the 1980s and a large number of students continue to enroll in law schools, competition for legal positions may be keen in the years ahead as more and more law graduates flood a shrinking job market. Contrary to most future job projections for lawyers, we believe opportunities for lawyers will not increase much during the 1990s. The demand for lawyers may actually decline due to substantial restructuring of the legal profession as lawyers become more competitive, promote more efficient legal services, hire more paralegals, change fee and billing practices, introduce more technology to traditional legal tasks, and develop more do-it-yourself legal approaches; as the criminal justice system undergoes restructuring; and as Americans become less litigious due to the high costs of pursuing legal action.

EXPECT JOB GROWTH IN MOST
OCCUPATIONS AND FOR MOST GROUPS

The growth in jobs has been steady during the past three to four decades. From 1955 to 1980, for example, the number of jobs increased from 68.7 to 105.6 million. This represented an average annual increase of about 1.5 million new jobs. During the 1970s the number of jobs increased by over 2 million per year. And between the years 1983 and 1988 the number of jobs increased by 16 million, a phenomenal annual growth rate of nearly 3 million!

Job growth during the 1990s is expected to slow but remain steady at about 1.5 million new jobs each year, reflecting the coming demographic changes in society. By the year 2000 the labor force should consist of nearly 140 million workers — up 15 percent from

1990.

Highlighting these patterns of job growth are 15 forecasts, based on U.S. Department of Labor data and projections, which represent the confluence of demographic, economic, and technological changes in society during the 1990s:

EMPLOYMENT FORECASTS FOR THE 1990s

1. **Growth of the labor force slows during the 1990s.**

   The growth in the labor force will slow to 139 million by the year 2000 — an 18 percent increase over the 1986 level. This represents half the rate of increase during the previous 14-year period, and it reflects the overall slow growth of the population, with a less than zero population birth rate of 0.7 percent per year.

2. **Labor force will be racially and ethnically more diverse.**

   The racial and ethnic mix of the work force in the year 2000 will be even more diverse than in the year 1990 given the differential birth and immigration rates of various racial and ethnic groups. Blacks, Hispanics, Asians, and other minority groups will represent 26 percent of the workforce. These groups also will account for 58 percent of the growth in the labor force from 1986 to 2000.

3. **Fewer young people will enter the job market.**

   The number of 16 to 24 year-olds entering the job market will continue to decline throughout the 1990s in the absence of a new baby boom generation entering the job market. The youth share of the labor force will fall to 16 percent by 2000. This represents a significant decline — down from 20 percent in 1986 and 23 percent in 1972. Businesses depending on this age group for students, recruits, customers, and part-time workers — especially colleges, the Armed Forces, eating and drinking establishments, and retail stores — must draw from a smaller pool of young people. Competition among young people for entry-level jobs will decline accordingly.

4. **The workforce will continue to gray as it becomes older and older.**

   As the baby-boom generation of the 1960s and 1970s becomes more middle-aged, the number of 25 to 54 year olds in the labor force will increase substantially by the year 2000 — with 3 of every 4 workers being between the ages of 25 and 54.

5. **Women will enter the labor force in growing numbers.**

   Women will represent 2 of every 3 new entrants into the labor force during the 1990s. While accounting for 39 percent of the labor force in 1972, women in the year 2000 will constitute over 47 percent of the labor force.

6. **Education requirements for most new jobs will continue to rise.**

   Most new jobs will require strong basic education skills, such as reading, writing, oral communication, and computation. Many of these jobs will include important high-tech components which will require previous specialized education and training as well as the demonstrated ability to learn and acquire nontraditional education and training to continuously re-tool skills.

7. **Employment will increase for most occupations in the 1990s.**

   As the population continues to grow and become more middle-aged and affluent, demands for more services will increase accordingly. Except in the cases of agriculture, mining, and traditional manufacturing, the 1990s will be a period of steady to significant job growth in all occupations.

8. **The fastest growing occupations will be in executive, managerial, professional, and technical fields — all requiring the highest levels of education and skill.**

   A combination of greater emphasis on productivity

in the workplace, increased automation, technological advances, innovations, changes in consumer demands, and import substitutions will decrease the need for workers with little formal education and few skills — helpers, laborers, assemblers, and machine operators.

9. **The greatest growth in jobs will take place in service industries and occupations.**

    Over 90 percent of all new jobs in the 1990s will be in the service-producing industries with services such as legal, business (advertising, accounting, word processing, and computer support), and health care leading the way. The number of jobs in services is expected to rise by 34 percent between 1986 and 2000, from 31.9 to 42.6 million. Services provided by hotels, barber shops, auto repair shops, hospitals, nonprofit organizations, and engineering firms will expand rapidly throughout the 1990s.

10. **Trade, both wholesale and retail, will be the second fastest growing industrial sector in the 1990s.**

    Employment in retail and wholesale trade is expected to increase by 27 percent, from 23.5 to 30.0 million during the 1986 to 2000 period.

11. **Government employment will increase at different rates for different levels of government as well as for governmental units in different regions of the country.**

    Federal government employment will remain relatively level, increasing by less than 1.0 percent each year as the federal government continues on a long-term trend to contract-out government services rather than increase in-house personnel. State and local government employment will increase by 2 to 3 percent each year with local governments in the rapidly developing and relatively affluent cities and counties of the West and Southwest experiencing the largest employment growth rates.

12. **Employment growth in education will slow at all**

levels.

Employment in education will increase slightly at the elementary level but decline for colleges and universities in response to the changing demographics of the 1990s. Employment in secondary education will remain steady, decline in some fields but increase in other fields, especially in science, math, technology, and communication.

13. **Jobs in manufacturing will decline throughout the 1990s.**

Manufacturing jobs are expected to decline by 4 percent, from 19.0 to 18.2 million. These declines will result from productivity gains achieved through automation and improved management as well as the closing of less efficient plants.

14. **Employment in agriculture and mining jobs will continue to decline.**

Employment in agriculture is expected to decline by 14 percent, from 3.3 to 2.9 million, reflecting a decrease of nearly 500,000 self-employed workers. Wage and salary positions in agricultural services will increase by 150,000. Much of the self-employment decline will be due to the closing of lucrative export markets as the productivity of agriculture abroad improves and new hybrid crops are introduced from genetic engineering breakthroughs to solve many of the world's food problems. Employment in mining will fall by 7 percent, from 783,000 to 725,000, due to a combination of improvements in mining technology and import competition.

15. **Glamorous new occupations, responding to new technological developments and consumer demands, will offer exciting new careering and re-careering opportunities for future job seekers who are well educated and skilled in the jobs of tomorrow.**

New occupations, created through a combination of technological innovations and new service demands, will provide excellent career opportunities for those who possess the necessary skills and drive to succeed in the 1990s. New occupations with such names as bionic-electronic technician, holographic inspector, cryonics technician, and aquaculturist will enter our occupational vocabulary during the 1990s.

PROJECT OCCUPATIONAL PROFILES INTO THE 1990s

The U.S. Department of Labor divides the economy into two types of industries and nine industrial sectors for projecting employment trends:

1. Service-producing industries

- Transportation
- Trade
- Finance
- Services
- Government

2. Goods-producing industries

- Agriculture
- Mining
- Construction
- Manufacturing

Throughout the 1990s most job growth will take place among service producing industries. Assuming the 1990s will be a decade of rising incomes and living standards, individuals will place greater demand on health care, entertainment, and business and financial services. With the continuing growth of cities and suburbs, the demand for local government services should increase.

The second largest service-producing industry generating jobs in the 1990s will be wholesale and retail trade. Again, if we assume incomes and living standards will rise throughout the 1990s, the largest number of new jobs in the trade sector will be found among eating and drinking establishments. Other retail trade firms that should generate large numbers of new jobs will be department stores, grocery stores, and new car dealerships. The largest contributors to new jobs in the wholesale trade will be firms handling machinery, electric goods, and motor vehicles.

Between 1986 and 2000 the Department of Labor anticipates the following occupational growth and decline patterns for service- and goods-producing industries, as shown on page 49.

─── TOMORROW'S JOBS BY INDUSTRIAL SECTOR ───

Industrial Profile

• **Service Producing Industries**: The long-term shift from goods-producing to service-producing employment will continue. By 2000, nearly 4 out of 5 jobs will be in industries that provide services — industries such as banking, insurance, health care, education, data processing, and management consulting.

1. **Services**. Employment in services — one of the subgroups within the service-producing sector — is expected to rise 34 percent, from 31.9 to 42.6 million — making it the fastest growing industry division. These jobs will be found in large corporations and government agencies as well as in one- or two-person firms, for the services industries are a diverse group. A few of these industries are expected to grow extremely fast and a few will grow very slowly, but most are projected to grow at a rate exceeding that for the economy as a whole.

    Job growth in legal services and business services (advertising, accounting, word processing, and computer support, for example) will be exceptionally rapid. Employment in health services also should make impressive gains as demand for health care continues to expand. Cost-containment policies are expected to slow employment growth in hospitals as services once performed in hospitals are shifted to outpatient care facilities. This will dramatically boost employment in outpatient settings such as clinics and physicians' offices.

2. **Retail and wholesale trade**. Employment in both retail and wholesale trade is expected to rise by 27 percent; from 17.8 to 22.7 million in retail trade, and from 5.7 to 7.3 million in wholesale trade. Over half the nearly 5 million new retail jobs will be in eating and drinking places. Substantial increases in retail employment are also anticipated in grocery stores, department stores, and miscellaneous shopping goods stores — chiefly establishments selling sporting goods, jewelry, books, cards, and stationery. About half of the 1.5 million new jobs in wholesale trade will occur in machinery and equipment distributors, reflecting large outlays for electronic machinery in the future by domestic manufacturers.

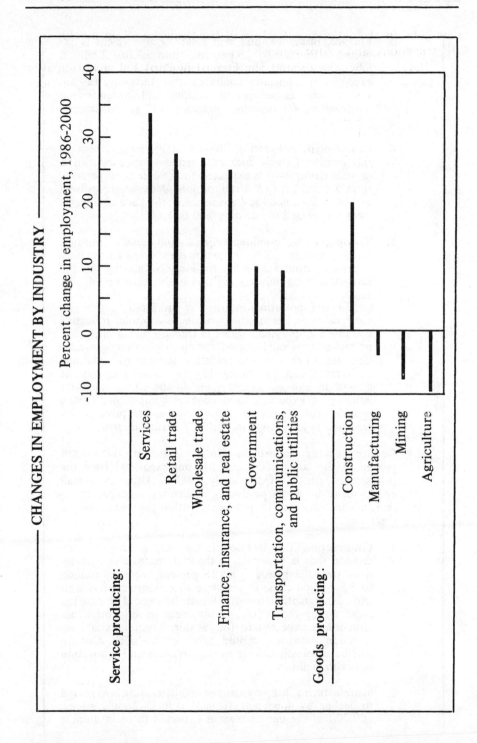

CHANGES IN EMPLOYMENT BY INDUSTRY

Percent change in employment, 1986-2000

Service producing:
Services
Retail trade
Wholesale trade
Finance, insurance, and real estate
Government
Transportation, communications, and public utilities

Goods producing:
Construction
Manufacturing
Mining
Agriculture

3. **Finance, insurance, and real estate.** Employment is expected to increase by 26 percent, from 6.3 to 7.2 million jobs. The demand for financial products and services is expected to continue unabated, but technological advances, such as automated banking and computerized underwriting for insurance agencies, will act to dampen job growth.

4. **Government.** Between 1986 and 2000, employment in this division (which does not include public education or public hospitals) is expected to increase by 9 percent, from 8.6 million to 9.4 million jobs. Most of the growth will be in State and local government; the Federal Government is expected to add only 100,000 jobs.

5. **Transportation, communications, and public utilities.** Employment in this broad sector is expected to rise only 9 percent, from 5.2 to 5.7 million jobs, making this the slowest growing industry division in the service-producing sector.

   The transportation industry is projected to grow almost twice as fast as the division as a whole, reflecting continued employment gains in trucking and airline transportation services. Demand for electric power, gas utilities, and water and transportation services will continue to increase, too, producing slow but steady employment growth in utilities. Employment in the communications industry is expected to decline as competition among providers of telephone service encourages productivity gains and as job growth in cable TV begins to taper.

• **Goods-Producing Industries:** Employment in this sector peaked in the late 1970's and has not recovered from the recessionary period of the early 1980's. Although overall employment in goods-producing industries is expected to remain constant, growth prospects within the sector vary a great deal.

1. **Construction.** Construction is the only goods-producing division that is expected to show an increase in employment over the period — up 18 percent, from 4.9 million to 5.8 million jobs, in response to economic conditions and demographic trends. When household formation slows during the 1990's, employment in residential construction is expected to follow suit. Nonresidential construction, however, should take up the slack. Growth will be especially strong in construction and renovation of health facilities.

2. **Manufacturing.** Employment in manufacturing is expected to decline by 4 percent, from 19.0 to 18.2 million jobs; 500,000 of the net decrease is expected to be in durable

goods manufacturing and 300,000 in nondurable goods. The projected loss of manufacturing jobs reflects productivity gains achieved from increased investment in manufacturing technologies as well as a winnowing out of less efficient operations.

Within durable goods manufacturing, job losses are projected to be greatest in blast furnaces, basic steel products, and the aircraft industry; within nondurable goods, in apparel and the weaving, finishing, and yarn and thread mills industries.

Not all manufacturing industries will decline, however. Those in which increases are expected include, among the durable goods industries, electronic computing equipment and medical instruments and supplies; and miscellaneous plastics products and commercial printing and business forms among nondurable goods.

The occupational composition of manufacturing employment is expected to shift since most of the jobs that will disappear will be production jobs. The number of professional, technical, and managerial positions in manufacturing firms will actually increase.

3. **Mining.** Mining employment is expected to drop from 783,000 to 725,000 — a 7-percent decline. Underlying this projection is the assumption that domestic oil production will drop and oil imports will rise sharply. Other mining industries are expected to experience decreases in employment because of improvements in mining technology as well as import competition.

4. **Agriculture.** Employment in agriculture has been declining for many decades and this trend is expected to continue — the number of jobs is projected to decline by 14 percent, from 3.3 to 2.9 million.

The decline in agricultural jobs reflects a decrease of almost 500,000 in the number of self-employed workers. Wage and salary positions will increase by about 150,000 — with especially strong growth in the agricultural services industry.

EXAMINE GROWING AND DECLINING OCCUPATIONS

In addition to the industrial classification, the Department of Labor divides occupations into 16 broad groups based on the Standard Occupation Classification, the classification system used by all government agencies for collecting occupational employment information:

- Executive, administrative, and managerial occupations
- Engineers, scientists, and related occupations
- Social science, social service, and related occupations
- Teachers, librarians, and counselors
- Health-related occupations
- Writers, artists, and entertainers
- Technologists and technicians
- Marketing and sales occupations
- Administrative support occupations, including clerical
- Service occupations
- Agricultural and forestry occupations
- Mechanics and repairers
- Construction occupations
- Production occupations
- Transportation and material moving occupations
- Handlers, equipment cleaners, helpers, and laborers

Assuming a moderate rate of economic growth throughout the 1990s — not boom and bust cycles — the U.S. Department of Labor projects an average growth rate of 19 percent for all occupations. Technical and service occupations will grow the fastest between 1986-2000:

PROJECTED EMPLOYMENT CHANGES IN BROAD OCCUPATIONAL GROUPS, 1986-2000

Occupational group	Total increase/decrease in new jobs	Percent change
• Service workers	5,381,000	+31
• Sales workers	3,728,000	+30
• Professional workers	3,655,000	+27
• Executive, administrative, and managerial workers	3,033,000	+29
• Administrative support workers, including clerical	2,258,000	+11
• Precision production, craft, and repair workers	1,669,000	+12

• Technicians and related support workers	1,403,000	+38
• Operators, fabricators, and laborers	443,000	+3
• Agriculture, forestry, and fishing workers	-163,000	-5

More than one-half of all job growth in the 1986-2000 period will be contributed by 27 fast growing occupations:

FASTEST GROWING OCCUPATIONS CONTRIBUTING MORE THAN 50% TO JOB GROWTH, 1986-2000

Occupation	Number of new jobs created	Percent growth
• Sales workers, retail	1,201,000	34
• Waiters and waitresses	752,000	44
• Registered nurses	612,000	44
• Janitors and cleaners	604,000	23
• General managers and top executives	582,000	24
• Cashiers	575,000	27
• Truckdrivers	525,000	24
• General office clerks	462,000	20
• Food counter and related workers	449,000	30
• Nursing aides, orderlies, and attendants	433,000	35
• Secretaries	424,000	13
• Guards	383,000	48
• Accountants and auditors	376,000	40
• Computer programmers	335,000	70
• Food preparation workers	324,000	34
• Teachers, kindergarten and elementary	299,000	20
• Receptionists and information clerks	262,000	41

• Computer systems analysts	251,000	76
• Cooks, restaurant	240,000	46
• Licensed practical nurses	238,000	38
• Gardeners and groundskeepers	238,000	31
• Maintenance repairers, general utility	232,000	22
• Stock clerks, sales floor	225,000	21
• Clerical supervisors and managers	205,000	21
• Dining room attendants and related workers	197,000	26
• Electrical and electronics engineers	192,000	48
• Lawyers	191,000	36

The patterns of growth and decline in industries and occupations during the 1990s generally follow the larger changes in the economy we discussed earlier. The U.S. Department of Labor studies have identified the fastest growing and declining occupations for years 1986-2000. Occupations, for example, contributing the largest job growth in terms of the actual number of new jobs generated will be in service industries requiring a wide range of skills. Twelve of the 20 fastest growing occupations will be in the health services alone, and most of the jobs will require advanced education and training:

20 FASTEST GROWING OCCUPATIONS, 1986-2000

Occupation	Percent growth	Numerical growth
• Paralegal personnel	101	64,000
• Medical assistants	90	119,000
• Physical therapists	87	53,000
• Physical and corrective therapy assistants and aids	82	29,000
• Data processing equipment repairers	80	56,000
• Home health aides	80	111,000
• Podiatrists	77	10,000
• Computer systems analysts	76	251,000

• Medical records technicians	75	30,000
• Employment interviewers	71	54,000
• Computer programmers	70	335,000
• Dental hygienists	63	54,000
• Dental assistants	57	88,000
• Physician assistants	57	15,000
• Operations and systems researchers	54	21,000
• Occupational therapists	52	15,000
• Peripheral electronic data processing equipment operators	51	24,000
• Data entry keyers, composing	51	15,000
• Optometrists	49	18,000

On the other hand, the 20 fastest declining occupations will be in the following fields:

——————— 20 FASTEST DECLINING OCCUPATIONS, ———————
1986-2000

Occupation	Percent decline	Numerical decline
• Electrical and electronic assemblers	54	133,000
• Electronic semiconductor processes	51	15,000
• Railroad conductors and yardmasters	41	12,000
• Railroad brake system and switch operators	40	17,000
• Gas and petroleum plant and system occupations	34	11,000
• Industrial truck and tractor operators	34	143,000
• Shoe sewing-machine operators and tenders	32	9,000
• Station installers and repairers, telephone	32	18,000
• Chemical equipment controllers, operators,		

and tenders	30	21,000
• Chemical plant and system operators	30	10,000
• Stenographers	28	50,000
• Farmers	28	332,000
• Statistical clerks	28	19,000
• Textile draw-out and winding machine operators	25	55,000
• Central office and PBX installers and repairers	23	17,000
• Farm workers	20	190,000
• Coil winders, tapers, and installers	19	6,000
• Central office operators	18	8,000
• Directory assistance operators	18	5,000
• Compositors, typesetters, and arrangers, precision	17	5,000

DETERMINE "THE BEST" JOB FOR YOU

The fastest growing occupational fields are not necessarily the best ones to enter. The best job and career for you will depend on your particular work and life style values. Money, for example, is only one of many determiners of whether or not a job and career is particularly desirable. A job may pay a great deal of money, but it also may be very stressful and insecure, or it is found in an undesirable location. "The best" job for you will be one you find very rewarding in terms of your own criteria and priorities.

Periodically some observers of the labor market attempt to identify what are the best, the worst, the hottest, the most lucrative, or the most promising jobs and careers of the decade. The latest and most objective attempt to assemble a list of "the best" jobs in America is presented in *The Jobs Rated Almanac*. Similar in methodology to *The Places Rated Almanac* for identifying the best places to live in America, *The Jobs Rated Almanac* evaluates and ranks 250 jobs in terms of six primary "job quality" criteria: income, stress, physical demands, environment, outlook, and security. According to their analysis, the 20 highest ranking jobs by accumulated score on each of these criteria are:

```
┌──────────────  "THE BEST" JOBS IN AMERICA  ──────────────┐
```

Job title	Overall rank	Cumulative score
• Actuary	1	73
• Computer programmer	2	185
• Computer systems analyst	3	187
• Mathematician	4	208
• Statistician	5	221
• Hospital administrator	6	223
• Industrial engineer	7	228
• Physicist	8	254
• Astrologer	9	257
• Paralegal (legal assistant)	10	264
• Bank officer	11	271
• Motion picture editor	12	283
• Biologist	13	285
• Technical/copy writer	14	288
• Accountant	15	289
• Civil engineer	16	309
• Print editor	17	316
• Pharmacist	18	325
• Political scientist	19	332
• Astronomer	20	334

For the relative rankings of the remaining 230 jobs as well as the ratings of each job on individual criteria, consult the latest edition of *The Jobs Rated Almanac*, which should be available in your local library or bookstore. It can also be ordered from Impact Publications by completing the order form at the end of this book.

LOOK FOR EXCITING NEW OCCUPATIONS IN THE 21st CENTURY

In the early 1970s the auto and related industries — steel, rubber, glass, aluminum, railroads and auto dealers — accounted for one-fifth of all employment in the United States. Today that percentage continues to decline as service occupations further dominate America's occupational structure.

New occupations for the 1990s and beyond will center around information, energy, high-tech, health, and financial industries. They promise to create a new occupational structure and vocabulary relating to computers, robotics, biotechnology, lasers, and fiber optics. And as these fields begin to apply new technologies to developing new innovations, they in turn will generate other new occupations in the 21st century. While most new occupations are not major growth fields, because they do not initially generate a large number of new jobs, they will present individuals with fascinating new opportunities to become leaders in pioneering new fields and industries.

Futurists identify several emerging occupations for the coming decades. Most tend to brainstorm lists of occupational titles they feel will emerge in the next decade based on present trends. Others identify additional occupations which may be created from new, unforeseen technological breakthroughs. Feingold and Miller (*Emerging Careers*), for example, see 30 new careers emerging for the 21st century:

EMERGING CAREERS FOR THE 21st CENTURY

1. artificial intelligence technician
2. aquaculturist
3. automotive fuel cell battery technician
4. benefits analyst
5. bionic electron technician
6. computational linguist
7. computer microprocessor
8. cryonics technician
9. dialysis technologist
10. electronic mail technician
11. fiber optic technician
12. fusion engineer
13. hazardous waste technician
14. horticulture therapy assistant
15. image consultant
16. information broker
17. information center manager
18. job developer
19. leisure consultant
20. materials utilization specialist
21. medical diagnostic imaging technician
22. myotherapist
23. relocation counselor
24. retirement counselor
25. robot technician
26. shyness consultant
27. software club director
28. space mechanic
29. underwater archaeologist
30. water quality specialist

The World Future Society projects the emergence of 10 new jobs requiring specialized education and training:

FUTURE JOBS

Occupational title	Qualifications required
Industrial Laser Process Technicians	High-school, technical training, and retraining requirements will vary with levels of skill required under a severe system of job revolution.
Housing Rehabilitation Technician	Technicians, inspectors, and supervisors will require a high-school education and equivalent of two years of technical-college education plus appropriate experience (such as formal apprenticeship).
Energy Technician	Technicians, inspectors, and supervisory positions will require high-school education and the equivalent of two years of technical college.
Hazardous Waste Management Technician	Highly specialized technical training will be required for workers, supervisors, and managers in this very hazardous occupation.
Industrial Robot Production Technician	Knowledge and skills requirements will compare with present-day computer programmers and electronics technicians.
Materials Utilization Technician	An education level equivalent to that of an electronics technician, tool and die maker, nondestructive materials testing specialist, or industrial inspector will be minimum requirement.
Battery Technician	The processes within this occupa-

	tion include potential hazards, but they can be safely performed by technicians with a vocational high school education.
Bionic-Electronic Technicians	These technicians will require appropriate technical knowledge of microprocessors and specialized accredited education in the respective anatomical, physiological, and psychiatric disciplines equivalent to a minimum of four years of college work. Medical professionals who establish a reputation will move into the higher six-figure levels of earnings.
Holographic Inspection Specialist	Specialist working in this new technology will require a minimum of two years of post-secondary technical education and training, with emphasis on optical fibers characteristics and transmission, photography, optical physics, and computer programming.
Genetic Engineering Technician	A bachelor's degree in chemistry, biology, or medicine will be helpful in the initial industrial production work, but production operations will be accomplished by "process technicians" with high-school and two-year post-secondary technical education and training.

Most futurists agree that such new occupations will have two dominant characteristics during the 1990s:

- **They will generate a small number of new jobs** in comparison to the overall growth of jobs in hundreds of more traditional service fields.

- *They require a high level of education and skills* for entry into the fields as well as continuing training and retraining as each field transforms itself into additional growth fields.

If you plan to pursue any of these occupations, expect to first acquire highly specialized skills which may require years of higher education and training.

CONSIDER THE IMPLICATIONS OF FUTURE TRENDS FOR YOU

Most growth industries and occupations require skills training and experience. Moving into one of these fields will require knowledge of job qualifications, the nature of the work, and sources of employment. Fortunately, the Department of Labor publishes several useful sources of information to help you. These include the *Dictionary of Occupational Titles*, which identifies nearly 20,000 job titles. The *Occupational Outlook Handbook* provides an overview of current labor market conditions and projections as well as discusses 225 occupations that account for 80 percent of today's jobs according to several useful informational categories: nature of work; working conditions; employment; training, other qualifications, and achievement; job outlook; earnings; related occupations; and sources of additional information. Anyone seeking to enter the job market or change careers should initially consult these publications for information on trends and occupations.

However, remember that labor market statistics are for industries and occupations *as a whole*. They tell you little about the shift in employment emphasis *within the industry*, and nothing about the outlook of particular jobs for you, *the individual*. For example, employment in agriculture is expected to decline by 14 percent between 1985 and 2000, but the decline consists of an important shift in employment emphasis within the industry: there will be 500,000 fewer self-employed workers but 150,000 more wage and salary earners in the service end of agriculture. The employment statistics also assume a steady-state of economic growth with consumers having more and more disposable income to stimulate a wide variety of service and trade industries.

Therefore, be careful in how you interpret and use this information in making your own job and career decisions. If, for example, you want to become a college teacher, and the data indeed tells you there will be a 10 percent decline in this occupation during the next 10 years, this does not mean you could not find employment, as well as advance, in this field. It merely means that, on the whole, competition may be keen for these jobs, and that future advancement and mobility in this occupation may not be very good — on the whole. At the same time, there may be numerous job opportunities available in a declining occupational field as many individuals abandon the field for more attractive occupations. In fact, you may do much better in this declining occupation than in a growing field, depending on your interests, motivation, abilities, job search savvy, and the level of competition. And if the 1990s becomes a decade of boom and bust cycles, expect most of these U.S. Department of Labor statistics and projections to be invalid for the economic realities of this decade.

As we emphasized earlier, use this industrial and occupational data to expand your awareness of various job and career options. By no means should you make critical education, training, and occupational choices based upon this information alone. Such choices require additional types of information — subjects of the next eight chapters on you, the individual.

Chapter Four

ACQUIRE THE NECESSARY SKILLS THROUGH EDUCATION AND TRAINING

The American economy and workforce have faced numerous crises in the past. Most crises related to occasional economic downturns that generated temporary high unemployment rates. During bad economic times, unemployment increased; during good economic times, unemployment decreased. This cyclical nature of unemployment seemed to be a permanent feature of America's unplanned economic system.

The coming crisis for the economy and workforce in the 1990s will be quite different from the previous cyclical patterns of growth and decline. The cyclical patterns will continue in a boom/bust economy. But structural unemployment will increase due to transformations in the economy brought about with the introduction of new technology in the workplace and the decline of traditional industries. The new crisis will be the imbalance between skills workers possess and those employers need. Widening in recent years, this imbalance is expected to continue, if not increase, into the 21st century.

The skills imbalance is due to several training failures — and failures to train — on the part of both government and industry. Traditional educational institutions fail to teach the skills needed for the new jobs of today and tomorrow. Government policies, emphasizing redistributive subsidy and welfare programs designed for the economies of the 1960s and 1970s, provide little incentive for individuals to seek retraining. And present training programs offered by the private sector tend to be oriented toward managers in the soft skill areas; training of production workers in the hard technical skill areas is relatively neglected.

In the meantime, a large segment of the workforce is still oriented to the job market with skills and expectations best suited for the past three decades. Rather than take initiative to acquire new skills, many people do nothing; they remain unemployed, under-employed, or unhappy with their work. Others, unwilling to accept responsibility, seek scapegoats for their plight.

In this chapter we address the problem of training as well as outline how individuals can acquire the necessary education and training for the jobs and careers of tomorrow. This knowledge is essential information for careering and re-careering in the decades ahead.

ON YOUR OWN IN A
SEA OF GOOD INTENTIONS

The structure of education and training in the United States is highly fragmented, and its scope, quality, and effectiveness vary greatly among regions, communities, and institutions. As a result, many people have difficulty understanding and using education and training opportunities.

Federal government-sponsored training programs consist of a maze of over 20 programs ranging from Trade Adjustment Assistance to programs for redwood forest lumberjacks. The major federal program, which replaced the controversial Comprehensive Employment and Training Act (CETA) program in 1982, is the Jobs Training Partnership Act (JTPA). This program, like its predecessor, is limited in scope, focusing primarily on providing training and employment assistance for the poor and hardcore unemployed.

Employment observers and policy analysts Pat Choate and Noel Epstein best characterize federal training programs as being subject to "confusion, fragmentation, bureaucracy and the political pork barrel." While much needed, such programs will not have a great effect on the overall training and retraining needs of the nation.

But politicians, journalists, employment specialists, and many other "experts" continue to propose more government-sponsored training and retraining programs to deal with the problems of unemployment and displaced workers. Such well-meaning proposals have limitations. They fail to take into account the capabilities of the government to develop and manage such programs. First, the costs of training and retraining are so massive that the government could not sustain them for long. Second, the intergovernmental system through which retraining must take place — state and local governments — is already too fragmented, decentralized, and political to allow for effective *implementation* of a government-sponsored program. Third, given these constraints, any realistic government-sponsored program would be small in scale; consequently, it would have little impact on the overall training and retraining needs of the country. These are real — not ideological or philosophical — constraints.

Despite its failures and limitations, government still has a major role to play in promoting training and retraining. For instance, it would be ideal if both government and the private sector provided new *incentives* to encourage more people to re-career by acquiring new skills and relocating to new jobs and communities. These incentives might include tax breaks for individuals engaged in retraining and for corporations sponsoring training programs. Another incentive, outlined by Choate and Epstein, would be to create Individual Training Accounts (ITA), structured similarly to a pension fund. Jointly financed by employers and employees, the innovative ITA would provide money for retraining displaced workers. The individual could use this money — perhaps in the form of a retraining voucher — to enroll in a specialized program of his or her own choosing. The problem of *how to finance retraining* will have to be addressed with these and other public policy options in the not-too-distant future.

The problem with most government policies and programs is that they are inevitably political. They are controversial, reflecting competing values in American society. They take time to develop and implement. And they often fail. In the meantime, individuals must be responsible for their own employment fate by taking appropriate actions to solve their own employment and career problems. Government is not likely to solve these problems.

The old cliche that "there is no such thing as a free lunch" should be reinforced with a new saying for the coming re-careering era: "Times will be tough for those who don't get off their duff!" At the very least, re-careering requires individuals to:

- take risks
- invest time and money in their future
- learn something new and usable
- apply new skills to changing employment situations

TRAIN AND RETRAIN
FOR AN UNCERTAIN FUTURE

Retraining needs in the decade ahead are difficult to estimate. Indeed, conducting a survey on the present state of training is difficult, if not impossible, given the fragmented nature of organizations in America. Nonetheless, certain trends are evident in the workplace, and some statistics are available on the scope and depth of training in the United States. For example, during the past 30 years, blue-collar employment has steadily declined to the point where the traditional distinction between blue-collar and white-collar workers has become somewhat meaningless for describing critical characteristics of the labor force.

Changes have been evident during the past decade, and they will likely accelerate in the decade ahead. For example, Bluestone and Harrison (*The Decentralization of America*) found that between 35 and 40 million Americans lost their jobs in the 1970s; many were forced to relocate as plants closed and industries moved South. The U.S. Department of Labor found that 11.5 million Americans lost their jobs between 1979 and 1984 due to plant shut downs or relocation, rising productivity, and shrinking output. A study by Carnegie-Mellon University predicts that robots will supplant 3 million factory workers by the year 2000. Many factories may be completely automated — requiring only a handful of technicians to supervise the robots. In fact, the Japanese have already completed the first totally automated factory.

Where will the displaced workers of today and tomorrow go? The fear — justifiably so — is that many workers will be permanently displaced by the new technology. For example, Harvard University economist James L. Medoff points to Commerce Department statistics; between 1969 and 1978 job-related training provided by employers for workers aged 25 to 49 increased 6 percent from 5.2 percent. A further indication of a growing skills imbalance in the labor market since 1969 is found in Medoff's study of unemployment. Prior to 1969, when unemployment increased among 25 to 64 year-old men, the number of help-wanted ads declined as employers hired from the excess pool of skilled unemployed workers. However, since 1969 the number of help-wanted ads has not declined proportionately during a period of high unemployment. Medoff believes this indicates there is now a decreasing demand for the skills of present unemployed workers, a clear sign of worsening structural unemployment.

On the other hand, the emphasis on productivity and the introduction of new technology promise to create new jobs and career opportunities. Many people hope these changes will create a sufficient number of new jobs to absorb displaced workers and that employers will retrain them for the new technology.

Both the fear and the hope will probably come true, but for different groups in the society. The fears are indeed real. For example, at present 21 million Americans are estimated to be functionally illiterate — they can't read or write. Add to this number the fact that nearly 1 million students drop out of high school each year, and the U.S. Department of Education Secretary's warning to Congress: "up to 75 percent of the unemployed lack the basic skills of communication, personal relations, motivation, self-confidence, reading and computing that would enable employers to train them for the jobs that will open up in the next few years." Therefore, a large segment of the population will require remedial training *prior to* receiving job skills training.

For poor inner city and rural people, the consequences of productivity improvements and the introduction of new technology in the workplace are frightening. Many of these people may become hopeless wards of the state, ill-equipped to function in a highly literate and efficient information society. Facing a vicious circle of circumstances which prevent them from taking initiative, they will constitute a major problem for society. In the end, government may be the only institution willing and able to provide basic training in functional skills for these individuals.

The worldwide problem of unemployment is even more frightening. Third World nations, with nearly 500 million unemployed at present, are expected to have nearly 1 billion unemployed in the year 2000. Twice this number are underemployed — performing jobs at low productivity and skill levels. Not surprising, jobs are increasingly becoming the top priority problem for all nations.

QUESTION PUBLIC EDUCATION PERFORMANCE

Public educational institutions have been slow in responding to the obvious training and retraining needs of employers. Despite billions of dollars expended on university education, the quality of reading, writing, and communication skills, as well as analytical and problem-solving abilities, seems to be declining compared to previous generations of graduates. The critical high-tech programs of engineering and computer science are not producing enough graduates to meet the demands of private industry. The result is a mismatch of college and university educational programs with the employment needs of companies.

Colleges and universities continue to graduate students in fields where there are few job opportunities. For example, while most college graduates in the 1960s found jobs in their chosen occupations, more graduates in the 1970s and 1980s were forced to seek employment outside their fields.

The transition for public education will be slow and difficult. Many public schools are too tradition-laden as well as insulated from the realities of the labor market to place a major emphasis on vocational-skills training within their academic programs. Lacking accountability, many public colleges and universities continue to teach a disproportionate number of subjects, courses, and disciplines which are favorites of the faculty, simply considered necessary for a "well-rounded" graduate, or at best "interesting" rather than emphasize skills for a turbulent job market.

On the other hand, community colleges, business colleges, vocational-technical schools, specialized training institutes, and university-sponsored conferences and workshops have been more responsive to training individuals in relation to job market needs. Many of these institutions provide practical, intensive skills training programs as well as placement services for their graduates. Over 25 million people participate in these programs each year.

KNOW MORE ABOUT PRIVATE EFFORTS

If public educational institutions fail to respond to real needs, the private sector will have to provide the bulk of the training and retraining necessary for the decades ahead. More private educational and professional training organizations will be required to provide short two to five-day workshops, four-week refresher courses, or 15-week intensive training programs.

The private sector is equipped to provide training alternatives. Thousands of private organizations already provide off-the-shelf, custom-designed, and generic training seminars. Most of these programs last one to five days and stress intensive training in particular subject and skill areas.

A few companies are preparing for the future with their own in-house training programs. For example, Ford Motor Company and the United Auto Workers work with a nationwide network of community colleges in providing retraining for displaced automakers. Polaroid Corporation conducts reading labs and math tutorials for assembly line workers in order to prepare them for new technology in the workplace. AT&T maintains the largest number of in-house trainers for a trainer-to-employee ratio of 1:100. The U.S. Navy maintains the highest train-to-employee ratio: 26,000 full-time trainers for 565,000 enlisted personnel or a 1:21 ratio. Altogether, the private sector spends over $200 billion a year on training and retraining. This figure is likely to increase as the skills required in the workplace change in response to the changing technology.

Most training takes place within organizations as either on-the-job or classroom training. Most firms with 500 or more employees have at least one full-time trainer in their organization; many of these organizations also have training departments. Organizations with more than 25,000 employees have an average of 50 full-time trainers. Organizations with 100 or fewer employees normally use part-time trainers or contract with private firms to conduct specific training programs for their employees.

While billions of dollars are spent each year on training and education, neither the public nor private sectors are adequately meeting the new retraining needs of society. From the perspective of training professionals, we are rapidly approaching a "human capital crisis."

BECOME A GENERALIST-SPECIALIST

As we noted earlier, individuals must take the initiative to acquire the training and retraining necessary for a turbulent job market. No longer will knowledge of job hunting techniques alone be sufficient to function in such a job market. Specific work-content skills — mostly technical in nature — must accompany well-defined job search strategies. And promising trends have begun. For example, each year over 3 million Americans enroll in courses specifically designed to help them change careers.

So where do you go for skills training in a highly fragmented, decentralized, and chaotic educational and training market? While many organizations provide their own in-service training and retraining programs, they assume one possesses a certain level of skill proficiency prior to being hired. In other words, they expect the employee is easily *trainable*. For many jobs, this means one needs a well-rounded educational background which develops basic reading, writing, and communication skills as well as interpersonal, analytical, organizational, and problem-solving abilities — the major thrust of a good generalist liberal arts education. Given the changing nature of the job market, such an educational background can best prepare you for the flexibility you will need in the future.

At the same time, while providing a good foundation, a generalist background is insufficient for functioning in today's job market. Individuals need a strong background in scientific-technical skills. These skills are in math, science, computers, and technical fields. In addition, individuals are expected to have developed basic work attitudes which translate into positive behaviors such as: coming to work, being on time, managing time, meeting deadlines, getting along with superiors and co-workers, and being courteous to the public.

The changing job market requires more generalist-specialists who are trainable and thus can adapt to rapidly changing workplaces. For example, it is estimated that 40 million office workers will be using some type of electronic equipment in the 1990s — an increase of 30 million from the 1980s. Given the rapidly changing office technologies, employers may need to retrain the same workers five to ten times during a 20 year period. Therefore, regardless of what type of word processor an individual is trained on in a secretarial school today, the same individual can expect to operate one of a new generation of word processors five years from now. The important question for employers will be: *"Is this individual, who is now a specialist in technology X, flexible enough to learn and adapt to technology Y tomorrow?"* The answers require a merging of the generalist and specialist traditions in individuals' educational and training programs.

IDENTIFY YOUR MAJOR TRAINING OPTIONS

The Department of Labor identifies nine structured training programs individuals should familiarize themselves with prior to making educational and training choices. Most of these sources emphasize practical hands-on training in specific occupational fields. Private trade schools, for example, are flourishing at a time when university enrollments are stagnant and declining — an indication of the shift to practical skills training in education.

1.   Public vocational education

Public vocational education is provided through secondary, postsecondary, and adult vocational and technical programs. The emphasis in many secondary schools is to give high school students vocational training in addition to the regular academic program. Postsecondary vocational education is provided for individuals who have left high school but who are not seeking a baccalaureate degree.

Adult vocational and technical programs emphasize retraining or upgrading the skills of individuals in the labor force. The traditional agricultural, trade, and industrial emphasis of vocational education has been vastly expanded to include training in distribution, health, home economics, office, and technical occupations. Most programs train individuals for specific occupations, which are outlined in the *Occupational Outlook Handbook*. Each year over 20 million people enroll in public vocational education programs.

2. **Noncollegiate postsecondary vocational education**

Nearly 2 million people enroll in over 6,500 noncollegiate postsecondary schools with occupational programs each year. Most of these schools specialize in one of eight vocational areas: cosmetology/barber, business/commercial, trade, hospital, vocational/technical, allied health, arts/design, and technical. They offer programs in seven major areas: agribusiness, marketing and distribution, health, home economics, technical, business and office, and trade and industrial. Over 75 percent of these schools are proprietary institutions. And over 70 percent of the proprietary schools are either cosmetology/barber schools or business/commercial schools. Over 75 percent of the independent nonprofit schools are hospital schools. Over 1 million people complete occupational programs in noncollegiate postsecondary schools each year.

3. **Employer training**

Employer training usually involves training new employees, improving employee performance, or preparing employees for new jobs. Skilled and semi-skilled workers are trained through apprenticeships, learning by doing, and structured on-the-job instruction. Structured classroom training is increasingly offered to skilled workers by in-house trainers, professional associations, private firms, or colleges and universities. Tuition-aid programs are used frequently among firms lacking in-house training capabilities.

4. **Apprenticeship programs**

Apprenticeship programs normally range from one to six

years, depending on the particular trade and organization. These programs are used most extensively in the trade occupations, especially in construction and metalworking. They involve planned on-the-job training in conjunction with classroom instruction and supervision. Over 500,000 individuals are involved in apprenticeship programs each year.

5. **Federal employment and training programs**

Federal employment and training programs largely function through state and local governments. The major federal program is the Job Training Partnership Act (JTPA) program. Working through Private Industry Councils (PIC's), the JTPA program is designed to train the economically disadvantaged as well as displaced workers who need assistance with skills training, job search, and job relocation. JTPA also operates two youth programs — The Job Corps and the Summer Youth Employment Program. Other major federal programs include two administered through the Employment and Training Administration: The Trade Adjustment Act program to assist workers displaced by foreign competition, and the Work Incentive (WIN) program for employable recipients of Aid to Families with Dependent Children, migrant and seasonal farm workers, Native Americans, and workers 55 and over.

6. **Armed Forces training**

The Armed Forces provides training in numerous occupational skills that may or may not be directly transferred to civilian occupations. Thousands of military recruits complete training programs in several transferable areas each year, such as computer repair, medical care, food service, metalworking, communications, and administration. Occupations unique to the military, such as infantry and guncrew, are less transferable to civilian occupations.

7. **Home study (correspondence) schools**

Home study or correspondence schools provide a variety of training options. Most programs concentrate on acquiring a single skill; others may even offer a BA, MA, or Ph.D. by mail! Some programs are of questionable quality while others may be revolutionizing the education and training landscape of America. For many people, this is a convenient, inexpensive, and effective way to acquire new skills. Over five million people enroll in home study courses each year. Colleges and universities are quickly moving into the home study business by offering numerous televised courses for academic credit. The Public Broadcast System (PBS) offers several home study courses through its Adult Learning Service: computer literacy and applications, basic skills and personal enrichment, sales and customer service, effective communication skills, and management skills.

8.   **Community and junior colleges**

Community and junior colleges in recent years have broadened their missions from primarily preparing individuals for university degree programs to preparing them with skills for the job market. Accordingly, more of their programs emphasize vocational and occupational curriculums, such as data processing or dental hygiene, which are typically two-year programs resulting in an associate degree. Community and junior colleges will probably continue to expand their program offerings as they further adjust to the employment needs of communities. Nearly 5 million students enroll in community and junior college programs each year.

9.   **Colleges and universities**

Colleges and universities continue to provide the traditional four-year and graduate degree programs in various subject fields. While many of the fields are occupational-specific, such as engineering, law, medicine, and business, many other fields are not. The exact relationship of the degree program to the job market varies with different disciplines. As noted earlier, in recent years graduates of many programs have had difficulty finding employment in their chosen fields. This is particularly true for students who only have a generalist background in the liberal arts. During the past decade many colleges and universities have adjusted to declining enrollments by offering several non-traditional occupational-related courses and programs. Continuing education, special skills training courses, short courses, evening course offerings, "telecourses", and work-shops and seminars on job-related matters have become popular with nontraditional, older students who seek specific skills training rather than degrees. At the same time, traditional academic programs are placing greater emphasis on internships and cooperative education pro-grams in order to give students work experience related to their academic programs.

Additional training programs may be sponsored by local govern-ments, professional associations, women's centers, YWCA's, and religious and civic groups. As training and retraining become more acceptable to the general public, we can expect different forms and types of training programs to be sponsored by various groups.

We also can expect a revolution in the training field, closely related to high-tech developments. Televised education and training courses should continue to increase in number and scope. Computer-based training, similar in some respects to traditional home study programs, will become more prevalent as computer software and interactive video training packages are developed in response to the new technology and the rising demand for skills training. Individuals in tomorrow's education and training markets will become examples of Toffler's "prosumer society": in a decentralized information market, individuals will choose what training they most desire as well as control when and where they will receive it. With the de-velopment of interactive video and computer training programs, individuals will manage the training process in a more efficient and effective manner than with the more centralized, time consuming, and expensive use of traditional student-teacher classroom instruc-tion. This type of training may eventually make many of the previ-ously discussed categories of education and training obsolete.

MAKE INFORMED CHOICES

Choosing a skills training program presupposes you know what you want to do. As we will see later, knowing what it is you want to do is the key to doing it. The fact that many organizations offer a multiplicity of training options gives you little comfort in choosing the specific training and retraining that are right for you.

Should you go to college to get a degree or go for a certificate program? Should you enroll in a public vocational school or the Armed Forces for skills training? What about a home study course or a two-year community college program? We cannot answer these questions for you. You must first know what it is you want to do. Perhaps you don't need to enter a structured program after all. Maybe you first need to get a job, based on your present work-content skills, and then take advantage of training opportunities provided by the employer.

Whatever you do, you must engage in some soul searching about yourself. Start by taking an inventory of your present skills, as discussed in Chapter Six. What, for example, do you do well and enjoy doing? Next, find out what you would like to do with the rest of your life, as outlined in Chapter Seven. Moreover, what is it you would like to do but you don't have sufficient skills to do? Chart a course of action for career building, however vague, and begin filling in the blanks by doing the research we specify in Chapter Nine. Once you have answered these questions, you should be ready to research your educational and training options.

You should begin your search for useful education and training information by consulting publications on these subjects. The major sources will be found in the reference section of libraries as well as in guidance offices and career planning centers of schools, colleges, universities, and specialized employment assistance centers. Most of these organizations maintain catalogues, directories, and files listing educational and training opportunities.

Two useful sources for information on education and training programs are *Peterson's Guides* and *Barron's Educational Series* which publish several excellent directories. Most of the directories are updated annually and include basic information on choosing programs and institutions best suited to your interests. Among the many titles offered by Peterson's and Barron's are:

- *Guide to Four-Year Colleges*
- *Guide to Two-Year Colleges*
- *The College Money Handbook*
- *Guides to Graduate Study:*
  - *Graduate and Professional Programs*
  - *Humanities and Social Sciences*
  - *Biological Agricultural and Health Sciences*
  - *Physical Sciences and Mathematics*
  - *Engineering and Applied Sciences*
- *Regional Guides to Colleges:*
  - *Middle Atlantic*
  - *Midwest*
  - *New England*
  - *New York*
  - *Southeast*

　　　　　　— Southwest
　　　　　　— West
- *Winning Money for College*
- *How to Write Your Way into College*
- *Engineering, Science, and Computer Jobs*
- *Business and Management Jobs*
- *Guide to Medical and Dental Schools*
- *How to Prepare for the SAT*
- *Guide to Law Schools*
- *Profiles of American Colleges*
- *Guide to Graduate Business Schools*
- *Applying to Colleges and Universities in the United States*
- *Applying to Graduate School in the United States*
- *Competitive Colleges*
- *Colleges with Programs for Learning-Disabled Students*
- *National College Databank*
- *Handbook for College Admissions*
- *Guide to College Admissions*
- *How the Military Will Help You Pay for College*
- *Corporate Tuition Aid Programs*
- *Graduate Education Directory*

Most major libraries have copies of these publications in their reference section. If you cannot find them in your local library, check with your local bookstore or contact the publishers directly: Peterson's Guides, P.O. Box 2123, Princeton, NJ 08543-2123, Tel. 609/924-5338; and Barron's Educational Series, 250 Wireless Blvd., Hauppauge, NY 11788, Tel. 516/434-3311.

　　　　Many professional and trade associations provide information on institutions providing training in particular fields. Look for copies of the *Encyclopedia of Associations* (Gale Publishers) and *National Trade and Professional Associations* (Columbia Books) — two excellent directories listing contact information for most such associations. You can find copies of these two directories in the reference section of most libraries. The *National Trade and Professional Associations* directory also can be purchased from Impact Publications by completing the order form at the end of this book.

　　　　The U.S. Department of Labor's *Occupational Outlook Handbook* also lists useful names and addresses relating to employment training in specific fields. Consult the "Where to Go For More Information" section in the latest edition of this biannual directory. This book is also available in most libraries and can be purchased from Impact Publications by completing the order form at the end of this book.

If you are contemplating a program in business, for example, consult the *Directory of Educational Institutions* for a listing of schools accredited by the Association of Independent Colleges and Universities (AICS). Institutions accredited by AICS offer programs in secretarial sciences, business administration, accounting, data processing, court reporting, paralegal studies, fashion merchandising, culinary arts, drafting, electronics, and more. You can get a copy of the *Directory* by contacting: Association of Independent Colleges and Schools, 1 Dupont Circle NW, Suite 350, Washington, DC 20036, Tel. 202/659-2460.

For information on *private trade and technical schools*, contact the National Association of Trade and Technical Schools (NATTS). They produce three publications you may find useful: *Handbook of Accredited Private Trade and Technical Schools* and a series of pamphlets, including *How to Choose A Career and a Career School* Write or call NATTS for information on these publications: NATTS, 2251 Wisconsin Ave. NW, Washington, DC 20007, Tel. 202/333-1021.

For information on *apprenticeship programs*, contact the Bureau of Apprenticeship and Training (BAT), U.S. Department of Labor, 200 Constitution Ave. NW, Washington, DC 20210, Tel. 202/535-0545. BAT offices are also found in each state. To find if there is a BAT office near you, consult the White Pages of your telephone directory under "United States Government – Department of Labor". Your local library and public employment service office should also have information on apprenticeship programs. For women interested in apprenticeship opportunities, send a self-addressed mailing label to the Women's Bureau, U.S. Department of Labor (200 Constitution Ave. NW, Washington, DC 20210, Tel. 202/523-6631) to receive a free copy of their useful publication, *A Woman's Guide to Apprenticeship*.

If you are interested in *home study and correspondence courses*, contact the National Home Study Council (NHSC) for information on home study programs. NHSC distributes copies of a useful publication entitled *Directory of Accredited Home Student Programs*. For information on this and other NHSC publications, contact: National Home Study Council, 1601 18th St. NW, Washington, DC 20009, Tel. 202/234-5100.

In addition to familiarizing yourself with these options, you need to determine the quality of the programs and their suitability to your needs. When contacting a particular institution, ask to speak to former students and graduates, and write to the Council on Post-secondary Accreditation (One Dupont Circle, Suite 760, Washington, DC 20036) to inquire about the school's credentials. Focus your attention on the *results* or *outcomes* the institution achieves. Instead of asking how many faculty have MA or Ph.D. degrees, or how many students are enrolled, ask:

- What happened to last year's graduates?
- Where do they work?
- How much do they earn?
- How many were placed in jobs through this institution?

Institutions that can answer these questions focus on **performance**. Beware of those that can't answer these questions, for they may not be doing an adequate job to meet your needs.

Most colleges and universities will provide assistance to adult learners. Contact student services, continuing education, academic advising, adult services, or women's offices at your local community college, college, or university. Be sure to talk to present and former students about the **expectations and results** of the programs for them. Always remember that educators are first in the business of keeping themselves employed and, second, in the business of delivering educational services. And today, more than ever, educational institutions need students to keep their programs alive. Don't necessarily expect professional educators to be objective about your future vis-a-vis their interests, skills, and programs. At the very least, you must do a critical evaluation of their programs and services.

If you need further assistance, contact a local branch of the National Center for Educational Brokering. While there is no national clearinghouse to help you match your goals with appropriate educational programs, NCEB can assist you nonetheless. NCEB counselors will help you identify your goals and career alternatives. For information on the center nearest you, write to the National Center for Educational Brokering, 329 9th St., San Francisco, CA 94103, Tel. 415/626-2378.

Other useful sources of information on education and training programs are your telephone book and employers. Look under "Schools" in the Yellow Pages of your telephone directory. Call the schools and ask them to send you literature and application forms and discuss the relevance of their programs to the job market. You should also talk to employers and individuals who have work experience in the field that interests you. Ask them how best to acquire the necessary skills for particular occupations. Most important, *thoroughly research education and training alternatives before you invest any money, time, or effort*.

KNOW HOW TO FINANCE YOUR FUTURE

Most people can take advantage of training opportunities in order to better function in today's job market. Lack of information and money are often excuses based upon ignorance of available resources and costs. Education and training may not be cheap, but neither need they be excessively expensive. It is best to view education and training as good investments in your future.

You will find many alternatives to expensive training. For example, adult education programs sponsored by the public school system as well as community colleges are relatively inexpensive to attend. If you have the will, you usually can find the way in the American education and training systems.

Financial aid for education and training is somewhat bewildering and confusing. It requires research and perseverance on your part. You should begin by contacting the financial aid officers at various institutions that offer the training you desire for advice on financial aid. The particular institutions as well as many other organizations provide scholarships, fellowships, grants, loans, and work-study programs. The American Legion, for example, publishes a useful booklet — *Need a Lift?* — on careers and scholarships for undergraduate and graduate students. To get a copy, send $1.00, which also covers postage, to: American Legion, ATTN: Need a Lift?, P.O.Box 1050, Indianapolis, IN 46206. The College Board also publishes information on student aid. Among its many publications is its annual *Meeting College Costs*. For information on this and other College Board publications, contact: College Board Publications, Box 886, New York, NY 10101.

Information on federal government financial aid programs — grants, loans, work-study, and benefits — can be obtained by writing to the U.S. Department of Education for a pamphlet entitled *The Student Guide to Federal Financial Aid Programs*. Revised yearly, this publication can be obtained by calling or writing to: Federal Student Aid Programs, P.O. Box 84, Washington, DC, Tel. 301/984-4070.

For information on financial assistance for specific groups, such as Hispanics, blacks, Native Americans, and women, get a copy of the U.S. Department of Education's *Higher Educational Opportunities for Minorities and Women* (Superintendent of Documents, U.S. Government Printing Office, Washington, DC 20402, Tel. 202/783-3238 for order information). You should also consider examining several useful books relevant to minorities and women which are published by Garrett Park Press:

- *Directory of Special Programs for Minority Group Members: Career Information Services, Employment Skills Banks, Financial Aid Sources*, Willis L. Johnson (ed.)

- *Financial Aid for Minority Students* (a series of booklets on Allied Health, Business, Education, Engineering, Law, Journalism/Communications, Medicine, Science), Ruth V. Swann (ed.)

- *Minority Organizations: A National Directory*, Katherine W. Cole (ed.)

- *Directory of Special Opportunities for Women*, Martha Merrill Doss (ed.)

- *Women's Organizations: A National Directory*, Martha Merrill Doss

These books can be ordered directly from Impact Publications by completing the order information at the end of this book.

COMPARE COST AND PERFORMANCE OPTIONS

Don't forget to compare the different costs of various educational and training programs. Many are inexpensive whereas others are extremely costly. Keep in mind that there is no necessary correlation between educational costs and performance; you may well get your best performance at the lowest cost and the worst performance at the highest cost — and vice versa. Indeed, one of the major characteristics of the American education and training system is the variety of *options* it offers individuals. These include different choices in terms of programs, quality, costs, and expected outcomes. Therefore, you must do your research in order to identify your options and make informed choices.

BEWARE OF MYTHS

Let us emphasize once again the importance of being an *informed consumer* in today's education and training markets. Beware of education and training myths. Remember, education is a big $300 billion a year business. Exhibiting a great deal of inertia, few educational institutions are prepared to describe their performance in relation to today's job market. At best, educational institutions are most adept at keeping their businesses well and alive through the marketing of degree programs to relatively uninformed, accepting consumers.

Contrary to what educators may tell you, *additional education and training may not be necessary for entering or advancing within today's job market*. But it is a good investment for the job markets of tomorrow. To determine if you need additional education and training, you should first learn what it is you do well and enjoy doing (through self-assessment) and then identify what it is you need to do to get what you want (through research). Education and training may be only one of several things you need to do. You may, for example, determine that you need to change your behavior by setting goals, becoming more focused on achieving results, and improving your dress and appearance. Or you may need to develop effective job search skills as well as relocate to a new community. Indeed, employers spend more than $200 billion each year on employee training and retraining — much of which is spent because of the failure of traditional educational institutions.

You may learn it is best to find an apprenticeship program or get into a particular organization that provides excellent training for its employees. Such training will be both up-to-date and relevant to the job market. Most of the best run corporations rely on their own in-house training rather than on institutions outside the corporation. When making hiring decisions, such organizations are more concerned about your ability to learn, acquire new skills, and grow within the organization than with the specific work-content skills you initially bring to the job — our basic careering and re-careering concerns for the 1990s!

Chapter Five

UNDERSTAND PROCESSES FOR SUCCESS

Making future occupational projections and knowing "what" jobs are available and "where" to find them in society as a whole tells you little about the critical "how" to find a job in your particular situation. Answers to general "what" and "where" questions may be interesting in describing and explaining reality, but they may or may not be useful in developing specific strategies for taking action. If you are to be effective in the job markets of the 1990s, you must link the "how" to the "what" and "where". At the very least, you must plan and organize specific activities in relation to your future goals.

IDENTIFY THE PREREQUISITES TO SUCCESS

Achieving job and career success in the 1990s will depend on how well you understand and implement key *processes* for planning your future. Directly related to on-going job market realities, these processes constitute a set of how-to strategies for developing an effective job search, managing time, organizing specific job search activities, and achieving success. Examined separately, they are important prerequisites for developing effective careering and re-careering skills. Taken together, they constitute a well-organized framework for achieving successful careering and re-careering for the 1990s.

This chapter relates our previous overview of careering and re-careering to the practical aspects of planning and implementing an effective job search. Here we examine the basic *prerequisites* for launching a successful job search. Each constitutes a skill that you can learn and apply with success:

- Understand job market realities
- Develop a well-organized job search
- Identify your careering and re-careering competencies
- Seek assistance when necessary
- Manage your time
- Organize a plan of action
- Follow principles for achieving success
- Take risks
- Handle rejections
- Form a support group

Above all, you must *organize and implement* to achieve success. You must translate your understanding of problems, approaches, and solutions into concrete action steps for achieving results.

UNDERSTAND JOB MARKET MYTHS AND REALITIES

What do you know about the job market? Is it a place that has jobs for you? How will you approach it? What do you do when you get there? Whom do you talk to? What do you say?

The notion of "a job market" generates several images of structures, processes, and outcomes. In one sense it appears to be well structured for dispensing job information and assistance. After all, you will find various elements that supposedly make up the structure of the job market: classified ads listing job vacancies; personnel offices with vacancy announcements; employment agencies linking candidates to job openings; and a variety of helpers known as career counselors, employment specialists, and headhunters who make a living by serving as gatekeepers to a "job market." At the same time, we know various processes are key to making this job market function: self-assessment, applications, resume and letter writing, networking, interviewing, negotiating, and hiring.

Understanding the job market is like the blind person exploring an elephant: you may recognize a trunk, a leg, and a tail, but you're not sure what it is as a whole. As we will see shortly, the job market is anything but organized, centralized, and coherent. It is more an abstraction, or convenient short-hand way of talking about finding jobs, than a set of well defined and related structures.

Most people have an image of how the job market works as well as how they should relate to it. This image is based upon a combination of facts, stereotypes, and myths learned from experience and from the advice of well-meaning individuals. It's an unfortunate image when it guides people into unproductive job search channels by advising them to spend most of their time responding to vacancy announcements and waiting to hear from employers. In so doing, it reconfirms the often-heard lament of the unsuccessful job searcher — *"What more can I do — there are no jobs out there for me."*

Let's examine ten myths about jobs, careers, and the job search before you proceed to organize yourself for today's and tomorrow's employment realities. These myths illustrate important points for organizing your job search:

MYTH 1:   **Anyone can find a job; all you need to know is how to find a job.**

REALITY: This is the "form versus substance" myth developed and perpetuated by some career counselors as well as leading career writers during the past two decades. They have been more concerned with promoting a job search philosophy which emphasizes process skills than with urging more job generation, the development of job content skills, and relocation. It reflects a disturbing preference for style and image rather than substance and performance in the workplace. This myth was most likely a reality in an industrial society with low unemployment — the 1950s and 1960s — or in certain high turnover service sectors requiring low level skills — the 1980s. But it is a myth for the post-industrial, high-tech society of the 1990s. In a society that requires more and more highly skilled labor, knowing how to find a job is not enough to get a good job. Getting a job in such a society also requires that (1) jobs be available (job generation), (2) individuals have the proper mix of skills to perform those jobs (work-content skills), and (3) individuals be willing to go where the jobs are located (relocation). While it is extremely important to learn job search skills, these skills are no substitute for concrete work-content skills, job generation, and relocation.

MYTH 2: The best way to find a job is to respond to classified ads, use employment agencies, submit applications, and mail resumes and cover letters to personnel offices.

REALITY: This is one of the most serious myths preventing many individuals from finding a good job. Many people do get jobs by following such formalized application and recruitment procedures. However, these are not the best ways to get the best jobs — those offering good pay, advancement opportunities, and an appropriate "fit" with one's abilities, goals, and values. This approach makes two questionable assumptions about the structure of the job market and how you should relate to it. The first assumption deals with how the job market does or should operate:

> **Assumption #1:** There is an organized, coherent, and centralized job market "out there" where one can go to get information on available job vacancies.

In reality no such market exists. It is a highly decentralized, fragmented, and chaotic job market where job vacancy information is at best incomplete, skewed, and unrepresentative of available job opportunities at any particular moment. Classified ads, agencies, and personnel offices tend to list low paying yet highly competitive jobs. Most of the best jobs — high level, excellent pay, least competitive — are neither listed nor advertised; they are uncovered through word-of-mouth. When seeking employment, your most fruitful strategy will be to conduct research and informational interviews on what is called the "hidden job market" — a loosely structured network which informally exchanges job vacancy and hiring information.

The second assumption deals with how you should relate to this job market:

> **Assumption #2:** You should try to fit your goals and abilities into existing vacancies

rather than find a job designed around your
strengths.

This may be a formula for future job unhappiness.
If you want to find a job fit for you rather than
try to fit yourself into a job, you must use another
job search strategy based upon a different set of
assumptions regarding how you should relate your
goals and abilities to the world of work.

MYTH 3: **In a tight job market with high unemployment,
few jobs are available for me.**

REALITY: This may be true if the entire economy is in a
depression, you lack marketable skills, or you in-
sist on applying for jobs only listed in newspapers,
employment agencies, or personnel offices. Competition in the advertised job market increases
during periods of high unemployment, but mainly
for jobs requiring few skills. Many jobs will be
available on the hidden job market during hard
times. Many jobs requiring advanced technical
skills, for example, may go begging during such
times. There may be less competition for many
jobs during a high unemployment period because
many people become discouraged and quit job
hunting after a few weeks of disappointing efforts
to find work through the advertised job market.

MYTH 4: **I know how to find a job but opportunities are not
available for me.**

REALITY: Most people don't know how to best find a job,
they lack marketable work-content skills to communicate their value to employers, or they look in
the wrong places where jobs are not being generated. They continue to use the most ineffective
methods — responding to job listings, sending
resumes, and contacting employment agencies.
Opportunities are readily available for those who
understand the structure and operation of the job
market, have appropriate work-content skills, are
willing to relocate, and use job search methods
designed for the hidden job market.

MYTH 5: **Employers are in the driver's seat; they have the upper hand with applicants.**

REALITY: Employers often do not know what they want and they make numerous hiring mistakes. Their problems begin from the very moment they decide to hire someone. Few employers know what the job entails, many write weak job descriptions, and few know how to properly interview and evaluate candidates. Many employers are notorious for making poor hiring decisions! Unclear as to what they want, they instead let applicants define their hiring needs. The candidate who gets the job is likely to be someone who makes the employer "feel good" rather than has a perfect job-skill fit. If you can help employers define their needs as being your skills, talents, and personality, you should end up in the driver's seat.

MYTH 6: **Employers hire the best qualified candidates — those with the most education, skills, and experience. Without a great deal of experience and numerous qualifications, I don't have a chance.**

REALITY: Employers hire individuals for many different reasons. Education, skills, and experience — major information categories appearing on application forms and resumes — are only a few of several hiring criteria. Employers seldom hire the best qualified individual because "qualifications" are difficult to measure. Employers normally seek competent, intelligent, honest, and likeable individuals — qualities that cannot be communicated effectively on application forms and resumes. Moreover, education, skills, and experience may not be the most important hiring criteria in the eyes of many employers. If, for example, employers only hired on the basis of education, skills, and experience, they would not need to interview candidates. Such static information is available in applications and resumes. Employers interview because they want to see a warm body — how you look and interact with them and how you will fit into their organization. They can get other information from additional sources. Indeed, the most important reason for hiring you is that the employer "likes" you. How "likes" is defined will vary from one employer and organization to another. In some cases the employer "likes" you because of your educational background, demonstrated skills, and experience. In other cases, the employer "likes" you because of your style and personality as well as a gut feeling that you are the right person for the job. The employer will determine or confirm these feelings in the actual job interview. So be prepared in the interview to communicate a great deal of information about yourself other than what the employer already knows — your education, skills, and experience. By all means communicate your *future value* to employers. You must learn how to overcome employers' objections to any lack of experience or qualifications. In the end, the best qualified person is the one who knows how to get the job — convince employers they will *like* him or her the most.

MYTH 7: **It is best to go into a growing field where jobs are plentiful.**

REALITY: It depends on several factors. First, so-called growth fields can quickly become no-growth fields, such as aerospace engineering and nuclear energy. Second, by the time you acquire the necessary skills for entering a growth field, you may experience the "disappearing job" phenomenon: too many people did the same thing you did at the same time. Third, since many people may be leaving a no-growth field, you may see new opportunities arising for you. Fourth, going after a growth field is another way of trying to fit into a job rather than find one that is fit for you. You should first find out what it is you do well and enjoy doing (Chapter Six), what additional training you may need, and then find a job or career which is conducive to your skills and interests. You will be better off in the long run if you go after what *you* want to do.

MYTH 8:   **People over 40 have difficulty finding a good job.**

REALITY: Yes, if they apply for youth jobs. If they conduct a well organized job search, they should find their age no barrier to employment. The major problem will be the time involved in landing a new job. The job search of experienced individuals may take longer because they are more selective in the types of jobs they wish to pursue. Employers want experience, maturity, and stability. People over 40 have these qualities. But they must clearly communicate these qualities to employers rather than dwell upon their age. In fact, as the population continues to age and birth rates decline, it should become easier for older individuals to change jobs and careers if they are willing to re-career.

MYTH 9:   **You should not change jobs and careers more than once or twice; job-hoppers are discriminated against in hiring.**

REALITY: While this may have been true 30 years ago, it is not true today. America is a skills-based society where individuals market their skills to different organizations in exchange for money. Most organizations are small businesses with limited advancement opportunities. In such a society, often the only way to advance your career is to change jobs frequently. Job-hopping is okay as long as you don't make a bad habit of it. Most individuals entering the job market today will undergo several job and career changes during their lifetime.

MYTH 10:   **You can plan all you want, but getting a job is really a function of good luck.**

REALITY: Luck is a function of being in the right place at the right time to take advantage of opportunities that come your way. Therefore, the best way to have luck come your way in a job search is to plan to be in many different places at many different times. You can do this by putting together an excellent resume and network with it in both the advertised and hidden job markets. If you are persistent in implementing your plans, luck may strike you many times!

You also should be aware of several other realities which will affect your job search or which you might find helpful in developing your plan of action for finding a job or changing a career:

ADDITIONAL REALITIES

- **You will find less competition for high-level jobs than for middle and low-level jobs.** If you aim high yet are realistic, you may be pleasantly surprised with the results.

- **Personnel offices seldom hire.** They primarily screen candidates for employers who are found in operating units of organizations. Knowing this, you should focus your job search efforts on those who do the actual hiring.

- **Politics are both ubiquitous and dangerous in many organizations.** If you think you are above politics, you may quickly become one of its victims. Unfortunately, you only learn about "local politics" *after* you accept a position and begin relating to the different players in the organization.

- **It is best to narrow or "rifle" your job search** on particular organizations and individuals rather than broaden or "shotgun" it to many alternatives. If you remain focused, you will be better able to accomplish your goals.

- **Employment firms and personnel agencies may not help you.** Most work for employers and themselves rather than for applicants. Few have your best interests at heart. Use them only after you have investigated their effectiveness. Avoid firms that require up-front money for a promise of performance.

- **Most people can make satisfying job and career changes.** They should minimize efforts in the advertised job market and concentrate instead on planning and implementing a well organized job search tailored to the

---

realities of the hidden job market.

- **Jobs and careers tend to be fluid and changing.** Knowing this, you should concentrate on acquiring and marketing skills, talents, and abilities which can be transferred from one job to another.

- **"Connections" or "pull" can be very effective in finding a job or changing careers.** You should use whatever "connections" and "pull" you have developed over the years and can mobilize to make a job or career change.

- **Millions of job vacancies are available every day** because new jobs are created every day, and people resign, retire, get fired, or die.

- **Most people, regardless of their position or status, love to talk about their work and give advice** to both friends and strangers. You can learn the most about job opportunities and alternative careers by talking to such people.

As you conduct your job search, you will encounter many of these and other myths and realities about how you should relate to the job market. Several people will give you advice. While much of this advice will be useful, a great deal of it will be useless and misleading. You should be skeptical of well-meaning individuals who most likely will reiterate the same job and career myths. You should be particularly leary of those who try to *sell* you their advice. Always remember you are entering a relatively disorganized and chaotic job market where you can find numerous job opportunities. Your task is to organize the chaos around your skills and interests. You must convince prospective employers that they will like you more than other "qualified" candidates.

FIND JOBS AND CHANGE CAREERS

If you are looking for your first job, reentering the job market after a lengthy absence, or planning a job or career change, you will join an army of millions of individuals who do so each year. Indeed, more than 15 million people find themselves unemployed each year.

Millions of others try to increase their satisfaction within the workplace as well as advance their careers by looking for alternative jobs and careers. If you are like most other Americans, you will make more than 10 job changes and between 3 and 5 career changes during your lifetime.

Most people make job or career transitions by accident. They do little other than take advantage of opportunities that may arise unexpectedly. While chance and luck do play important roles in finding employment, we recommend that you *plan* for future job and career changes so that you will experience even greater degrees of chance and luck!

Finding a job or changing a career in a systematic and well-planned manner is hard yet rewarding work. The task should first be based upon a clear understanding of the key ingredients that define jobs and careers. Starting with this understanding, you should next convert key concepts into action steps for implementing your job search.

A career is a series of related jobs which have common skill, interest, and motivational bases. You may change jobs several times without changing careers. But once you change skills, interests, and motivations, you change careers.

It's not easy to find a job given the present structure of the job market. You will find the job market to be relatively disorganized, although it projects an outward appearance of coherence. If you seek comprehensive, accurate, and timely job information, the job market will frustrate you with its poor communication. While you will find many employment services ready to assist you, such services tend to be fragmented and their performance is often disappointing. Job search methods are controversial and many are ineffective.

No system is organized to give people jobs. At best you will encounter a *decentralized and fragmented system* consisting of job listings in newspapers, trade journals, employment offices, or computerized job data banks — all designed to link potential candidates with available job openings. Many people will try to sell you job information as well as questionable job search services. While efforts are underway to create a nationwide computerized job bank which would list available job vacancies on a daily basis, don't expect such data to become available soon nor to be very useful. Many of the listed jobs may be nonexistent, at a low skill and salary level, or represent only a few employers. In the end, most of the systems organized to help you find a job do not provide you with the information you need in order to land a job that is most related to your skills and interests.

UNDERSTAND AND IMPLEMENT
CAREER DEVELOPMENT

Finding a job is both an art and a science; it encompasses a variety of basic facts, principles, and skills which can be learned but which also must be adapted to individual situations. Thus, *learning how to find a job* can be as important to career success as *knowing how to perform a job*. However, having marketable skills is essential to making job search strategies work effectively for you.

Our understanding of how to find jobs and change careers is illustrated on pages 95 and 96. As outlined on page 95, you should involve yourself in a four-step career development process as you prepare to move from one job to another.

FOUR STEP CAREER DEVELOPMENT PROCESS

1. **Conduct a self-assessment**

   This first step involves assessing your skills, abilities, motivations, interests, values, temperament, experience, and accomplishments. Your basic strategy is to develop a firm foundation of information about *yourself* before proceeding to other stages in the career development process. This self-assessment develops the necessary self-awareness upon which you can effectively communicate your qualifications to employers as well as focus and build your career.

2. **Gather career information**

   Closely related to the first step, this second step is an exploratory, research phase of your career development. Here you need to formulate goals, gather information about alternative jobs and careers through reading and talking to informed people, and then narrow your alternatives to specific job targets.

3. **Develop job search skills**

   The third step focuses your career around specific job search skills for landing the job you want. As further outlined on page 96, these job search skills are closely related to one another as a series of *job search steps*.

They involve conducting research, writing resumes and letters, prospecting and networking, conducting informational interviews, interviewing for a job, and negotiating salary and terms of employment. Each of these job search skills involves well-defined strategies and tactics you must learn in order to be effective in the job market.

4. **Implement each job search step**

The final career development step emphasizes the importance of transforming understanding into *action*. You do this by implementing each job search step which already incorporates the knowledge, skills, and abilities you acquired in Steps 1, 2, and 3.

ORGANIZE AND SEQUENCE YOUR JOB SEARCH

The figure on page 96 further expands our career development process by examining the key elements in a successful job search. Consisting of a seven-step process which relates your past, present, and future, each step is examined in a separate chapter of this book (Chapters Six to Twelve). Notice that *your past* is well integrated into the process of finding a job or changing your career. Therefore, you should feel comfortable conducting your job search: it represents the best of what you are in terms of your past and present accomplishments as these relate to your present and future goals. If you follow this type of job search, you will communicate your *best self* to employers.

Since the individual job search steps are interrelated, they should be followed in sequence. If you fail to properly complete the initial self-assessment steps, your job search may become haphazard, aimless, and costly. For example, you should never write a resume (Step 3) before first conducting an assessment of your skills (Step 1) and identifying your objective (Step 2). Relating Step 1 to Step 2 is especially critical to the successful implementation of all other job search steps. You *must* complete Steps 1 and 2 *before* continuing on to the other steps. Steps 3 to 6 can be conducted simultaneously because they complement and reinforce one another.

Try to sequence your job search as close to these steps as possible. The true value of this sequencing will become very apparent as you implement your plan.

THE CAREER DEVELOPMENT PROCESS

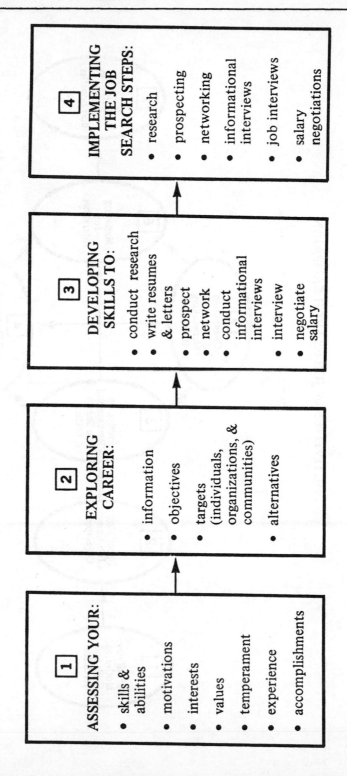

1 ASSESSING YOUR:

- skills & abilities
- motivations
- interests
- values
- temperament
- experience
- accomplishments

2 EXPLORING CAREER:

- information
- objectives
- targets (individuals, organizations, & communities)
- alternatives

3 DEVELOPING SKILLS TO:

- conduct research
- write resumes & letters
- prospect
- network
- conduct informational interviews
- interview
- negotiate salary

4 IMPLEMENTING THE JOB SEARCH STEPS:

- research
- prospecting
- networking
- informational interviews
- job interviews
- salary negotiations

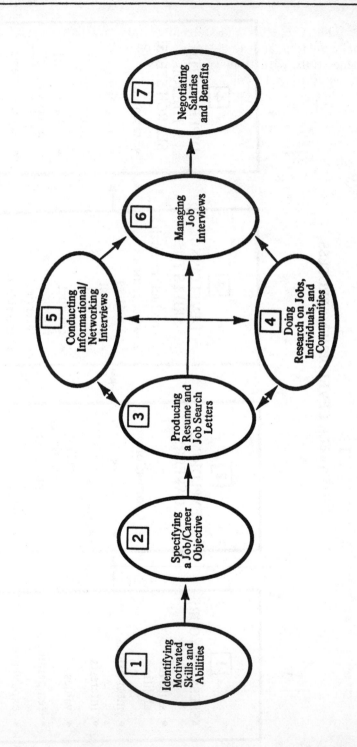

ACTIVITIES IN JOB SEARCH CAMPAIGN

1 Identifying Motivated Skills and Abilities

2 Specifying a Job/Career Objective

3 Producing a Resume and Job Search Letters

4 Doing Research on Jobs, Individuals, and Communities

5 Conducting Informational/ Networking Interviews

6 Managing Job Interviews

7 Negotiating Salaries and Benefits

The processes and steps identified on pages 95 and 96 represent the careering and re-careering processes we and others have used successfully with thousands of clients during the past 30 years. They are equally applicable as careering and re-careering processes for the 1990s as long as you recognize the importance of acquiring work-content skills along with job search skills. You must do much more than just know how to find a job. In the job markets of today and tomorrow, you need to constantly review your work-content skills to make sure they are appropriate for the changing job market. Once you have acquired the necessary skills through training and retraining, you will be ready to target your skills on particular jobs and careers that you do well and enjoy doing. You will be able to avoid the trap of trying to fit into jobs that are not conducive to your particular mix of skills, motivations, and abilities.

IDENTIFY YOUR CAREERING COMPETENCIES

Just how well prepared are you for planning and implementing an effective job search? Successful job seekers use a great deal of information and skills in getting the jobs they want. Test yourself to see what job search information and skills you currently possess and which ones you most need to concentrate upon improving. Identify your level of job search competence by responding to each of the statements that follow:

```
┌──── TESTING YOUR CAREERING COMPETENCIES ────┐

  SCALE:          1 = strongly agree
                  2 = agree
                  3 = maybe, not certain
                  4 = disagree
                  5 = strongly disagree

  1.  I know what skills I can offer employers in
      different occupations.                    1  2  3  4  5

  2.  I know what skills employers most seek in
      candidates.                               1  2  3  4  5

  3.  I can clearly explain to employers what
      I do well and enjoy doing.                1  2  3  4  5

  4.  I can specify why an employer should hire me.  1  2  3  4  5
```

5. I can gain support of family and friends for
   making a job or career change.   1 2 3 4 5

6. I can find 10 to 20 hours of time each week
   to conduct a part-time job search.   1 2 3 4 5

7. I have the financial ability to sustain a
   three-month job search.   1 2 3 4 5

8. I can conduct library and interview research
   on different occupations, employers
   organizations, and communities.   1 2 3 4 5

9. I can write different types of effective
   resumes, job search letters, and
   thank-you notes.   1 2 3 4 5

10. I can produce and distribute resumes and
    letters to the right people.   1 2 3 4 5

11. I can list my major accomplishments in
    action terms.   1 2 3 4 5

12. I can identify and target employers I
    want to interview.   1 2 3 4 5

13. I can develop a job referral network.   1 2 3 4 5

14. I can persuade others to join in forming
    a job search support group.   1 2 3 4 5

15. I can prospect for job leads.   1 2 3 4 5

16. I can use the telephone to develop
    prospects and get referrals and
    interviews.   1 2 3 4 5

17. I can plan and implement an
    effective direct-mail job search
    campaign.   1 2 3 4 5

18. I can generate one job interview for
    every 10 job search contacts I make.   1 2 3 4 5

19. I can follow up on job interviews.   1   2   3   4   5

20. I can negotiate a salary 10-20% above
what an employer initially offers.   1   2   3   4   5

21. I can persuade an employer to
renegotiate my salary after six
months on the job.   1   2   3   4   5

22. I can create a position for myself
in an organization.   1   2   3   4   5

Add the numbers you circled for a total composite score. If your total score is more than 60 points, you need to work on developing your careering skills. If you score under 40 points, you don't need this book!

The following chapters focus on developing these careering competencies in order to better prepare you for planning and implementing your own careering and re-careering campaign. By the time you finish this book, you should be able to score under 40 points on this exercise.

SEEK PROFESSIONAL HELP

The remaining chapters in this book are designed to be self-directed. If you use them as suggested, you should be able to organize and implement your own careering and re-careering plan. You need not pay someone to do this work for you.

However, we also are realistic. We know many people will purchase this book, read a few chapters, and do nothing. After a while they will seek professional assistance and pay good money to be told that they should do exactly what this book tells them to do. Some people need this type of expensive motivation.

At the same time, we recognize the value of professional assistance. Especially with the critical skills identification (Chapter Six) and objective setting (Chapter Seven) steps, some individuals may need more assistance than our advice and exercises can give them. If this is the case for you, by all means seek professional help.

But beware of the pitfalls in seeking such advice. There are excellent as well as useless and fraudulent services available. Career planning and job assistance are big businesses involving millions of dollars each year. Many people enter these businesses without expertise. Others major in their own problems — can't find a job so they become job-finding specialists. And still others are frauds and hucksters who will take your money in exchange for broken promises. You should know something about these professional services before you venture beyond this book.

If you look in the Yellow Pages of your telephone directory, you will find several career planning and employment services listed under the following headings: Management Consultants, Employment, Resumes, Career Planning, and Social Services. Some services help everyone regardless of occupational or skill specialties. Other services are highly specialized for groups such as oil riggers, computer specialists, or engineers. Most will tell you they can help. If they promise to find you a job, be careful. You should seek some very specific services you need, and these are outlined in subsequent chapters. If you read these chapters, you will know what questions to ask. Not surprisingly, you may discover you know more about finding a job than some of the so-called professionals! This is because there is a high turnover of personnel in the career planning field. Many counselors are in "training" when they meet you — and many may be reading this book as part of their "homework."

You will encounter at least 10 different career planning and employment services for assisting you with your job search. Again, approach them with caution. Don't sign a contract before reading the fine print, getting a second opinion, and talking to former clients about *results*. With these words of caution in mind, let's take a look at the variety of services available.

1. **Public employment services**

    Public employment services usually consist of a state agency which provides employment assistance as well as dispenses unemployment compensation benefits. Employment assistance largely consists of job listings and counseling services. However, counseling services often are a front to screen individuals for employers who list with the public employment agency. If you are looking for entry-level jobs in the $10,000 to $16,000 range, contact this service. Most employers do not list with this service, especially for positions requiring skills in the $18,000 plus range. If you walk through one of these offices, you will find that most people are unemployed and look poor; they will likely remain so for some time. In fact, some experts believe we should abolish these offices altogether because they exacerbate unemployment; they take people away from the more productive channels for employment — personal contacts — and put them in a line with other hopeless individuals. We recommend avoiding these offices unless you are really down on your luck and want some company.

2. **Private employment agencies**

Private employment agencies work for money, either from applicants or employers. Approximately 8,000 such agencies operate nationwide. Many are highly specialized in technical, scientific, and financial fields. The majority of these firms serve the interests of employers since employers — not applicants — represent repeat business. While employers normally pay the placement fee, many agencies charge applicants 10 to 15 percent of their first year salary. These firms have one major advantage: job leads which you may have difficulty uncovering elsewhere. Especially highly specialized fields, a good firm can be extremely helpful. The major disadvantages are that they can be costly and the quality of the firms varies. Be careful in how you deal with them. Make sure you understand the fee structure and what they will do for you before you sign anything.

3. **College and university placement offices**

College and university placement offices provide in-house career planning services for graduating students. While some give assistance to alumni, don't expect too much help if you already graduated. Many of these offices are understaffed or provide only rudimentary services, such as maintaining a career planning library, coordinating on-campus interviews for graduating seniors, and conducting workshops on how to write resumes and interview. Others provide a full range of well supported services including testing and one-on-one counseling. Check with your local campus to see what services you might use.

4. **Private career and job search firms**

Private career and job search firms are organized to help individuals acquire job search skills. They do not find you a job. In other words, they teach you much — maybe more but possibly less — of what is outlined in this book. Expect to pay anywhere from $1,500 to $10,000 for this service. If you need a monetary incentive to conduct your job search, contract with one of these firms. The most highly respected and innovative firm is Haldane Associates. Many of their pioneering career planning and job search methods are incorporated in this book.

5. **Executive search firms**

Executive search firms work for employers in finding employees to fill critical positions in the $35,000 plus salary range. They also are called "Headhunters," "management consultants," and "executive recruiters." These firms play an important role in linking high level technical and managerial talent to organizations. Don't expect to contract for these services. Executive recruiters work for employers — not applicants. If a friend or relative is in this business or you have relevant skills, let them know you are available — and ask for their advice.

6. **Marketing services**

Marketing services represent an interesting combination of job search and executive search activities. They can cost $2,500 or more, and they work with individuals anticipating a starting salary of at least $30,000. These firms try to minimize the time and risk of applying for jobs. A typical operation begins with a client paying a $150 fee for developing psychological, skills, and interests profiles. Next, a marketing plan is outlined and a contract signed for specific services. Using word processing equipment, the firm normally develops a slick "professional" resume and mails it along with a cover letter, to hundreds — maybe thousands — of firms. Clients are then briefed and sent to interview with interested employers. While you can save money and achieve the same results on your own, these firms do have one major advantage. They save you *time* by doing most of the work for you. Again, approach these services with caution.

7. **Women's Centers and special career services**

Women's Centers and special career services have been established to respond to the employment needs of special groups. Women's Centers are particularly active in sponsoring career planning workshops and job information networks. These centers tend to be geared toward elementary job search activities because their clientele largely consists of housewives who are entering or re-entering the workforce with little knowledge of the job market. Special career services arise at times for different categories of employees. Unemployed aerospace engineers, teachers, veterans, air traffic controllers, and government employees have formed special groups for developing job search skills and sharing job leads.

8. **Testing and assessment centers**

Testing and assessment centers provide assistance for identifying vocational skills, interests, and objectives. Usually staffed by trained professionals, these centers administer several types of tests and charge from $500 to $800 per person. You may wish to use some of these services if you feel our activities in Chapters Six and Seven do not give you enough information on your skills and interests to formulate your job objective. Try our exercises before you hire a psychologist.

9. **Job fairs or career conferences**

Job fairs or career conferences are organized by employment agencies to link applicants to employers. Consisting of one or two day meetings in a hotel, employers meet with applicants as a group and on a one-to-one basis. Employers give presentations on their companies, resumes are circulated, and candidates are interviewed. Many of these conferences are organized around particular skill areas, such as engineering and computers. These are excellent sources for job leads and information — if you get invited to the meetings. Employers pay for this service — not applicants.

10. **Professional associations**

Professional associations often provide placement assistance. This usually consists of listing job vacancies and organizing a job information exchange at annual conferences. These meetings are good sources for making job contacts in different geographic locations within a particular professional field. But don't expect much from these services. Talking to people at professional conferences will probably yield better results than reading job listings and interviewing at conference placement centers.

Other types of career planning and employment services are growing and specializing in particular occupational fields. We recommend using these services as a supplement to this book. Again, proceed with caution and know exactly what you are getting. Remember, there is no such thing as a free lunch, and you often get less than what you pay for. After reading the next six chapters, you should be able to make intelligent decisions about what, when, where, and with what results you can use professional assistance. Shop around, compare services, ask questions, talk to former clients, and read the fine print with your lawyer before giving a professional a job!

USE TIME EFFECTIVELY

If you decide to conduct your own job search with minimum assistance from professionals, your major cost will be your time. Therefore, you must find sufficient time to devote to your job search. Ask yourself: How valuable is my time in relation to finding a job or changing my career? Assign a dollar value to your time; compare it to what you might pay a professional for doing much of the job search work for you. Figure on a $2,000 to $12,000 range if you hired a professional.

The time you devote to your job search will depend on whether you want to work at it on a full-time or part-time basis. If you are unemployed, by all means make this a full-time endeavor — 40 to 80 hours per week. If you are presently employed, we do not recommend quitting your job in order to look for employment. You will probably need the steady income and attendant health benefits during your transition period. Furthermore, it is easier to find new employment by appearing employed. Unemployed people project a negative image in the eyes of many employers — they appear to need a job. *Your goal is to find a job based on your strengths rather than your needs*.

However, if you go back to school for skills retraining, your present employment status may be less relevant to employers. Your major strength is the fact that you have acquired a skill the employer needs. If you quit your job and spend money retraining, you will communicate a certain degree of risk-taking, drive, responsibility, and dedication which employers readily seek, but seldom find, in candidates today.

Assuming you will be conducting a job search on a part-time basis - 15 to 25 hours per week — you will need to find the necessary time for these job activities. Unfortunately, most people are busy, having programmed every hour to "important" personal and professional activities. Thus, conducting a job search for 15 or more hours a week means that some things will have to go or receive low priority in relation to your job search.

This is easier said than done. The job search often gets low priority. It competes with other important daily routines, such as attending meetings, taking children to games, going shopping, and watching favorite TV programs. Rather than fight with your routines — and create family disharmony and stress — make your job search part of your daily routines by improving your overall management of time.

Certain time management techniques will help you make your job search a high priority activity in your daily schedule. These practices may actually lower your present stress level and thus enhance your overall effectiveness.

Time management experts estimate that most people waste their time on unimportant matters. Lacking priorities, people spend 80 percent of their time on trivia and 20 percent of their time on the important matters which should get most of their attention. If you reverse this emphasis, you could have a great deal of excess time — and probably experience less stress attendant with the common practice of crisis managing the critical 20 percent.

Before reorganizing your time, you must know how you normally use your time. Therefore, complete the statements on pages 106-107 for a preliminary assessment of your time management behavior. While many of these statements especially pertain to individuals in managerial positions, respond to those statements that are most relevant to your employment situation.

YOUR TIME MANAGEMENT INVENTORY

Respond to each statement by circling "yes" or "no," depending on which response best represents your normal pattern of behavior.

1. I have a written set of long, intermediate, and short-range goals for myself (and my family). Yes No
2. I have a clear idea of what I will do today at work and at home. Yes No
3. I have a clear idea of what I want to accomplish at work this coming week and month. Yes No
4. I set priorities and follow-through on the most important tasks first. Yes No
5. I judge my success by the results I produce in relation to my goals. Yes No
6. I use a daily, weekly, and monthly calendar for scheduling appointments and setting work targets. Yes No
7. I delegate as much work as possible. Yes No
8. I get my subordinates to organize their time in relation to mine. Yes No
9. I file only those things which are essential to my work. When in doubt, I throw it out. Yes No
10. I throw away junk mail. Yes No
11. My briefcase is uncluttered, including only essential materials; it serves as my office away from the office. Yes No
12. I minimize the number of meetings and concentrate on making decisions rather than discussing aimlessly. Yes No
13. I make frequent use of the telephone and face-to-face encounters rather than written communication. Yes No
14. I make minor decisions quickly. Yes No
15. I concentrate on accomplishing one thing at a time. Yes No
16. I handle each piece of paper once. Yes No
17. I answer most letters on the letter I receive. Yes No
18. I set deadlines for myself and others and follow-through in meeting them. Yes No
19. I reserve time each week to plan. Yes No
20. My desk and work area are well organized and clear. Yes No
21. I know how to say "no" and do so. Yes No
22. I first skim books, articles, and other forms of written communication for ideas before reading further. Yes No
23. I monitor my time use during the day by asking myself "How can I best use my time at present?" Yes No

24. I deal with the present by getting things done   Yes   No
    that need to be done.
25. I maintain a time log to monitor the best use   Yes   No
    of my time.
26. I place a dollar value on my time and behave   Yes   No
    accordingly.
27. I — not others — control my time.   Yes   No
28. My briefcase includes items I can work on   Yes   No
    during spare time in waiting rooms, lines, and
    airports.
29. I keep my door shut when I'm working.   Yes   No
30. I regularly evaluate to what degree I am achiev-   Yes   No
    ing my stated goals.

If you answered "no" to many of these statements, you should consider incorporating a few basic time management principles into your daily schedule.

Don't go to extremes by drastically restructuring your life around the "religion" of time management. If you followed all the advice of time management experts, you would probably alienate your family, friends, and colleagues with your narrow efficiency mentality! A realistic approach is to start monitoring your time use and then gradually re-organize your time according to goals and priorities. This is all you need to do. Forget the elaborate flow charts that are the stuff of expensive time management workshops and consultants. Start by developing a time management log. Keep daily records of how you use your time over a two week period. Identify who controls your time and the results of your time utilization. Within two weeks clear patterns will emerge. You may learn that you have an "open door" policy that enables others to control your time; you have little time to do your own work. Based on this information, you may need to close your door and be more selective about access. You may find from your analysis that most of your time is used for activities that have few if any important outcomes. If this is the case, then you may need to set goals and prioritize daily activities.

A simple yet effective technique for improving your time management practices is to complete a "to do" list for each day. You can purchase tablets of these forms in many stationery and office supply stores, or you can develop your own "Things To Do Today" list. This list also should prioritize which activities are most important to accomplish each day. Include at the top of your list a particular job search activity or several activities that should be completed on each day. If you follow this simple time management practice, you will find the necessary time needed to include your job search in your daily routines. You can give your job search top priority, and accomplish more in less time, with better results.

PLAN TO TAKE ACTION

While we recommend that you plan your job search, we want you to avoid the excesses of too much planning. Like time management, planning should not be all-consuming. Planning makes sense because it requires that you set goals and develop strategies for achieving the goals. However, too much planning can blind you to unexpected occurrences and opportunities. Be flexible enough to take advantage of new opportunities.

We outline a hypothetical plan for conducting an effective job search. This plan, as illustrated on page 109, incorporates the individual job search activities over a six month period. If you phase in the first five job search steps during the initial three to four weeks and continue the final four steps in subsequent weeks and months, you should begin receiving job offers within two to three months after initiating your job search. Interviews and job offers can come anytime — often unexpectedly — as you conduct your job search. An average time is three months, but it can occur within a week or take as long as five months. If you plan, prepare, and persist at the job search, the pay-off will be job interviews and offers.

While three months may seem a long time, especially if you have just lost your job and you need work immediately, you can shorten your job search time by increasing the frequency of your individual job search activities. If you are job hunting on a full-time basis, you may be able to cut your job search time in half. But don't expect to get a job within a week or two. It requires time and hard work — perhaps the hardest work you will ever do — but it pays off with a job that is right for you.

FOLLOW SUCCESS PRINCIPLES

Success is determined by more than just a good plan getting implemented. We know success is not determined primarily by intelligence, thinking big, time management, or luck. Based upon experience, theory, research, and common sense, we believe you will achieve careering and re-careering success if you follow many of these 20 principles:

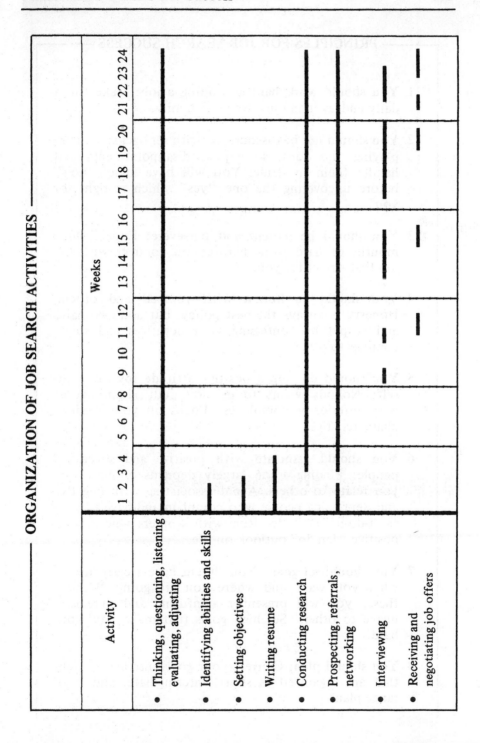

ORGANIZATION OF JOB SEARCH ACTIVITIES

─────── PRINCIPLES FOR JOB SEARCH SUCCESS ───────

1. **You should work hard at finding a job**: Make this a daily endeavor and involve your family.

2. **You should not be discouraged with set-backs**: You are playing the odds, so expect disappointments and handle them in stride. You will have many "no's" before uncovering the one "yes" which is right for you.

3. **You should be patient and persevere**: Expect three months of hard work before you connect with the job that's right for you.

4. **You should be honest with yourself and others**: Honesty is always the best policy, but don't be naive and stupid by confessing your negatives and short-comings to others.

5. **You should develop a positive attitude toward yourself**: Nobody wants to employ guilt-ridden people with inferiority complexes. Focus on your positive characteristics.

6. **You should associate with positive and successful people**: Finding a job largely depends on how well you relate to others. Avoid associating with negative and depressing people who complain and have a "you-can't-do-it" attitude. Run with winners who have a positive "can-do" outlook on life.

7. **You should set goals**: You should have a clear idea of what you want and where you are going. Without these, you will present a confusing and indecisive image to others. Set high goals that make you work hard.

8. **You should plan**: Convert your goals into action steps that are organized as short, intermediate, and long-range plans.

9. **You should get organized**: Translate your plans into activities, targets, names, addresses, telephone numbers, and materials. Develop an efficient and effective filing system and use a large calendar for setting time targets and recording appointments and useful information.

10. **You should be a good communicator**: Take stock of your oral, written, and nonverbal communication skills. How well do you communicate? Since most aspects of your job search involve communicating with others, and communication skills are one of the most sought-after skills, always present yourself well both verbally and nonverbally.

11. **You should be energetic and enthusiastic**: Employers are attracted to positive people. They don't like negative and depressing people who toil at their work. Generate enthusiasm both verbally and nonverbally. Check on your telephone voice – it may be more unenthusiastic than your voice in face-to-face situations.

12. **You should ask questions**: Your best information comes from asking questions. Learn to develop intelligent questions that are non-aggressive, polite, and interesting to others. But don't ask too many questions.

13. **You should be a good listener**: Being a good listener is often more important than being a good questioner and talker. Learn to improve your face-to-face listening behavior (nonverbal cues) as well as remember and use information gained from others – if they need improving. Make others feel they enjoyed talking with you i.e., you are one of the few people who actually *listens* to what they say.

14. **You should be polite, courteous, and thoughtful**: Treat gatekeepers, especially receptionists and secretaries, like human beings. Avoid being aggressive or too assertive. Try to be polite, courteous, and gracious. Your social graces are being observed. Remember to send thank-you letters – a very thoughtful thing to do

in a job search. Even if rejected, thank employers for the "opportunity" given to you. After all, they may later have additional opportunities, and they will remember you.

15. **You should be tactful**: Watch what you say to others about other people and your background. Don't be a gossip, back-stabber, or confessor.

16. **You should maintain a professional stance**: Be neat in what you do and wear, and speak with the confidence, authority and maturity of a professional.

17. **You should demonstrate your intelligence and competence**: Present yourself as someone who gets things done and achieves results — a ***producer***. Employers generally seek people who are bright, hard working, responsible, can communicate well, have positive personalities, maintain good interpersonal relations, are likeable, observe dress and social codes, take initiative, are talented, possess expertise in particular areas, use good judgment, are cooperative, trustworthy, and loyal, generate confidence and credibility, and are conventional. In other words, they like people who can score in the "excellent" to "outstanding" categories of the annual performance evaluation. Many want God!

18. **You should not overdo your job search**: Don't engage in overkill and bore everyone with your "job search" stories. Achieve balance in everything you do. Occasionally take a few days off to do nothing related to your job search. Develop a system of incentives and rewards — such as two non-job search days a week, if you accomplish targets A, B, C, and D.

19. **You should be open-minded and keep an eye open for "luck"**: Too much planning can blind you to unexpected and fruitful opportunities. You should welcome serendipity. Learn to re-evaluate your goals and strategies. Seize new opportunities if they appear appropriate.

> 20. **You should evaluate your progress and adjust**: Take two hours once every two weeks and evaluate what you are doing and accomplishing. If necessary, tinker with your plans and reorganize your activities and priorities. Don't become too routinized and therefore kill creativity and innovation.

These principles should provide you with an initial orientation for starting your job search. As you acquire job search experience, develop your own operating principles. As you immerse yourself in the task of structuring your career future, only you will know what works best for you.

TAKE RISKS AND HANDLE REJECTIONS

You can approach a job or career change in various ways. Some actions have higher pay-offs than others. Many people waste time by doing nothing, reconstructing the past, worrying about the future, and thinking about what they should have done. This negative approach impedes rather than advances careers.

A second approach is to do what most people do when looking for a job. They examine classified ads, respond to vacancy announcements, and complete applications in personnel offices. While this approach is better than doing nothing, it is relatively inefficient as well as ineffective. You compete with many others who are using the same approach. Furthermore, the vacancy announcements do not represent the true number of job vacancies nor do they offer the best opportunities. As we will see in Chapter Ten, you should use this approach to some degree, but it should not preoccupy your time. Responding to vacancy announcements is a game of chance, and the odds are usually against you. It makes you too dependent upon others to give you a job.

The third approach to making a job change requires *taking creative action* on your part. You must become a self-reliant risk-taker. You identify what it is you want to do, what you have acquired skills to do, and organize yourself accordingly by following the methods in subsequent chapters. You don't need to spend much time with classified ads, employment agencies, and personnel offices. And you don't need to worry about your future. You take charge of your future by initiating a job search which pays off with job offers. Your major investment is *time*. Your major risk is being turned down or rejected.

Job hunting is an ego-involving activity. You place your past, abilities, and self-image before strangers who don't know who you are or what you can do. ***Being rejected or having someone say "no" to you will probably be your greatest job hunting difficulty***. We know most people can handle two or three "no's" before they get discouraged. If you approach your job search from a less ego-involved perspective, you can take "no's" in stride; they are a normal aspect of your job search experience. Be prepared to encounter 10, 20, or 50 "no's." Remember, the odds are in your favor. For every 20 "no's" you get, you also should uncover one or two "yeses." The more rejections you get, the more acceptances you also will get. Therefore, you must encounter rejection ***before*** you get acceptances.

This third approach is the approach of this book. Experience with thousands of clients shows that the most successful job seekers are those who develop a high degree of self-reliance, maintain a positive self-image, and are willing to risk being rejected time after time without becoming discouraged. This approach will work for you if you follow our advice on how to become a self-reliant risk-taker in today's job market.

FORM A SUPPORT GROUP

We believe most people can conduct a successful job search on their own by following the step-by-step procedures of this book. We know they work because these methods have been used by thousands of successful job hunters. But we know it is difficult to become a risk-taker, especially in an area where few people have a base of experience and knowledge from which to begin. Therefore, we recommend that you share the risks with others.

Our self-directed methods work well when you team up with others in forming a job search group or club. The group provides a certain degree of security which is often necessary when launching a new and unknown adventure. In addition, the group can provide important information on job leads. Members will critique your approach and progress. They will provide you with psychological supports as you experience the frustration of rejections and the joys of success. You also will be helping others who will be helping you. Some career counselors estimate that membership in such groups can cut one's job search time by as much as 50 percent!

You can form your own group by working with your spouse or by finding friends who are interested in looking for a new job. Your friends may know other friends or colleagues who are interested in doing the same. Some of your friends may surprise you by indicating they would like to join your group out of curiosity. If you are over 40 years of age, check to see if there is a chapter of the 40-Plus Club in your community. This group is organized as a job search club.

Your group should meet regularly — once a week. At the meetings discuss your experiences, critique each other's approaches and progress, and share information on what you are learning or what you feel you need to know more about and do more effectively. Include your spouse as part of this group. We will return to this subject in Chapter Ten when we discuss how to develop your networks for uncovering job leads.

One other aspect of this self-directed book should be clarified. While we do not urge you to seek professional assistance, such as a career counselor, this assistance can be useful at certain stages and depending on individual circumstances. For example, the next chapter focuses on skills identification. While we present the necessary information and exercises for you to identify your skills, some individuals may wish to enhance this step of their job search by seeking the assistance of a professional career counselor who may have more sophisticated testing instruments for meeting their needs.

On the other hand, if you bring to your job search certain health and psychological problems which affect your job performance, you should seek professional help rather than try to solve your problems with this book. This is especially true for those with alcohol or drug problems who really need some form of professional therapy before practicing this book. If you are in serious financial trouble or a separation or divorce is greatly troubling you, seek professional help. Only after you get yourself together physically and mentally will this book produce its intended results for you. Remember, no employer wants to hire alcohol, drug, financial, or marital problems. They want productive, job-centered individuals who are capable of handling their personal problems.

You must be honest with yourself before you can be honest with others. The whole philosophy underlying this book is one of personal honesty and integrity in everything you do related to your job search.

PART II

DEVELOP POWERFUL CAREERING AND RE-CAREERING SKILLS

Chapter Six

IDENTIFY AND COMMUNICATE YOUR SKILLS

We live in a skills-based society where individuals market their skills to employers in exchange for money, position, and power. The ease by which individuals change jobs and careers is directly related to their ability to communicate their skills to employers and then transfer their skills to new work settings. To best position yourself in the job markets of today and tomorrow, you should pay particular attention to refining your present skills as well as acquiring new and more marketable skills.

What skills do you already have to offer employers? If you have just completed an educational program relevant to today's job market, the skills you have to offer are most likley related to the subject matter you studied. If you are changing jobs or careers, the skills you wish to communicate to employers will be those things you already have demonstrated you can do in specific jobs.

We earlier addressed the question of how to acquire skills training for careering and re-careering in the years ahead by noting that the skills required for *finding a job* are no substitute for the skills necessary for *doing the job*. Learning new skills requires a major investment of time, money, and effort. Nonetheless, the long-term pay-off should more than justify the initial costs. Indeed, research continues to show that well selected education and training provide the best returns on individual and societal investments.

ASSESS YOUR WORK-CONTENT
AND FUNCTIONAL SKILLS

Most people possess two types of skills that define their accomplishments and strengths as well as enable them to enter and
advance within the job market: work-content and functional skills.
You need to acquaint yourselves with these skills before communicating them to employers.

We assume you have already acquired certain **work-content**
skills necessary to function effectively in today's job market. These
"hard skills" are easy to recognize since they are often identified as
"qualifications" for specific jobs, and they are the subject of most
educational and training programs. Work-content skills tend to be
technical and job-specific in nature. Examples of such skills include
proficiency in typing, programming computers, repairing air conditioners, or operating an x-ray machine. They may require formal
training, are associated with specific trades or professions, are used
only in certain job and career settings, and use a separate skills
vocabulary, jargon, and subject matter for specifying technical
qualifications for individuals entering and advancing in an occupation. While these skills do not transfer well from one occupation to
another, they are critical for entering and advancing within certain
occupations.

At the same time, you possess numerous **functional/transfer-**
able skills employers readily seek along with your work-content
skills. These "soft skills" are associated with numerous job settings,
are mainly acquired through experience rather than formal training,
and can be communicated through a general vocabulary. Functional/
transferable skills are less easy to recognize since they tend to be
linked to **dealing with processes** (communicating, problem solving,
motivating) rather than **doing things** (programming a computer,
building a house, repairing air conditioners). While most people have
only a few work-content skills, they have numerous – perhaps as
many as 300 – functional/transferable skills. These skills enable
job seekers to more easily change jobs. But you must first be aware
of your functional skills before you can adequately relate them to
the job market.

Most people view the world of work in traditional occupational-
job-skill terms. This is a **structural view** of occupational realities.
Occupational fields are seen as consisting of separate and distinct
jobs which, in turn, require specific work-content skills. From this
perspective, occupations and jobs are relatively self-contained enti-
ties. Social work, for example, is seen as being different from paralegal work; social workers, therefore, are not "qualified" to seek

paralegal work.

On the other hand, a *functional view* of occupations and jobs emphasizes similar characteristics among jobs as well as common linkages between different occupations. Although the structure of occupations and jobs may differ, they have similar functions. They involve working with people, data, processes, and objects. If you work with people, data, processes, and objects in one occupation, you can transfer that experience to other occupations which have similar functions. Once you understand how your skills relate to the functions as well as investigate the structure of different occupations, you should be prepared to make job changes from one occupational field to another. Whether you possess the necessary work-content skills to qualify for entry into the other occupational field is another question altogether.

The skills we identify and help you organize in this chapter are the functional skills career counselors normally emphasize when advising clients to assess their *strengths*. In contrast to work-content skills, functional skills can be transferred from one job or career to another. They enable individuals to make some job and career changes without the need to acquire additional education and training. They constitute an important bridge for moving from one occupation to another.

Before you decide if you need more education or training, you should first assess both your functional and work-content skills to see how they can be transferred to other jobs and occupations. Once you do this, you should be better prepared to make careering and re-careering decisions as well as relate your functional skills to your work-content skills.

KNOW YOUR STRENGTHS

Regardless of what combination of work-content and functional skills you possess, a job search must begin with identifying your strengths. Without knowing these, your job search will lack content and focus. *Your goal should be to find a job that is fit for you rather than one you think you might be able to fit into*. Of course, you also want to find a job for which there is a demand. This particular focus requires a well-defined approach to identifying and communicating your skills to others. You can best do this by asking the right questions about your strengths and then conducting a systematic self-assessment of *what you do best as well as enjoy doing*. This chapter gets you started with your job search by raising the key questions and outlining alternative self-assessment techniques.

ASK THE RIGHT QUESTIONS TO KNOW YOURSELF

Knowing the right questions to ask will save you time and steer you into productive job search channels from the very beginning. Asking the wrong questions can cripple your job search efforts and leave you frustrated. The questions must be understood from the perspectives of both employers and applicants.

Two of the most humbling questions you will encounter in your job search are *"Why should I hire you?"* and *"What are your weaknesses?"* While employers may not directly ask these questions, feel assured they are asking them nonetheless. If these questions are not answered in a positive manner — directly, indirectly, verbally, or nonverbally — your job search will likely flounder and you will join the ranks of the unsuccessful and disillusioned job searchers who feel something is wrong with them. Individuals who have lost their jobs are particularly vulnerable to these questions since many lack self esteem and a positive self-image. Many such people focus on what is wrong rather than *what is right* about themselves. Such thinking creates self-fulfilling prophecies and is self-destructive in the job market. By all means avoid such negative thinking.

Employers want to hire your *value or strengths* — not your weaknesses. Since it is easier to identify and interpret weaknesses, employers look for indicators of your strengths by trying to identify your weaknesses. *Your job is to communicate your strengths to employers.* The more successful you are in doing this, the better off you will be in relation to both employers and fellow applicants.

Therefore, you should organize your questions around the concerns of employers. Above all, don't dwell on your weaknesses — past or present. Start from a position of strength by learning to communicate your strengths to others.

The best approach to identifying your strengths is to ask two related questions:

- What do I do well?
- What do I enjoy doing?

What do you do well and enjoy doing? These questions must be answered prior to deciding on alternative jobs and careers. The questions identify the skills, abilities, and talents you have to offer potential employers.

Unfortunately, many people work against their own best interests. Not knowing their strengths, they market their weaknesses by first identifying job vacancies and then trying to fit their "qualifications" to job descriptions. This approach often frustrates applicants; it presents a picture of a job market which is not interested in the applicant's strengths. This leads some people toward acquiring new skills which they hope will be marketable, even though they do not enjoy using them. Millions of individuals find themselves in such misplaced situations. Your task is to avoid joining the ranks of the misplaced and unhappy work force.

COMMUNICATE YOUR
FUNCTIONAL/TRANSFERABLE SKILLS

We know most people stumble into jobs by accident. Some are at the right place at the right time to take advantage of a job or career opportunity. Others work hard at trying to fit into jobs listed in classified ads, employment agencies, and personnel offices; identified through friends, acquaintances; or found by knocking on doors. After 15 to 20 years in the work world, many people wish they had better planned their careers from the very start. All of a sudden they are unhappily locked into jobs because of retirement benefits and the family responsibilities of raising children and meeting monthly mortgage payments. Re-careering is an option they fail to pursue because they lack knowledge of how to do it or they fear taking the risks of pursuing a new career.

After 10 or 20 years of work experience, most people have a good idea of what they don't like to do. While their values are more set than when they first began working, many people are still unclear as to what they do well and enjoy doing as well as how their skills fit into the job market. If they have the opportunity to change jobs or careers — either voluntarily or forced through termination — and find the time to plan the change, they can move into jobs and careers which fit their skills and motivational patterns.

The key to understanding your non-technical strengths is to *identify your transferable or functional skills*. Once you have done this, you will be better prepared to identify what it is you want to do. Moreover, your self-image and self-esteem will improve and you will be prepared to communicate your strengths to others through a rich skills vocabulary. These outcomes are critically important for writing your resume and letters as well as for conducting interviews.

Let's illustrate the concept of functional/transferable skills for careering and re-careering by examining the case of educators. Many educators view their skills in strict work-content terms — knowledge of a particular subject matter such as math, history, English, physics, or music. When looking outside education for employment, many educators seek jobs which will use their subject matter skills. However, they soon discover that non-educational institutions are not a ready market for such "skills."

On the other hand, educators possess many other skills that are directly transferable to business and industry. Most educators are not aware of these skills and thus they fail to communicate their strengths to others. For example, research shows that graduate students in the humanities most frequently possess these transferable skills, in order to importance:

- critical thinking
- research techniques
- perseverance
- self-discipline
- insight
- writing

- general knowledge
- cultural perspective
- teaching ability
- self-confidence
- imagination
- leadership ability

Most functional/transferable skills can be classified into two general skills and trait categories:

TYPES OF TRANSFERABLE SKILLS

Organizational and Interpersonal Skills

_____ communicating	_____ trouble shooting
_____ problem solving	_____ implementing
_____ analyzing/assessing	_____ self-understanding
_____ planning	_____ understanding
_____ decision-making	_____ setting goals
_____ innovating	_____ conceptualizing
_____ thinking logically	_____ generalizing
_____ evaluating	_____ managing time
_____ identifying problems	_____ creating
_____ synthesizing	_____ judging
_____ forecasting	_____ controlling
_____ tolerating ambiguity	_____ organizing
_____ motivating	_____ persuading
_____ leading	_____ encouraging
_____ selling	_____ improving
_____ performing	_____ designing
_____ reviewing	_____ consulting
_____ attaining	_____ teaching
_____ team building	_____ cultivating
_____ updating	_____ advising
_____ coaching	_____ training

_____ supervising	_____ interpreting
_____ estimating	_____ achieving
_____ negotiating	_____ reporting
_____ administering	_____ managing

Personality and Work-Style Traits

_____ diligent	_____ honest
_____ patient	_____ reliable
_____ innovative	_____ perceptive
_____ persistent	_____ assertive
_____ tactful	_____ sensitive
_____ loyal	_____ astute
_____ successful	_____ risk taker
_____ versatile	_____ easy going
_____ enthusiastic	_____ calm
_____ out-going	_____ flexible
_____ expressive	_____ competent
_____ adaptable	_____ punctual
_____ democratic	_____ receptive
_____ resourceful	_____ diplomatic
_____ determining	_____ self-confident
_____ creative	_____ tenacious
_____ open	_____ discrete
_____ objective	_____ talented
_____ warm	_____ empathic
_____ orderly	_____ tidy
_____ tolerant	_____ candid
_____ frank	_____ adventuresome
_____ cooperative	_____ firm
_____ dynamic	_____ sincere
_____ self-starter	_____ initiator
_____ precise	_____ competent
_____ sophisticated	_____ diplomatic
_____ effective	_____ efficient

These are the types of skills you need to identify for yourself and then communicate to employers in your resumes and letters as well as during informational and job interviews.

IDENTIFY YOUR SKILLS

If you are just graduating from high school or college and do not know what you want to do, you probably should take a battery of vocational tests and psychological inventories to identify your interests and skills. These tests are listed in Chapter Seven. If you don't fall into these categories of job seekers, chances are you don't need complex testing. You have experience, you have well defined values, and you know what you don't like in a job. Therefore, we outline several alternative skills identification exercises — from simple to complex — for assisting you at this stage.

Use the following exercises to identify both your work-content and transferable skills. These self-assessment techniques stress your positives or strengths rather than identify your negatives or weaknesses. They should generate a rich vocabulary for communicating your "qualifications" to employers. Each exercise requires different investments of your time and effort as well as varying degrees of assistance from other people. We recommend using the most complete and extensive activity — the Motivated Skills Exercise — to gain a thorough understanding of your strengths.

These exercises, however, should be used with caution. There is nothing magical or particularly profound about them. Most are based upon a very simple and somewhat naive *deterministic theory of behavior* — understanding your past patterns of behavior are good predictors of your future behavior. Not a bad theory for most individuals, but it is rather simplistic and disheartening for individuals who wish to and can break out of past patterns as they embark on a new future. Furthermore, most exercises are *historical devices*. They provide you with a clear picture of your past, which may or may not be particularly useful for charting your future. Nonetheless, these exercises do help individuals (1) organize data on themselves, (2) target their job search around clear objectives and skills, and (3) generate a rich vocabulary of skills and accomplishments for communicating strengths to potential employers.

If you feel these exercises are inadequate for your needs, by all means seek professional assistance from a testing or assessment center staffed by a licensed psychologist (Chapter 5). These centers do in-depth testing which goes further than our self-directed, historical motivated skill exercises. For most people the following exercises will be sufficient. But also keep in mind that some individuals can and do change — often very dramatically — their behavior regardless of such deterministic and historical assessment devices. Much of the "motivation and success", "power of positive thinking", and "thinking big" literature, for example, challenges the validity of these standardized assessment tests that are used to predict or pattern future individual behavior. So be careful how you use such information for charting your career future. You *can* change your future. But at least get to know yourself before making the changes.

1. Checklist Method

Your first skills identification alternative is the most simple. Review the list of skills on pages 124-125. Place a "1" in front of the skills that *strongly* characterize you; a "2" before those that describe you to a *large extent*; and a "3" before those that describe you to *some extent*. After completing this exercise, review the lists and rank order the 10 characteristics that best describe you on each list.

2. Self-Directed Search

The second exercise also is relatively simple. Acquire a copy of John Holland's "The Self-Directed Search." You can find it in his book, *Making Vocational Choices: A Theory of Careers* or purchase it from Consulting Psychologists Press, 577 College Avenue, Palo Alto, California 94306. Most career counselors have copies of it. "The Self-Directed Search" is particularly good for quickly identifying what type of work environment you are motivated to seek — realistic, investigative, artistic, social, enterprising, or conventional — and aligns these work environments with lists of common, although somewhat dated, occupational titles. The exercise is extremely simple and gives you a quick overview of your orientation toward different types of work settings.

3. Skills Map

Richard N. Bolles has produced two useful exercises for identifying transferable skills. In his book, *The Three Boxes of Life*, he develops a checklist of 100 transferable skills which is based on Holland's self-directed search. They are organized into 12 categories or types of skills: using hands, body, words, senses, numbers, intuition, analytical thinking, creativity, helpfulness, artistic abilities, leadership, and follow-through. Bolles' second exercise, "The Quick Job Hunting Map," expands upon this first one. The "Map" is a checklist of 222 skills organized according to Holland's typology of skills. This exercise requires you to identify seven of your most satisfying accomplishments, achievements, jobs, or roles. After writing a page about each experience, you relate each experience to the checklist of 222 skills. After completing all this for the seven experiences, the "Map" gives you a comprehensive picture of what skills you (1) use most frequently, and (2) enjoy using in satisfying and successful settings. While this exercise may take you six hours to complete, it yields an enormous amount of data on your past strengths. In addition, the "Map" represents a rich skills vocabulary for communicating your skills to others. The "Map" is found in the appendix of Bolles' *What Color is Your Parachute?* or it can be purchased separately in beginning, advanced or "new" versions from the publisher, Ten Speed Press. Order information on this assessment instrument is included in the resource section of this book.

4. Career Analysis Worksheet

Richard Lathrop has developed a useful "Career Analysis Worksheet" for identifying skills. With this exercise you identify your general, strongest, and specific abilities as well as assess and determine your ideal job, personal relationships, flexibility, working environment, pay goals, and fields of work. Lathrop outlines the procedure for developing a "Career Analysis Worksheet" in his book, *Who's Hiring Who*.

5. Autobiography of Accomplishments

A fifth exercise consists of writing a lengthy essay about your life accomplishments. This could range from 20 to 100 pages. After completing the essay, go through it page by page to identify what you most enjoyed doing (working with different kinds of data, people, processes, and objects) and what skills you used most frequently as well as enjoyed using. Finally, identify those skills you wish to continue using. After analyzing and synthesizing this data, you should have a relatively clear picture of your strongest skills.

6. Motivated Skills Exercise

Our final exercise is one of the most complex and time consuming self-assessment exercises. However, it yields some of the best data on skills, and it is especially useful for those who feel they need a more thorough analysis of their skills. Developed by Haldane Associates, this particular exercise is variously referred to as "Success Factor Analysis" or "System to Identify Motivated Skills". While you can use this technique on your own, it is best to work with someone else. Be prepared to devote from six to eight hours to this exercise. It is divided into five steps. The steps follow the basic pattern of generating raw data, identifying patterns, analyzing the data through reduction techniques, and synthesizing the patterns into a transferable skills vocabulary. You need strong analytical skills to complete this exercise on your own. The five steps are as follows:

STEP 1: Take 15 to 20 sheets of paper and at the top of each sheet write one achievement. Your achievements consist of those things you enjoyed doing and felt a sense of accomplishment in doing. These include childhood experiences as well as educational, military, recreational, home, or work-related achievements. For example, at the top of the paper you might state:

> *"I learned to play the guitar and joined a rock group while in high school."*
>
> ---
>
> *"I received an 'A' in physics from the toughest teacher in school."*
>
> ---
>
> *"I reorganized the files of our office which improved the efficiency of operations."*
>
> ---
>
> *"I competed in the marathon and finished in the upper third."*
>
> ---
>
> *"I organized a committee to investigate reducing the number of customer complaints."*
>
> ---
>
> *"I sang a solo in our church choir."*

STEP 2: Select from among your achievements the seven most important ones and prioritize them. Identify the factors that explain your success in each achievement. Examples of these success factors might include various aspects of managing, communicating, creating, analyzing, designing, supervising, coordinating, and problem solving. On each page write the details of your achievements — how you got involved, what you did, how you did it, and what the outcome was.

STEP 3: Further detail the "what" and "how" of your achievements by having your spouse or a friend interview you over a 60-minute period. Have them ask you to elaborate on each of your achievements and note the terminology you use to elaborate on your skills and abilities. Record your answers for each achievement on separate pieces of paper.

STEP 4: Combine the self-generated and interview data on your achievements into a single master list of success factors. Group the factors into related categories beginning with the most important factor. For example, if "supervising" is your strongest achievement, "decision-making" and "delegating" may be related to this factor. Therefore, the factors would cluster as follow:

supervising decision-making delegating	selling promoting demonstrating
creating designing initiating	decision-making managing strategizing

STEP 5: Synthesize the clusters into new combinations for projecting your past skills into the future. For example, the clusters "supervising — decision-making — delegating" and "creating — designing — initiating" may combine into a new skill category called "creative management." This is the key step in this exercise, because it begins to relate your past strengths to your future goals. It functions as a ***bridge*** between your skills and your stated objective.

USE REDUNDANCY

Knowing your strengths is the key to launching a successful job search. We recommend starting with the simple techniques for generating data on your transferable skills. If you don't feel comfortable with the results, try a more complex and thorough technique. Indeed, redundancy is a virtue at this stage; it will help reinforce understanding of your strengths. If our exercises still leave you uncertain about your strengths, by all means seek professional help.

Our self-assessment techniques stress your positives or strengths rather than dwell on your negatives or weaknesses. This is precisely the way you should communicate your "qualifications" to prospective employers. You should use the rich skills vocabulary from these exercises for communicating to employers that you have numerous skills which will produce concrete results for them.

As you complete these exercises, your self-image and self-esteem may well improve. You should be able to say *"Yes, that is me; I'm good at doing this, and I really enjoy it."* At the same time, you might note that you have been misplaced in previous jobs; you did things which you disliked as well as demonstrated your weaknesses. These exercises should put you on the right path for renewed career satisfaction and success.

But beware of one potential problem when completing these exercises. Don't expect them to outline a new future for you. These strength identification exercises are historical techniques. They examine your past experiences — from childhood to the present — in order to identify your past motivated patterns for success. They are compatible with most employers' assumptions: your past performance best predicts your future performance. You bridge your past and present when you integrate these motivated skills into your job and career objective — the subject of the next chapter.

ACHIEVE SUCCESS

Experience shows that individuals who know and can communicate their functional skills are better able to get jobs than those who don't view their capabilities in these terms. This is especially true for individuals seeking to change careers. Therefore, these skills play a central role in careering and re-careering for the 1990s.

However, as noted earlier, functional skills have their limitations in today's job market. These general process skills lack the specificness of work-content skills. While they are important skills to know and target, **functional skills will not substitute for specific** *work-content skills*. As jobs become more specialized and technical in nature, changing jobs and careers on the basis of functional skills alone will become increasingly difficult. More and more jobs require specialized knowledge and technical abilities which are beyond the scope of functional skills. Consequently, you may need to acquire new work-content skills *in addition* to learning how to best communicate your transferable skills to employers.

While training takes time, it may be a wise investment for you in the long run. In the meantime, if you find yourself suddenly unemployed or you need to change jobs and careers within a six to twelve month period, the best way to deal with the job market is to focus on your transferable skills in developing a job search campaign based upon your past and present strengths. Once you land a job, continue to develop new work-content skills as well as improve your functional skills for future careering and re-careering. By stressing *both* functional and work-content skills, you will have an advantage over other job seekers who only emphasize functional or work-content skills.

Chapter Seven

STATE YOUR OBJECTIVE RIGHT

Once you identify your skills and accomplishments, you should be well prepared to develop a clear and purposeful objective for targeting your job search. With a renewed sense of direction and versed in an appropriate language, you should be able to communicate to employers that you are a talented and purposeful individual who **achieves results**. Your objective must tell employers what you will **do for them** rather than what you want from them. It targets your accomplishments around employers' needs. In other words, your objective should become **employer-centered** rather than self-centered.

GIVE YOUR JOB SEARCH DIRECTION

Without a clear objective, your job search will most likely flounder. You will wander aimlessly in a highly decentralized, fragmented, and chaotic job market looking for interesting jobs you might fit into. Your goal, instead, should be to find a job or career that is compatible with your interests, motivations, skills, and talents.

Job hunters with clearly stated objectives have several advantages over those who do not. Their job search is much easier and enjoyable because they approach it with confidence and optimism.

133

They gain greater control over the job market because they structure the job market around their goals. They communicate a reassuring sense of purpose and self-confidence to employers who worry about hiring individuals who don't know what they want. They write well designed resumes and letters that help employers make clear choices. For employers lacking basic hiring criteria, such applicants help them better define their "needs" as the applicant's job objective.

If you want to achieve the best results, you must have an objective *before* conducting your job search. With a clear objective, you can target your job search at specific high pay-offs in the job market. A clear objective will help you organize your job search into a coherent and manageable whole.

TARGET EMPLOYERS' NEEDS

Knowing the advantages and importance of a job objective does not tell you what an objective is. "Objective" is one of those elusive terms which has as many definitions as definers. In its simplist form, an objective is a statement of *what you want to do*. However, this self-centered view of an objective may not impress employers whose primary interest is *what you will do for them*.

Souerwine in *Career Strategies* develops one of the more complex and exhaustive definitions. He sees career objectives as having four major components:

1. **What you *might* do**. This requires identifying job and career opportunities.

2. **What you *can* do**. You did this already in Chapter Six when you identified your strengths or competencies.

3. **What you *want* to do**. This relates to your values and priorities.

4. **What you *should* do**. This is your sense of obligation to various individuals and groups within society regardless of their expectations.

The components in this definition require you to conduct an extensive self-assessment of your past, present, and future.

We have no problems with these differing definitions. Their usefulness depends on your needs and purposes. Our preference, however, is to orient a job or career objective toward its intended audience — employers. We prefer defining an objective as a statement of *what you can and will do for employers* at present and in the future. Such a statement synthesizes as well as gives direction to what you might do, can do, and should do.

BE REALISTIC

The problem of historical determinism — your past determining your future — often arises when identifying objectives. Many people know their past strengths but they want to do other things in the future. For example, the secretary who makes $14,000 a year and enjoys her work, may have other goals which cannot be met by remaining a secretary. Those goals may be life-long dreams, such as acquiring a vacation home in the mountains, traveling to exciting places, owning a Mercedes-Benz, or receiving media recognition. Meeting these goals requires a healthy income from a new type of occupation.

At the same time, your ideals and fantasies may be unrealistic and thus you must temper them with a heavy dose of reality. For example, going directly from a $14,000 a year secretarial job to a $80,000 a year corporate management position is unrealistic. It may be realistic for the long term if you target your job search initially for an entry-level management position which leads to such advancement.

Many job seekers have unrealistic goals such as doubling their salaries and moving into executive positions overnight. Government employees are a case in point. Contrary to public perceptions, many public employees feel underpaid and thus anticipate making a major salary jump by leaving government for the private sector. But reality tells them a different story. For example, a GS-14 federal government employee making $50,000 a year as a grants specialist may have to initially lower his or her monetary expectations in order to change jobs or careers. This may mean taking a $25,000 a year job in order to begin a new career. The same is true for the postal worker making $35,000 a year. Since the job market does not have many high salary opportunities for people with their experience, these individuals should be prepared to take salary cuts in order to learn new skills for reinvesting in their future. If all goes well, they may meet and surpass their previous salaries within three to five years. But they should not expect to substantially advance their careers over a few months or in a single year. They must be realistic in relation to the job market and honest with themselves. Only then can they direct their job search in a purposeful, positive, and enthusiastic manner.

SET ASIDE SUFFICIENT TIME

When developing your objective, keep in mind that you can state it over different time periods. Objectives can reflect your immediate, intermediate, and long-range goals. For example, if you have been terminated, your immediate goal will be to find a job in order to generate sufficient cash flow to pay bills and maintain a certain life style. This may require a stopgap job search strategy — take a part-time or full-time position which normally has high employee turnover with few expectations concerning employee loyalty. If you do this, try to find a job which permits spare time to conduct your job search. Many sales positions or jobs with evening shifts will give you enough flexibility to conduct your job search during the day. Avoid stopgap jobs which will lock you into an 8 a.m. to 5:00 p.m. work routine; you need some of this time frame for conducting your job search. If not, such jobs may turn into new and most unpromising careers!

You also should set intermediate and long-range goals. Your intermediate goal should state what you want to be doing or have achieved 5 to 10 years from today. Your long-range goals address the same consideration for 10 to 20 years from now.

Knowing exactly what they want to do, some people need little or no assistance in identifying their work objective. Others find identifying and stating an objective to be the most difficult and frustrating task in the whole job search process. If you need assistance, here are some approaches you can use to help formulate a clear and effective objective.

DEVELOP A DATA BASE

Several practical self-directed exercises can alleviate the frustrating aspects of developing a job objective. The exercises require you to generate and analyze data about yourself. Begin thinking of your objective as being composed of several ingredients relating to your work values, skills, and knowledge of work environments. Five activities or steps will help you generate a complete set of data for stating your objective.

The first step is to *identify your work and career values* by completing several exercises:

1. List 10 things you would like to achieve before you die. Alternatively, write your obituary for the year 2010 stressing highlights or achievements of your career and life.

2. Think of 10 answers to this question: "If I had $1,000,000 I would. . ."

3. List 10 things you prefer and enjoy doing. Prioritize each item.

4. Identify 10 working conditions which you view as negative. Prioritize each condition.

5. List 10 working conditions which you view as positive. Prioritize each item.

6. Check as many of the following work values you feel are desirable in your employment:

_____ contribute to society	_____	be creative
_____ have contact with people	_____	supervise others
_____ work alone	_____	work with details
_____ work with a team	_____	gain recognition
_____ compete with others	_____	acquire security
_____ make decisions	_____	make a lot of money
_____ work under pressure	_____	help others
_____ use power and authority	_____	solve problems
_____ acquire new knowledge	_____	take risks
_____ be a recognized expert	_____	work at own pace

7. Write an essay on your ideal job. Include a weekly calendar of daily activities divided into one-hour segments. Specify your duties, responsibilities, authority, salary, working conditions, and opportunities.

The second step is to **gather information on how others see you and your goals**. Ask your spouse or two or three close friends to frankly critique both your strengths and weaknesses. You want them to respond to these questions:

- What are my strengths and weaknesses?
- How can they be improved?
- What working conditions do I enjoy?
- What are my career goals?

The third step is to examine the data you generated in the previous section of this chapter on your strengths. Include it with the information you just generated yourself and received from your spouse and friends. *Rank order which skills you most and least prefer to use in your job or career.*

The fourth step is optional, depending on whether you feel you need more information on your work values, interests, and skills. *Take one or two psychological, aptitude, or vocational tests.* Your options include:

- Strong-Campbell Interest Inventory
- Career Assessment Inventory
- The Self-Directed Search
- Temperament and Values Inventory
- Sixteen Personality Factor Questionnaire
- Edwards Personal Preference Schedule
- Myers-Briggs Type Indicators
- The Occupational View Deck
- Self-Description Inventory
- Kuder Occupational Interest Survey

Information from these tests should reinforce and validate the information you gathered from the self-assessment exercises. See a career counselor or a licensed psychologist for identifying and administering the proper tests.

The fifth step is to *test the information concerning your objective against reality and the future* by asking yourself these questions:

- Is my objective realistic?
- Can it be achieved within the next year, 5 years, or 10 years?
- Who needs my skills?
- What factors might help me or hinder me in achieving my objective?

You will further clarify your objective as you expose yourself to more job market information while conducting library research and talking to people about your skills, different jobs, and career opportunities as outlined in Chapter Nine.

FOCUS ON SKILLS AND OUTCOMES

You now should be prepared to develop a one sentence statement of your job objective. Begin by stating your objective at a general level. Next, restate it at a more specific level on your resume.

We recommend developing a *functional job objective*. Recommended by Germann and Arnold in *Bernard Haldane Associates Job and Career Building*, this type of objective includes *skills* and *outcomes*. At a general level it would appear in the following skills-outcomes framework:

> *"I would like a job where I can use my ability to (a primary skill) which will result in (an outcome)."*

If, for example, you wish to write grant and research proposals, you might state the general objective in these terms:

> *"I would like a job where my technical research and writing experience will result in new and expanded programs."*

In this example "technical research and writing experience" is the primary skill; "new and expanded programs" is the outcome of using the primary skill.

The same objective should be re-written at a more specific level for your resume:

> *"A management consulting position where strong grantsmanship, research, and writing abilities will be used for expanding human resource development operations."*

Including both skills and outcomes, this objective is targeted toward particular employers.

As you develop your objective statement, keep in mind that employers want to know how you will achieve *their* goals. Always remember to develop a work-related objective responsive to the needs of your audience. Tell employers what you have to offer — strengths, skills, competencies — and what you will do for them. Emphasize that you are a *doer* who produces concrete results.

While you have certain self-centered goals you wish to achieve for yourself, employers are less interested in what they can do for you. As many employees quickly learn, they are expendible commodities. Employers feel no need to love them, take care of them, and become sensitive to their personal and professional needs. Employment is a business transaction — their money for your talent. *"You're fired!"* are two words which stress that the employer did not get what he or she wanted — your value for their money. Communicate that value loud and clear from the very beginning.

REFORMULATE YOUR OBJECTIVE

While you initially develop a job objective for orienting your job search and organizing your resume, your objective should not be set in stone. You may want to reformulate your objective from time to time. You will continually reality-test your objective as you conduct various phases of your job search. Your library research will be one important component; conversations, informational interviews, and job interviews will be other important sources for refining your objective. By all means do not expect to live and die with this objective! Be flexible and open to changing it as you absorb more useful job and career information. Your objective should focus — not fossilize — your job search!

Chapter Eight

COMMUNICATE YOUR QUALIFICATIONS WITH HIGH IMPACT RESUMES

Now that you know (1) what you do well, (2) what you enjoy doing, and (3) what you want to do in the future — the three key subjects of Chapters Six and Seven — you have the basic information necessary for communicating your qualifications to employers. But what will you do with this information? Let's be more specific. What messages, for example, do you want to send to employers about yourself? How will you convey these messages — by telephone, letter, or in face-to-face meetings?

Your choice of both the message and the medium will have important consequences for your job search. This and subsequent chapters are designed to assist you in sharpening the content of your communication as well as in developing effective communication strategies.

WRITE HIGH IMPACT RESUMES AND LETTERS

Resumes and letters are traditional means of communicating qualifications to employers. Most resumes and job search letters, however, are ineffective because they fail to relate work objectives and skills to the needs of employers. They lack impact because they are treated by most writers as writing rituals rather than as important products for furthering a communication process. Upon

141

completing this chapter you should be able to develop, target, and distribute high impact resumes and job search letters that clearly communicate your *purpose* and *capabilities* to prospective employers. High impact resumes and letters are ones that move employers to invite you to a job interview.

This chapter is your primer for developing key communication skills for probing the job market. Examples of effective resumes and letters are included in Appendices A and B (pages 285-300). A more extensive and complementary treatment of this subject and chapter, including worksheets and examples, is found in Ronald L. Krannich and William J. Banis, *High Impact Resumes and Letters* (see resource section for order information).

UNDERSTAND WHAT YOU ARE DOING

Resumes and job search letters are some of the most misunderstood and abused forms of communication. Many people overrate their purpose and effectiveness. Concentrating most of their efforts on mailing resumes and letters to numerous employers, they waste valuable job search time which should be devoted to other higher pay-off activities.

While few jobs can be acquired through the mail, it is difficult to pursue job opportunities without using the mail. Whether you like it or not, you will most likely need to write and distribute a resume and job search letters. Consequently, you need to know when, where, and how to send resumes and letters for maximum effectiveness.

Much misunderstanding of resumes relates to the definition and purpose of resumes. Many people still believe a resume should summarize their history. Others believe it will get them a job. Not so. In its simplist form, *a resume advertises your qualifications to prospective employers. It is your calling card for getting interviews.* For employers, resumes communicate applicants' *value* as well as serve as important *screening* devices for selecting candidates to interview. If you equate resumes with anything else, you will probably produce an ineffective resume.

AVOID COMMON MISTAKES

Perhaps 80 percent of all resumes in circulation are ineffective because people misunderstand their definition and purpose, as well as make numerous mistakes commonly associated with resumes.

Most resumes, for example, lack an objective, include unrelated categories of information, are too long, and appear unattractive. Other common resume problems identified by employers include:

- poor layout
- misspellings, punctuation errors, and poor grammar
- unclear purpose
- too much jargon
- include irrelevant data
- too long or too short
- poorly typed and reproduced
- unexplained time gaps
- too boastful
- deceptive or dishonest
- difficult to understand or interpret

You should avoid these problems by developing a resume that has enough impact to open the doors of prospective employers for interviews. At the very least your resume should:

PRINCIPLES OF HIGH IMPACT RESUMES

- clearly communicate your purpose and competencies in relation to employers' needs
- be concise and easy to read
- immediately motivate the reader to read it in-depth
- tell employers that you are a responsible and purpose-full individual — a doer who can solve their problems.

Knowing how to strengthen your resume is extremely important. Since many employers only glance at resumes, your resume must first be attractive or eye pleasing in order to motivate employers to spend more than the average 20 or 30 seconds reading it. Above all, your resume must clearly address employers' needs. It should answer a major question asked by employers:

Why should I read this or contact this person for an interview?

Always remember your audience; you are communicating to employers — not yourself, your mother, or your spouse. Once you know these critical points, you will be on the right road to developing an effective resume.

SELECT AN APPROPRIATE RESUME FORMAT

Resumes normally are produced in one of four different formats: chronological, functional, combination, or resume letter. Each format has advantages and disadvantages depending on your background and purpose. For example, someone first entering the job market or making a major career change should use a functional resume. On the other hand, a person who wants to target a particular job but doesn't want to rewrite the resume, may want to use a resume letter. Examples of these different types of resumes are included in Appendix A; they should be referred to as we outline the various characteristics of the different resumes.

Chronological Resumes

The chronological resume typifies 80 percent of all resumes. Among resume writing experts, this is the most controversial type of resume. It can be written in either traditional or improved chronological forms.

Some call the *traditional chronological resume* (see page 287) the "obituary resume" because it both "kills" your chances of getting a job and is a good source for writing a newspaper obituary. This resume summarizes your work history. It often lacks a job objective, lists dates and names first and duties and responsibilities second, and includes extraneous information such as height, weight, age, marital status, sex, and hobbies. While relatively easy to write, the traditional chronological resume is the most ineffective resume you can write. It has no purpose other than to inform people of what you have done in the past as well as where, when, and with whom. It tells employers little or nothing about what you want to do, can do, and will do for them.

The *improved chronological resume* (see page 288) avoids these problems. When you write this type of resume, you directly communicate to employers your purpose, past achievements, and probable future performance. You should use this type of resume when you have extensive experience directly related to a position. This resume should include a work objective which reflects both your work experience and professional goals. The work experience section should include the names and addresses of former employers followed by a brief description of your accomplishments, skills, and responsibilities; inclusive employment dates should appear at the end. Do not begin with the dates, since they are the least significant element in the descriptions. Be sure to stress your *accomplishments* and *skills* rather than your formal duties and responsibilities. You want to inform your audience that you are a productive and responsible person who gets things done.

However, a chronological resume may not be for you. If you are changing careers or have an unstable employment history, avoid the chronological resume. It communicates the wrong messages — you lack direct work experience, you are an unstable worker, or you have not advanced in your career. If you have such a career background, consider writing a functional or combination resume.

Functional Resumes

Functional resumes (see page 291) are designed to inform employers of applicants' work objectives and skills — especially their transferable skills as outlined in Chapter Six. This type of resume should be used by individuals making a significant career change, entering the workforce for the first time, or re-entering the job market after a lengthy absence. When using this resume, you should stress your accomplishments and skills regardless of your work settings. This could include accomplishments as a housewife or house husband, volunteer worker, or Sunday school teacher. Do not include names of employers or dates of employment since they will not strengthen your objective.

However, be careful with functional resumes. While they are important bridges for the inexperienced and for those making a career change, some employers have difficulty with these resumes. Like it or not, employers still look for names, dates, and direct experience; this resume doesn't meet these expectations. You should use a functional resume only if your past work experience does not strengthen your objective.

Combination Resumes

The *combination resume* (see page 289) is a good compromise between the chronological and functional resumes. This resume has more advantages than disadvantages, and it may be exactly what you need if you are making a career change with related experience from one career to another.

Combination resumes both *meet* and *raise* the expectations of employers. When writing this resume, you stress your accomplishments and skills as well as include work history. Your work history should appear as a separate section immediately following your presentation of accomplishments and skills in the "Areas of Effectiveness" or "Experience" section. It is not necessary to include dates unless they enhance your resume. This is the perfect resume for someone with work experience who wishes to change to a job in a related career field.

Resume Letters

The *resume letter* (see page 292) substitutes for a standard resume. Appearing as a job inquiry or application letter, a resume letter highlights one or two sections of what would normally appear in the body of your resume — work history, experience, areas of effectiveness, objective, or education. The resume letter should especially stress your objective, accomplishments and skills in relation to the employer's needs. This type of letter can be used at anytime. It is an ideal way to target a particular position for which you do not wish to send your more general resume. A resume letter has one major weakness: it may give some employers insufficient information and thus prematurely eliminate you from consideration.

After selecting an appropriate resume format, your next tasks are to generate and coordinate data, write drafts, produce the final copy, and distribute your resume into fruitful channels. Each stage requires particular knowledge and skills which you can develop.

STRUCTURE RESUME CONTENT

You should start by developing as much work-related information on yourself as possible. You generated much of this information in Chapters Six and Seven when you identified your strengths and specified your work objective. Now you need to round out this information with data for specific sections on your resume. Take several sheets of paper and include the following information categories and corresponding data on each sheet:

RESUME INFORMATION CATEGORIES

CONTACT INFORMATION:	name, address, telephone number.
WORK OBJECTIVE:	refer to Chapter Seven.
EDUCATION:	degrees, schools, dates, highlights, special training.
WORK EXPERIENCE:	paid, unpaid, civilian, military, and part-time employment. Include job

	titles, employers, locations, dates, skills, accomplishments, duties, and responsibilities. Use the functional language of Chapter Six.
OTHER EXPERIENCES:	volunteer, civic, and professional organizations. Include your contributions, demonstrated skills, offices held, names, and dates.
SPECIAL SKILLS OR LICENSES/ CERTIFICATES:	foreign languages, teaching, paramedical, etc. relevant to your objective.
MISCELLANEOUS INFORMATION:	references, expected salary, willingness to relocate and travel, availability dates.

Most of this information will appear on your resume while some information will only be used for reference to prepare you for interviews.

DRAFT IT INTELLIGENTLY

Your next task is to write two or three drafts of your resume in reference to the key information you just organized. If you will write a combination resume, for example, the internal organization of the resume should be as follows:

- contact information
- work objective
- qualifications or functional experience
- work history or employment
- education

You may want to include a personal statement at the end. However, we discourage including extraneous information, such as height, weight, age, marital status, state of health, sex, hobbies, references. Also avoid any negative information, such as being divorced, fired, or having medical problems, or a criminal record. You should never lie. But being honest does not mean you need to be naive or stupid by volunteering negatives. Such categories do not enhance your resume. As for references, do not list them on the resume; omit this category or simply state "References available upon request." Refer to the examples in Appendix A (pages 285-292) for illustrations of how these categories are organized.

While your first draft may run two or more pages, as you rewrite try to get all the information on one or two pages. The single page high impact resume is still the best even though some people may recommend longer resumes. Employers lose interest after one page. If you choose a longer resume, make sure to design the additional pages or attached supplemental materials so they are sufficiently eye catching to maintain the attention of the reader.

In completing your final draft, keep these "don'ts" and "dos" of effective resume writing in mind:

EFFECTIVE RESUME WRITING RULES

RESUME "DON'TS"

- *Don't* use abbreviations except for your middle initial.
- *Don't* make the resume cramped and crowded; it should be pleasing to the eyes.
- *Don't* make statements you can't document.
- *Don't* use the passive voice.
- *Don't* change tense of verbs.
- *Don't* use lengthy sentences and descriptions.
- *Don't* refer to yourself as "I".
- *Don't* include negative information.
- *Don't* include extraneous information.

RESUME "DOS"

- *Do* use action verbs and the active voice.
- *Do* be direct, succinct, and expressive with your language.
- *Do* appear neat, well organized, and professional.
- *Do* use ample spacing and highlighting (all caps or underlining) for different emphases.
- *Do* maintain an eye pleasing balance. Try centering your contact information at the top, keeping information categories on the left in all caps, and describing the categories in the center and on the right.
- *Do* check carefully your spelling, grammar, and punctuation.
- *Do* clearly communicate your purpose and value to employers.
- *Do* communicate your strongest points first.

If you incorporate these rules into your drafts and you have good content to offer, you should produce a first-class resume that will grab the attention of employers who will invite you for a job interview.

EVALUATE YOUR RESUME

After completing one or two drafts, you should thoroughly subject your resume to both internal and external evaluations. The *internal evaluation* consists of reviewing our lists of "dos" and "don'ts". The *external evaluation* involves circulating your resume to three or more individuals whom you believe will give you frank, objective, and useful feedback. Avoid people who tend to flatter you or make everyone feel good. The best evaluator would be someone in a hiring position similar to one you will encounter. Ask these people to critique your draft resume and suggest improvements in both form and content. This type of evaluation will serve as a dry-run for the final resume and will be your most important evaluation.

In the end, the only evaluation that counts is the one that helps get you an interview. Asking someone to critique your resume is one way to spread the word that you are job hunting; you may even get invited to an interview in the process!

REPRODUCING QUALITY RESUMES

There are several alternative ways to produce your final resume. You can have it typed, word processed or typeset. If you type it, be sure it looks professional. This can be done by using an electric typewriter with interchangeable elements and a carbon ribbon. Varying the typing elements produces attractive copy. Do not use a portable typewriter with a nylon ribbon; it does not produce professional copy. Many typists will do your resume on a typewriter with a carbon ribbon for less than $10.

If you have it word processed, be sure the final copy is printed on a letter quality printer using a carbon ribbon. Dot matrix and near letter quality printers make your resume look mass produced.

Alternatively, you can have a printer typeset your resume. This may cost anywhere from $20 to $50. The final product should look first-class. However, it may look *too* professional or *too* slick; some employers may think you had someone else write the resume for you.

Whichever method you use, be sure to proofread the final copy. It is disheartening to spend good money on typing and printing, and later find a typing error. Have two other people also proofread.

In reproducing the resume, you need to consider the quality and color of paper as well as the number of copies you need. By all means use good quality paper. You should use watermarked 20-pound or heavier bond paper. It costs 3¢ to 7¢ per sheet and can be purchased through stationery stores and printers. Don't be "penny wise but pound foolish" by cutting corners at this stage by using cheap paper or copy machine paper. You may save $5 on 100 copies but you also will communicate to employers that you are not particularly professional. What paper you choose may be just as important as how you present yourself on the paper. If you are presenting first-class resume content, complement it with first-class typing, paper, and printing. Remember, your major objective is to get an interview for a job — not to save $5.

In selecting paper color, use one of the following: white, off-white, light tan, light gray, or light blue. Avoid blue, yellow, green, pink, orange, red, or any other bright colors. Conservative, light muted colors are the best. Any of these colors can be complemented with black ink. In the case of light gray — our first choice — a navy blue ink looks best. Dark brown ink is especially attractive on light tan paper.

Your choices of paper quality and color say something about your personality and professional style. They are nonverbal cues to your strengths and weaknesses. Employers will use these as indicators for screening you in or out of an interview. At the same time, these choices may make your resume stand out from the crowd of standard black on white resumes.

You have two choices in reproducing your resume: a copy machine or an offset process. Many of the newer copy machines give good reproductions on the quality paper you need — nearly the same quality as the offset process. You should be able to make such copies for 10-20¢ per page. The offset process produces the best quality because it uses a printing plate. It also is relatively inexpensive — 5¢ to 10¢ per copy with a minimum run of 100 copies. The cost per copy decreases with larger runs of 300, 500, or 1000. In the end, you should be able to have your resume typed and 100 copies reproduced on high quality colored bond paper for less than $25. If you have it typeset, the same number of copies may cost you $50.

Whatever you do, don't try to cut costs when it comes to producing your resume. It simply is not worth it. Your resume is your calling card. You are putting your best foot forward at this stage. Go in style by spending a few dollars for producing a first-class resume.

WRITE DIFFERENT JOB SEARCH LETTERS

A resume is normally accompanied by a cover letter. In addition, you will write other job search letters — especially approach and thank-you letters. Examples of the different types of letters are found in Appendix B (pages 293-300).

Your letter writing should follow the principles of good resume and business writing. Job search letters are like resumes — they advertise you for interviews. As good advertisements these letters should:

- catch the reader's attention
- persuade the reader of your benefits or value
- convince the reader with more evidence
- move the reader to acquire the product — take action!

Effective Writing Principles

Before you write a letter, refer to this checklist of questions in order to clarify the content of your letters:

```
┌──── KEY QUESTIONS ORIENTING YOUR WRITING ────┐
│                                               │
│  ☐ What is the *purpose* of the letter?       │
│  ☐ What are the *needs* of my audience?       │
│  ☐ What *benefits* will my audience gain from me? │
│  ☐ What is a good opening sentence or paragraph for │
│    grabbing the *attention* of my audience?   │
│  ☐ How can I maintain the *interests* of my audience? │
│  ☐ How can I best end the letter so that the audience │
│    will be *persuaded* to contact me?         │
│  ☐ If a resume is enclosed, how can my letter best *ad-│
│    vertise the resume*?                        │
│  ☐ Have I spent enough *time* revising and proofreading │
│    the letter?                                 │
│  ☐ Does the letter represent my *best professional effort*? │
│                                               │
└───────────────────────────────────────────────┘
```

Since your letters are a form of business communication, they should conform to the rules of good business correspondence:

EFFECTIVE BUSINESS COMMUNICATION

- Plan and organize what you will say by outlining the content of your letter.
- Know your purpose and plan the elements of the letter accordingly.
- Communicate your message in a logical and sequential manner.
- State your purpose immediately in the first sentence and paragraph; main ideas always go first.
- End your letter by stating what your reader can expect next from you.
- Use short paragraphs and sentences; avoid overly complex sentences.
- Punctuate properly and use correct grammar and spelling.
- Use simple and straight forward language; avoid jargon.
- Communicate your message as directly and briefly as possible.

These rules stress how to both *organize and communicate* your message with impact. At the same time, you should always have a specific purpose in mind as well as know the needs of your audience.

Types of Letters

Cover letters (page 294) provide cover for your resume. Therefore, do not overwhelm your one-page resume with a two-page letter or repeat the contents of the resume in the letter. A short and succinct one-page letter which highlights one or two points in your resume is sufficient. Three paragraphs will suffice. The first paragraph should state your interests and purposes for writing. The second paragraph should highlight your possible value to the employer. The third paragraph should state that you will call the individual at a particular time to schedule an interview.

Don't expect much from cover letters. As many professional job search firms, using high speed word processing equipment, flood the job market with resumes and cover letters, employers are becoming increasingly suspicious of them.

Approach letters (pages 295-296) are written for the purpose of developing job contacts, leads, or information as well as for organizing networks (Chapter Ten) and getting interviews (Chapter Eleven). Your primary purposes should be to get employers to

1. Read your resume
2. Give you information and advice
3. Refer you to others
4. Remember you

These letters help you gain access to the hidden job market.

Approach letters can be sent out en masse to uncover job leads or they can be targeted to particular individuals or organizations. It is best to target these letters since they have maximum impact when personalized in reference to particular positions.

The organization of approach letters is similar to other letters. The first paragraph states your purpose. In so doing, you may want to use a personal statement for openers, such as *"John Everts recommended that I write to you. . ."* or *"I am familiar with your. . ."* State your purpose, but **do not suggest that you are asking for a job** — only career advice or information. In your final paragraph request a meeting and indicate you will call to schedule such a meeting at a mutually convenient time.

Thank-you letters (pages 297-300) may well become your most effective job search letters. They especially communicate your thoughtfulness. These letters come in different forms and are written for various occasions. The most common thank-you letter is written after receiving assistance, such as job search information or a critique of your resume. Other occasions include:

- **Immediately following an interview** — Thank the interviewer for the opportunity to interview for the position. Repeat your interest in the position.
- **Receive a job offer** — Thank the employer for his or her faith in you and express your appreciation.
- **Rejected for a job** — Thank the employer for giving you the "opportunity" to interview for the job. Ask to be remembered for future reference.
- **Terminate employment** — Thank the employer for the experience and ask to be remembered for future reference.

- **Begin a new job** — Thank the employer for giving you this new opportunity and express your confidence in producing the value he or she is expecting from you.

Examples of each type of letter are found in Appendix B.

Several of these thank-you letters are unusual, but they all have the same purpose in mind — to be remembered by potential employers in a positive light. In a job search, being remembered by employers is the closest thing to being invited to an interview and offered a job.

RESPOND EFFECTIVELY TO WANT ADS

While most of your writing activities should focus on the hidden job market, you will occasionally respond to job listings in newspapers and magazines. While this is largely a numbers game, you can increase your odds by the way you respond to the ads.

You should be selective in your responses. Since you know what you want to do, you will be looking for only certain types of positions. Once you identify them, your response entails little expenditure of time and effort — an envelope, letter, stamp, resume, and maybe 20 minutes of your time. Therefore, you have little to lose. While you have the potential to gain by sending a letter and resume in response to an ad, the odds are still against you.

It is difficult to interpret job listings. Some employers place blind ads with P.O. Box numbers in order to collect resumes for future reference. Others wish to avoid aggressive applicants who telephone or "drop-in" for interviews. Many employers work through professional recruiters who place these ads. While you may try to second guess the rationale behind such ads, respond to them as you would to ads which include the employer's name, address, or telephone number. Assume there is a real job behind the ad.

Most ads request a copy of your resume. You should respond with a cover letter and resume as soon as you see the ad. Depending on how much information on the position is revealed in the ad, your letter should be tailored to emphasize your qualifications vis-a-vis the ad. Examine the ad carefully. Underline any words or phrases which relate to your qualifications. In your cover letter you should use similar terminology in emphasizing your qualifications. Keep the letter brief and to the point.

If the ad asks you to state your salary history or salary requirements, state *"negotiable"* or include it by stating a salary range. For example, if you are making $30,000 a year, you can state this as *"in the $30,000 to $35,000 range."* You should address the salary question if this information is requested in the ad because some employers may screen you out if you "forget" to include it. By stating a salary range which goes above your present base salary, you establish some flexibility for future salary negotiations.

You may be able to increase your odds by sending a second copy of your letter and resume two or three weeks after your initial response. Ordinarily most applicants reply to an ad during the seven day period immediately after it appears in print. Since employers often are swamped with responses, your letter and resume may get lost in the crowd. If you send a second copy of your application two or three weeks later, the employer will have more time to give you special attention. By then, he also will have a better basis on which to compare you to the others.

Keep in mind that your cover letter and resume may be screened among 400 other resumes and letters. Thus, you want your cover letter to be eye catching and easy to read. Keep it brief and concise and highlight your qualifications as stated in the employer's ad. Above all, don't spend a great deal of time responding to an ad or waiting anxiously at your mailbox or telephone for a reply. You want to move on to the other potential opportunities as you play this numbers game.

DISTRIBUTE YOUR RESUMES AND LETTERS WITH IMPACT

Your letters and resumes can be distributed and managed in various ways. Many people shotgun hundreds of cover letters and resumes to prospective employers. This is a form of gambling where the odds are against you. For every 100 people you contact in this manner, expect that one or two might be interested in you. After all, direct-mail experts only expect a 2 percent return on their mass mailings to consider their efforts successful!

If you choose to use the shotgun method, you can increase your odds by *telephoning* a prospective employer within a week after he or she receives your letter. This technique will probably increase your effectiveness rate from 1 to 5 percent. However, many people are shotgunning their resumes today. As more resumes and letters descend on employers with the increased use of word processing equipment, the effectiveness rates may be even lower. This also can be an expensive marketing method.

Another generally ineffective distribution method, as noted previously, is to send resumes and letters in response to job listings. You will probably get better responses on your direct-mail efforts than in response to classified ads. The reasons are numerous. Many of the ads are blind ads. Competition is stiff; too many other people are applying in the same manner. Many positions are already filled with a friend or relative, but the job is listed to meet equal opportunity and affirmative action requirements.

Your best distribution strategy will be to:

1. Identify selectively whom you would be interested in working for

2. Send an approach letter

3. Follow up with a telephone call seeking an appointment for an interview.

In nearly 50 percent of the cases, you will get an interview. However, do not include your resume with the approach letter. Keep your resume for the interview; present it near the end of the interview. Chapter Ten on networking outlines the procedures for conducting this interview.

Once you begin distributing letters and resumes, you also will need to keep good records for managing your job search writing campaign. Purchase file folders for your correspondence and notes. Be sure to make copies of all letters you write since you may need to refer to them over the telephone or before interviews. Also, record your activities with each employer — letters, resumes, telephone calls, interviews — on a 4 x 6 card and file it according to the name of the organization or individual. These files will help you quickly access information and enable you to evaluate your job search progress.

Always remember the purpose of resumes and letters — advertisements for interviews. They do not get jobs. You are a stranger; most employers know nothing about you. Therefore, *you must effectively communicate your value in writing prior to the critical interview*. While you should not overestimate the importance of this written communication, neither should you underestimate it.

Chapter Nine
MAKE RESEARCH A TOP PRIORITY

The old adage that "knowledge is power" is especially true when conducting a job search. Your job search is only as good as the knowledge you acquire and use for finding the job you want.

Gathering, processing, and using information is the lifeblood of any job search. Given the numerous individuals and organizations involved in your job search, you must develop an information gathering strategy that will help you gain knowledge about, as well as access to, those individuals and organizations that will play the most important role in your job search.

Research is the key to gathering, processing, and using information in your job search. It is a skill that will point you in fruitful directions for minimizing job search frustrations and maximizing successes. Be sure to make research one of your top priorities.

Your research should focus on several questions relevant to three different opportunity levels within the job market:

- *Individuals* — those who have job information and the power to hire

- *Organizations* — groups with job vacancies and career opportunities

- *Communities* — the geographic location of your job

157

This chapter focuses primarily on how to do research on individuals and organizations. Chapter Fourteen examines research on communities.

CONDUCT RESEARCH

Assuming you have identified your skills, specified your job objective, and written your resume, what comes next? It depends on how well prepared you are for entering the job market. A *strong knowledge base* is required before taking the next critical steps — contacting individuals and interviewing.

You should be flexible and open to new information at all times while conducting your job search. As you acquire more information, weigh it in light of your previous experience; modify your job search if it seems appropriate. Doing this will help you stay on target and use your time efficiently.

Research, the process of uncovering information, is central to every step in your job search. It should be a continuous process aimed at developing two general areas of information. First, you must *understand the structure and operation of the job markets* — both the advertised and hidden job markets. Second, you must *develop specialized knowledge on the key elements in the job market* — individuals and organizations. You gather this information by conducting research in libraries, by mail and telephone, and through face-to-face conversations. This research should begin the first day of your job search and continue until the last day, and beyond.

Your research should focus on answering five major questions for organizing your job search:

1. What are the jobs?
2. Where are the jobs?
3. Who has the power to hire?
4. How does organization X operate?
5. What do I need to do to get a job with organization X?

The first two questions can be answered by consulting various directories and books found in most libraries as well as contacting specialized job listing services and job banks. The last three questions can only be answered by talking with knowledgeable people associated with the organization. You need to probe as much as possible for details in order to focus your job search on particular organizations, positions, and individuals.

Many people are reluctant to do research. Using a library intimidates some. Initiating contacts with strangers frightens others. But you do research every day as you acquire new information. If you want to become successful, you must overcome any reluctance to use unfamiliar sections of the library or initiate contacts with strangers. The best way to accomplish this is to *do it*! Get started immediately by visiting a library and by talking to friends, acquaintances, and strangers about your career plans.

TARGET BOTH THE ADVERTISED
AND HIDDEN JOB MARKETS

Your research should initially be directed toward better understanding the structure of the job market. The so-called job market actually consists of two structurally different arenas for locating job opportunities — one advertised and another hidden. Both are characterized by a high degree of decentralization, fragmentation, and chaos. Neither should be underestimated nor overestimated.

The *advertised job market* consists of job vacancy announcements and listings found in newspapers, professional and trade journals, newsletters, employment agencies, and personnel offices. Most people focus on this market because it is relatively easy to find, and because they believe it accurately reflects available job vacancies at any given moment. In reality, however, the advertised job market probably represents no more than 25 percent of actual job openings. Furthermore, this market tends to represent positions at the extreme ends of the job spectrum — low paid unskilled or high paid highly skilled jobs. The majority of positions lying between these two extremes are not well represented in the listings. Competition often is great for the low and middle level positions. Worst of all, many of these advertised jobs are either nonexistent or are filled prior to being advertised.

You should spend a minimum amount of time looking for employment in the advertised job markets. Monitor this market, but don't assume it represents the entire spectrum of job opportunities. Your job search time and money are better spent elsewhere — on the hidden job market. When, as we noted in Chapter Eight, you identify an advertised position that is right for you, send a cover letter and resume — but keep moving on to other potential opportunities.

However, you will find exceptions to this general rule of avoiding the advertised job market. Each occupational specialty has its own internal recruitment and job finding structure. Some occupations are represented more by professional listing and recruitment services than others. Indeed, as we move into the high-tech society of the 1990s, greater efforts will be made to increase the efficiency of employment communication by centralizing job listings and recruitment services for particular occupational specialties. These services will be designed to reduce the *lag time* between when a job becomes vacant and is filled. Computerized job banks may increasingly be used by employers to locate qualified candidates, and vice versa. Employers in a high-tech society need to reduce lag time as much as possible given the increasing interdependency of positions in high-tech industries. If and when such employment services and job banks become available for your occupational specialty, you should at least investigate them. In the meantime, since the job market will remain relatively disorganized in the foreseeable future, do your research and follow our careering and re-careering strategies.

Your research should center on one of the key dynamics to finding employment – helping employers solve their hiring problems. Many employers turn to the advertised job market *after* they fail to recruit candidates by other, less formal and public, means. The lag time between when a position becomes vacant, is listed, and then filled is a critical period for your attention and *intervention*. Your goal should be to locate high quality job vacancies before they are listed.

The *hidden job market* is where the action is. It is this job market that should occupy most of your attention. Although this job market lacks a formal structure, 75 percent or more of all job opportunities are found here. Your task is to give this market some semblance of structure and coherence so that you can effectively penetrate it. If you can do this, the hidden job market will yield numerous job interviews and offers that should be right for you.

Research is the key to penetrating the hidden job market. Consider, for example, the hiring problems of employers by putting yourself in their place. Suppose one of your employees suddenly gives you a two week notice, or you terminate someone. Now you have a problem – you must hire a new employee. It takes time and it is a risky business you would prefer to avoid. After hours of reading resumes and interviewing, you still will be hiring an unknown who might create new problems for you.

Like many other employers, you want to *minimize your time and risks*. You can do this by calling your friends and acquaintances and letting them know you are looking for someone; you would appreciate it if they could refer some good candidates to you. Based on these contacts, you should receive referrals. At the same time, you want to hedge your bets or fulfill affirmative action and equal opportunity requirements by listing the job vacancy in the newspaper or with your personnel office. While 300 people respond by mail to your want ad, you also get referrals from the trusted individuals in your network. In the end, you conduct 10 telephone interviews and three face-to-face interviews. You hire the *best* candidate — the one your former classmate recommended to you on the first day you informed her of your need to fill the vacancy. You are satisfied with your excellent choice of candidates; you are relatively certain this new employee will be a good addition to your organization.

This scenario is played out regularly in many organizations. It demonstrates the importance of getting into the hidden job market and devoting most of your time and energy there. If you let people know you are looking for employment, chances are they will keep you in mind and refer you to others who may have an unexpected vacancy. Your research will help you enter and maneuver within this job market of interpersonal networks and highly personalized information exchanges. Chapter Ten will show you how to do this with the maximum amount of impact.

CONSULT LIBRARIES AND LIBRARIANS

Libraries are filled with useful job and career relevant information. Reference and documents rooms of libraries have some of the best career resources. Career planning offices at colleges and universities have a wealth of job and career information in their specialized libraries — a wider selection than most general libraries.

Do seek out library personnel for assistance. Reference librarians know what indexes and reference books are available. Tell them you are doing research on job and career alternatives; you would appreciate their assistance in locating information, such as lists of names and addresses of employers. Most librarians will be happy to share their knowledge with you. Some may even overwhelm you with assistance!

Your goal should be to acquire as much written information as possible on individuals and organizations relating to your job objective. Normally this means examining directories, books, magazines, and reports. These publications will provide general surveys of occupational fields, information on particular individuals and organizations, as well as names, addresses, and telephone numbers of key individuals within organizations. At this stage you need to understand the organizations and collect many names, addresses, and telephone numbers for initiating your writing and telephoning activities. Use 4 x 6 cards to record this information to develop your data files.

You should start your research by examining several of the following resources normally found in the reference or documents sections of libraries:

KEY RESEARCH MATERIALS

Directories of Reference Materials:

- *Ayer Directory of Publications*
- *Applied Science and Technology*
- *Business Periodicals Index*
- *Directory of Directories*
- *Guide to American Directories* (Bernard Klein)
- *Readers' Guide to Periodical Literature*
- *Standard Periodical Directory*
- *Ulrich's International Periodicals Directory*
- *Working Press of the Nation*

Career and Job Alternatives

- *Ad Search*
- *Advance Job Listings*
- *Affirmative Action Register*
- *The College Placement Annual*
- *Dictionary of Occupational Titles*
- *Encyclopedia of Careers and Vocational Guidance*, William E. Hopke (ed.)
- *Guide for Occupational Exploration*
- *Occupational Outlook Handbook*
- *Occupational Outlook Quarterly*
- *Work Related Abstracts*

Business Sources

- *American Encyclopedia of International Information*
- *Career Guide to Professional Associations*
- *Directory of American Firms Operating in Foreign Countries*
- *The Directory of Corporate Affiliations: Who Owns Whom*
- *Dun & Bradstreet's Middle Market Directory*

- *Dun & Bradstreet's Million Dollar Directory*
- *Dun & Bradstreet's Reference Book of Corporate Managements*
- *Encyclopedia of Business Information Services*
- *Fitch's Corporation Reports*
- *Geographical Index*
- *Job Prospector*
- *MacRae's Blue Book — Corporate Index*
- *Moody's Manuals* (for various business fields)
- *The Multinational Marketing and Employment Directory*
- *Standard Directory of Advertisers*
- *The Standard Periodical Directory*
- *Standard & Poor's Industrial Index*
- *Standard Rate and Data Business Publications Directory*
- *Thomas' Register of American Manufacturers*

Associations

- *Directory of Professional and Trade Organizations*
- *Encyclopedia of Associations*

Individuals

- *American Men and Women in Science*
- *Standard & Poor's Register of Corporations, Directors, and Executives*
- *Who's Who in America*
- *Who's Who in Commerce and Industry*
- *Who's Who in the East*
- *Who's Who in the West*
- *Who's Who in the South*
- Directories of any professional or trade association

Government

- *The Book of the States*
- *Congressional Directory*
- *Congressional Staff Directory*
- *Congressional Yellow Book*
- *Federal Directory*
- *Federal Yellow Book*
- *Municipal Yearbook*

- *Taylor's Encyclopedia of Government Officials*
- *United Nations Yearbook*
- *United States Government Manual*
- *Washington Information Directory*
- Other sources listed in Chapter Sixteen

Newspapers

- *The Wall Street Journal*
- *The New York Times*
- *USA Today*
- *The Los Angeles Times*
- *The Houston Chronicle*
- *National Business Employment Weekly*
- *Washington Report*
- Trade newspapers
- Any newspaper — especially the Sunday edition for the area you are targeting

Business Publications

- *Barron's, Business Week, Business World, Forbes, Fortune, Harvard Business Review, Money, Newsweek, Nation's Business, Time, U.S. News and World Report*

Other Resources

- Trade journals (the *Directory of Libraries and Information Centers* and *Subject Collections: A Guide to Special Book Collections in Libraries* compiles information on specialized business, government, and association libraries)
- Publications of chambers of commerce; state manufacturing associations; federal, state and local government agencies
- Telephone books — especially the Yellow Pages (if not in library, contact your local telephone company which may have a telephone book collection)
- Trade books on "how to get a job"

As you accumulate names and addresses, write or call individuals and organizations for further information. Large public companies have annual reports which they freely distribute to interested individuals. Your local stock broker also may be able to get some reports for you or suggest other information sources. Small privately held companies will be more difficult to research.

If you plan to move from a nonbusiness occupation to one in business, you should read business publications in order to familiarize yourself with various fields as well as the concepts and terminology business people use. The more you read in a field related to your job objective, the more you will be able to intelligently ask and answer questions in the language of employers.

Libraries have several other publications you may wish to consult concerning various occupational fields as well as job search strategies and techniques. Many of these are listed according to subject categories in the resource section of Appendix C.

Let's return to the five major research questions we raised at the beginning of this chapter to illustrate some useful resources you may wish to consult when conducting your research.

WHAT ARE THE JOBS?

If you need to explore what types of jobs are available in today's job market for someone with your skills and interests, you should consult several books and directories in the reference section of your local library. The Department of Labor publishes several useful resources for surveying various job titles. At a minimum you should examine:

- *The Dictionary of Occupational Titles*
- *The Occupational Outlook Handbook*

Other books to consult include:

- *The Careers Encyclopedia*
- *The Encyclopedia of Careers and Vocational Guidance*

Your library should also have numerous career books which focus on individual careers and jobs. The most extensive collection is published by National Textbook and includes over 100 titles beginning with the title *Opportunities in. . ., Your Career in. . .*, and *Careers in. . .* Walker and Company publishes a series of 12 career books tied to specific college majors. These begin with the title *Career Choices*. Information on these titles is included in the resource section in Appendix C as well as in the order form at the end of this book.

In addition to conducting library research to identify different jobs, you may want to write to various professional and trade associations for detailed information on jobs and careers relevant to their members. For names, addresses, and telephone numbers of such associations, consult the following key directories which are available in many library reference sections:

- *The Encyclopedia of Associations*
- *National Trade and Professional Associations in the U.S.*

If you are interested in jobs with a particular organization, you should contact the personnel office for information on the types of jobs offered within the organization. You may be able to examine vacancy announcements which describe the duties and responsibilities of specific jobs. If you are interested in working for federal, state, or local governments, each agency will have a personnel office which can supply you with descriptions of their jobs. While gathering such information, be sure to ask people about their jobs.

For a good summary of what jobs are available on any particular day, consult the classified section of newspapers, especially the Sunday edition. These ads do not represent all available vacancies, but they do give you a handy directory of what types of jobs employers are advertising for at present.

WHERE ARE THE JOBS?

You also need to know where to find the jobs that interest you. Several "job bank" books provide such information on both communities and organizations. Organized nationally as well as by region, state, and city, the most popular job bank books are published by Bob Adams, Inc. and Surrey Books. They include such titles as:

- *How to Get a Job in New York*
- *How to Get a Job in Los Angeles*
- *The National Job Bank*
- *The Atlanta Job Bank*
- *The Greater Chicago Job Bank*
- *The Texas Job Bank*

Job bank books published by other companies include Boston, Pittsburgh, and San Francisco.

Telephone books provide a wealth of information on organizations in particular communities. Many libraries collect Yellow Page telephone books for major metropolitan areas. If you can't find the telephone book you need, call your local telephone company to see if they have a collection of telephone books that you could review.

If you are focusing on a particular organization, you should write the organization for information on their headquarters and field offices. The company's annual report may provide you with this and other valuable organizational information for organizing your job search.

WHO HAS THE POWER TO HIRE?

Finding out who has the power to hire may take some research effort on your part. Keep in mind that personnel offices normally do not have the power to hire. They handle much of the paper work involved in announcing vacancies, taking applications, testing candidates, screening credentials, and placing new employees on the payroll. In other words, personnel offices tend to perform auxiliary support functions for those who do the actual hiring — usually individuals in operating units.

If you want to learn who really has the power to hire, you need to conduct research on the particular organization that interests you. You should ask specific questions concerning who normally is responsible for various parts of the hiring process:

- Who describes the positions?
- Who announces vacancies?
- Who receives applications?
- Who administers tests?
- Who selects eligible candidates?
- Who chooses whom to interview?
- Who offers the jobs?

If you ask these questions about a specific position, you will quickly identify who has what powers to hire. Chances are the power to hire is *shared* between the personnel office and the operating unit. You should not neglect the personnel office, and in some cases it will play a powerful role in all aspects of the hiring. Your research will reveal to what degree the hiring function has been centralized, decentralized, or fragmented within a particular organization.

HOW DOES ORGANIZATION X OPERATE?

It's best to know something about the internal operation of an organization before becoming a member. Your research may uncover information that would convince you that a particular organization is not one in which you wish to invest your time and effort. You may learn, for example, that Company X has a history of terminating employees before they become vested in the company retirement system. Or Company X may be experiencing serious financial problems. Or advancement within Company X may be very political and company politics is vicious and debilitating.

You can get financial information about most companies by examining their annual reports as well as talking to individuals who know the organization well. Information on the internal operations, especially company politics and power, must come from individuals who work within the organization. Ask them. *"Is this a good organization to work for?"* and let them expand on specific areas you wish to probe — advancement opportunities, working conditions, relationships among co-workers and supervisors, growth patterns, internal politics, management style, work values, opportunities for taking initiative.

WHAT DO I NEED TO DO TO GET
A JOB WITH ORGANIZATION X?

The best way to find how to get a job in a particular organization is to follow the advice in the next chapter on prospecting, networking, and informational interviewing. This question can only be answered by talking to people who know both the formal and informal hiring practices.

You can get information on the formal hiring system by contacting the personnel office. A telephone call should be sufficient to get this information.

But you must go beyond the formal system and personnel office in order to learn how best to conduct your job search. This means contacting people who know how one really gets hired in the organization, which may or may not follow the formal procedures. The best source of information will be the individual or individuals who play a major role in the hiring process.

TALK TO PEOPLE

Reading and writing can take you only so far in your job search. Beware of becoming *too* preoccupied with library research. It never seems to end. Stop when you feel you have enough information to begin other types of research or start other job search steps. Two weeks or 40 hours in the library should get you off to a good start. If you are examining a highly specialized field where there are few names and addresses, you may achieve a high degree of redundancy within 10 hours. If you get carried away and are on your third week in the library, stop immediately and go on to more productive activities.

Your most productive research activity will be talking to people. Informal, word-of-mouth communication is still the most effective channel of job search information. In contrast to reading books, people have more current, and probably more accurate, information. In addition, most people are flattered to be asked for advice. They freely give it and will be happy to assist you with referrals to others. Don't hide the fact you are looking for a job, but don't ask for a job. Ask people about:

- Occupational fields
- Job requirements and training
- Interpersonal environments
- Performance expectations
- Their problems
- Salaries
- Advancement opportunities
- Future growth potential of the organization
- How best to acquire more information and contacts in a particular field
- How you can improve your resume

You may be surprised how willingly friends, acquaintances, and strangers will give you useful information. But before you talk to people, do your library research so that you are better able to ask thoughtful questions.

ACQUIRE AND USE POWER

Acquiring knowledge about the job market, individuals, and organizations does not assure job search success. Knowledge is power only when you use it. Research will help increase your power in the job market. You should always collect new information, revise previous conceptions, and adjust your job search efforts to new realities uncovered through your research. As you do this, your research will affect your original objective and resume as well as guide you in accomplishing the other job search steps. Your power to give some structure and coherence to the hidden job market in your particular area of interest should increase accordingly!

Chapter Ten

DEVELOP PROSPECTING, NETWORKING, AND INFORMATIONAL INTERVIEWING SKILLS

Now that you have identified your skills, specified your objective, written your resume, and conducted research, what should you do next? At this point let's examine where we are going so we don't get preoccupied with the trees and thus lose sight of the larger forest.

REMEMBER WHERE YOU ARE GOING

Everything you do up to this point in your job search should be aimed at *getting a job interview*. The skills you identified, the goals you set, the resume you wrote, and the information you gathered are carefully related to one another so you will have maximum impact for communicating your qualifications to employers who, in turn, will decide to invite you to a job interview.

But there are secrets to getting a job interview you should know before continuing further with your job search. The most important secret is the informational interview — a type of interview which yields useful job search information and may lead to job interviews and offers. Based on prospecting and networking techniques, these interviews minimize rejections and competition as well as quickly open the doors to organizations and employers. If you want a job interview, you first need to understand the informational interview and how to initiate and use it for maximum impact.

171

PROSPECT AND NETWORK FOR INTERVIEWS

What do you do after you complete your resume? Most people send cover letters and resumes in response to job listings; they then wait to be called for a job interview (THE RESPONSE APPROACH). Others mail numerous copies of their resume to employers in the hope that someone will invite them to an interview (THE SHOT-GUN APPROACH). Both approaches are relatively passive activities primarily involving written, clerical, and mailing skills. Viewing the job search as basically a direct-mail operation, many such job seekers are disappointed in discovering the realities of direct-mail — a 2 percent response rate is considered good!

Successful job seekers break out of this relatively passive job search role by orienting themselves toward face-to-face action. Being proactive, they develop *interpersonal strategies* in which the resume plays a supportive rather than a central role in the job search. They first present themselves to employers; the resume appears only at the end of a face-to-face conversation.

Throughout the job search you will acquire useful names and addresses as well as meet people who will assist you in contacting potential employers. Such information and contacts become key building blocks for generating job interviews and offers.

Since the best and most numerous jobs are found on the hidden job market, you must use methods appropriate for this job market. Indeed, research and experience clearly show the most effective means of communication are face-to-face and word-of-mouth. The informal, interpersonal system of communication is the central nervous system of the hidden job market. Your goal should be to penetrate this job market with proven methods of success. Appropriate methods for making important job contacts are *prospecting and networking*. Appropriate methods for getting these contacts to provide you with useful job information are *informational and referral interviews*.

HELP EMPLOYERS AND YOURSELF

Taken together, these interpersonal methods help you *communicate your qualifications to employers*. Although many job seekers may be reluctant to use this informal communication system, they greatly limit their potential for success if they do not.

Put yourself in the position of the employer for a moment. You have a job vacancy to fill. If you advertise the position, you may be bombarded with hundreds of applications, phone calls, and walk-ins. While you do want to hire the best qualified individual for the job, you simply don't have time nor patience to review scores of applications. Even if you use a P.O. Box number, the paperwork may be overwhelming. Furthermore, with limited information from application forms, cover letters, and resumes, you find it hard to identify the best qualified individuals to invite for an interview; many look the same on paper.

So what do you do? You might hire a professional job search firm to take on all of this additional work. On the other hand, you may want to better control the hiring process. Like many other employers, you begin by calling your friends, acquaintances, and other business associates and ask if they or someone else might know of any good candidates for the position. If they can't help, you ask them to give you a call should they learn of anyone qualified for your vacancy. You, in effect, create your own hidden job market — an informal information network for locating desirable candidates. Your trusted contacts initially screen the candidates in the process of referring them to you.

Based on this understanding of the employer's perspective, what should you do to best improve your chances of getting an interview and job offer? Remember, the employer needs to solve a personnel problem. By conducting *informational interviews and networking* you help the employer solve his or her problem by giving them a chance to examine what you can offer them. You gain several advantages by conducting these interviews:

ADVANTAGES OF INFORMATIONAL INTERVIEWS

1. You are less likely to encounter rejections since you are not asking for a job — only information, advice, referrals, and to be remembered.

2. You go after higher level positions.

3. You encounter little competition.

4. You go directly to the people who have the power to hire.

5. You are likely to be invited to job interviews based upon the referrals you receive.

This job search approach has a much higher probability of generating job interviews and offers than the more traditional shotgunning and advertised job market approaches.

DEVELOP AND LINK NETWORKS

Networking is the process of purposefully developing relations with others. Networking in the job search involves connecting and interacting with other individuals who can be helpful to you. Your network consists of you interacting with these other individuals. The more you develop, maintain, and expand your networks, the more successful should be your job search.

Your network is your interpersonal environment. While you know and interact with hundreds of people, on a day-to-day basis you probably encounter no more than 20 people. The figure on page 175 outlines a hypothetical network. You frequently contact these people in face-to-face situations. Some people are more *important* to you than others. You *like* some more than others. And some will be more *helpful* to you in your job search than others. Your basic network may encompass the following individuals and groups: friends, acquaintances, immediate family, distant relatives, professional colleagues, spouse, supervisor, fellow workers, close friends and colleagues, and local businessmen and professionals, such as your banker, lawyer, doctor, minister, and insurance agent. You should contact many of these individuals for advice relating to your job search.

You need to *identify everyone in your network* who might help you with your job search. You first need to expand your basic network to include individuals you know and have interacted with over the past 10 or more years. Make a list of at least 200 people you know. Include friends and relatives from your Christmas card list, past and present neighbors, former classmates, politicians, business persons, previous employers, professional associates, ministers, insurance agents, lawyers, bankers, doctors, dentists, accountants, and social acquaintances.

After identifying your extended network, you should try to *link your network to others' networks*. The figure on page 176 illustrates this linkage principle. Individuals in these other networks also have job information and contacts. Ask people in your basic network for referrals to individuals in their networks. This approach should greatly enlarge your basic job search network.

What do you do if individuals in your immediate and extended network can not provide you with certain job information and contacts? While it is much easier and more effective to meet new people through personal contacts, on occasion you may need to *approach strangers without prior contacts*. In this situation, try the "cold turkey" approach. Write a letter to someone you feel may be useful to your job search. Research this individual so you are acquainted

YOUR NETWORK OF RELATIONSHIPS

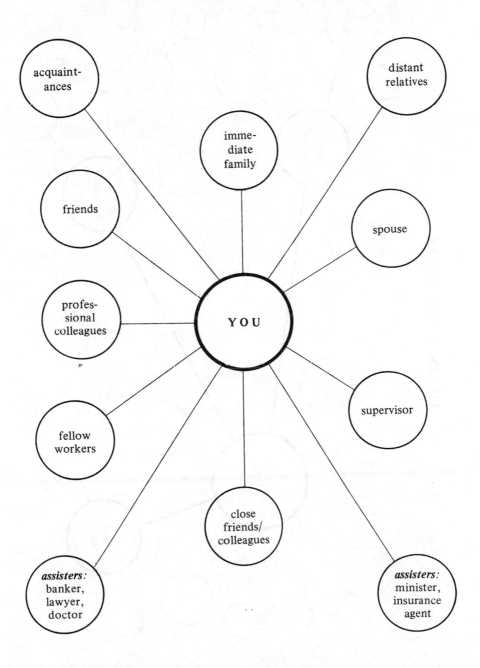

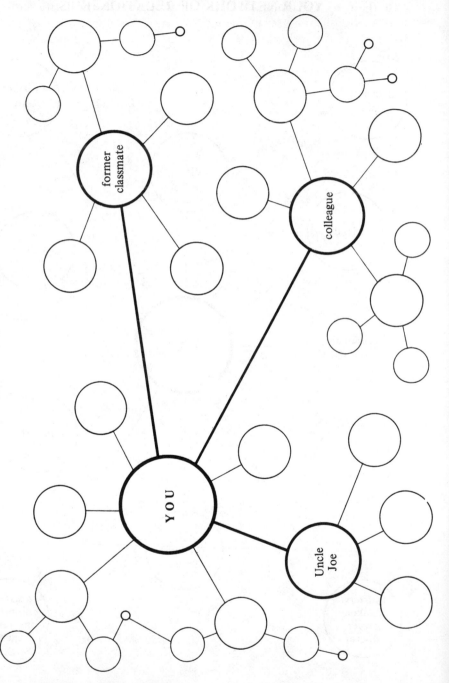

LINKING OF NETWORKS

with their background and accomplishments. In the letter, refer to their accomplishments, mention your need for job information, and specify a date and time you will call to schedule a meeting. An example of such a "cold turkey approach letter" is included in Appendix B. Another approach is to introduce yourself to someone by telephone and request a meeting and/or job information. While you may experience rejections in using these approaches, you also will experience successes. And those successes should lead to further expansion of your job search network.

PROSPECT FOR JOB LEADS

The key to successful networking is an active and routine *prospecting campaign*. Salespersons in insurance, real estate, Amway, Shaklee, and other direct-sales businesses understand the importance and principles of prospecting; indeed, many have turned the art of prospecting into a science! The basic operating principle is *probability:* the number of sales you make is a direct function of the amount of effort you put into developing new contacts and following-through. Expect no more than a 10 percent acceptance rate: for every 10 people you meet, 9 will reject you and 1 will accept you. Therefore, the more people you contact, the more acceptances you will receive. If you want to be successful, you must collect many more "nos" than "yeses." In a 10 percent probability situation, you need to contact 100 people for 10 successes.

These prospecting principles are extremely useful for your job search. Like sales situations, the job search is a highly ego-involved activity often characterized by numerous rejections accompanied by a few acceptances. While no one wants to be rejected, few people are willing and able to handle more than a few rejections. They take a "no" as a sign of personal failure — and quit prematurely. If they persisted longer, they would achieve success after a few more "nos." Furthermore, if their prospecting activities were focused on gathering information rather than making sales, they would considerably minimize the number of rejections. Knowing this, your best approach is to:

- Prospect for job leads.

- Accept rejections as part of the game.

- Link prospecting to informational interviewing.

- Keep prospecting for more information and "yeses" which will eventually translate into job interviews and offers.

A good prospecting pace to begin with is to make two new contacts each day. Start by contacting people in your immediate network. Let them know you are conducting a job search, but emphasize that you are only doing research. Ask for a few moments of their time to discuss your information needs. You are only seeking *information and advice* at this time — not a job.

It should take you about 20 minutes to make a contact by letter or telephone. If you make two contacts each day, by the end of the first week you will have 10 new contacts for a total investment of less than seven hours. By the second week you may want to increase your prospecting pace to four new contacts each day or 20 each week. The more contacts you make, the more useful information, advice, and job leads you will receive. If your job search bogs down, you probably need to increase your prospecting activities.

Expect each contact to refer you to two or three others who will also refer you to others. Consequently, your contacts should multiply considerably within only a few weeks.

MINIMIZE AND HANDLE REJECTIONS

These prospecting and networking methods are effective. While they are responsible for building, maintaining, and expanding multimillion dollar businesses, they work extremely well for job hunters. But they only work if you are patient and persist. *The key to networking success is to focus on gathering information while also learning to handle rejections*. Learn from rejections, forget them, and go on to more productive networking activities. The major reason direct-sales people fail is because they don't persist. The reason they don't persist is because they either can't take, or get tired of taking, rejections.

Rejections are no fun, especially in such an ego-involved activity as a job search. But you will encounter rejections as you travel on the road toward job search success. This road is strewn with individuals who quit prematurely because they were rejected four or five times. Don't be one of them!

Our prospecting and networking techniques differ from sales approaches in one major respect: we have special techniques for minimizing the number of rejections. If handled properly, at least 50 percent — maybe as many as 90 percent — of your prospects will turn into "yeses" rather than "nos." The reason for this un-usually high acceptance rate is how you introduce and handle your-self before your prospects. Many insurance agents and direct distribu-tors expect a 90 percent rejection rate, because they are trying to sell specific products potential clients may or may not need. Most people don't like to be put on the spot — especially when it is in their own home or office — to make a decision to buy a product.

SELL THROUGH HONESTY AND SINCERITY

The principles of selling yourself in the job market are similar. People don't want to be put on the spot. They feel uncomfortable if they think you expect them to give you a job. Thus, you should never introduce yourself to a prospect by asking them for a job or a job lead. You should do just the opposite: relieve their anxiety by mentioning that you are not looking for a job from them — only job information and advice. You must be honest and sincere in communicating these intentions to your contact. The biggest turn-off for individuals targeted for informational interviews is insincere job seekers who try to use this as a mechanism to get a job.

Your approach to prospects must be subtle, honest, and pro-fessional. You are seeking *information, advice, and referrals* relating to several subjects: job opportunities, your job search approach, your resume, and others who may have similar information, advice, and referrals. Most people gladly volunteer such information. They generally like to talk about themselves, their careers, and others. They like to give advice. This approach flatters individuals by placing them in the role of the expert-advisor. Who doesn't want to be recognized as an expert-advisor, especially on such a critical topic as one's employment?

This approach should yield a great deal of information, advice, and referrals from your prospects. One other important outcome should result from using this approach: people will *remember* you as the person who made them feel at ease and who received their valuable advice. If they hear of job opportunities for someone with your qualifications, chances are they will contact you with the in-formation. After contacting 100 prospects, you will have created 100 sets of eyes and ears to help you in your job search!

OBSERVE THE 5-R's OF INFORMATIONAL INTERVIEWING

The guiding principle behind prospecting, networking, and in-formational interviews is this: *the best way to get a job is to ask for job information, advice, and referrals; never ask for a job.* Remember, you want your prospects to engage in the 5-R's of informational interviewing:

- *Reveal* useful information and advice.
- *Refer* you to others.
- *Read* and *revise* your resume.
- *Remember* you for future reference.

If you follow this principle, you should join the ranks of thousands of successful job seekers who paid a great deal of money learning it from highly-paid professionals.

APPROACH THE RIGHT PEOPLE RIGHT

Whom should you contact within an organization for an informational interview? Contact people who are busy, who have the power to hire, and who are knowledgeable about the organization. The least likely candidate will be someone in the personnel department. Most often the heads of operating units are the most busy, powerful, and knowledgeable individuals in the organization. However, getting access to such individuals may be difficult. Some people at the top may appear to be informed and powerful, but they may lack information on the day-to-day personnel changes or their influence is limited in the hiring process. It is difficult to give one best answer to this question.

We recommend contacting a variety of people. Aim for the busy, powerful, and informed, but be prepared to settle for less. Secretaries, receptionists, and the person you want to meet may refer you to others. From a practical standpoint, you may have to take whomever you can schedule an appointment with. Sometimes people who are not busy can be helpful. Talk to a secretary or receptionist sometime about their boss or working in the organization. You may be surprised with what you learn!

Nonetheless, you will conduct informational interviews with different types of people. Some will be friends, relatives, or acquaintances. Others will be referrals or new contacts. You will gain the easiest access to people you already know. This can usually be done informally by telephone. You might meet at their home or office or at a restaurant.

You should use a more formal approach to gain access to referrals and new contacts. The best approach is to write an approach letter and follow it up with a phone call. Examples of approach letters are found in Appendix **B**. Your Approach letter should include the following elements:

```
┌──── KEY ELEMENTS IN THE APPROACH LETTER ────┐
```

OPENERS: If you have a referral, tell the individual you are considering a career in _____ _____ . His or her name was given to you by _____ who suggested he or she might be a good person to give you useful information about careers in _____ .

If you lack a referral to the individual and thus must use a "cold turkey" approach to making this contact, you might begin your letter by stating that you are aware he or she has been at the forefront of _____ business — or whatever is both truthful and appropriate for the situation. A subtle form of flattery will be helpful at this stage.

THE REQUEST: Demonstrate your thoughtfulness and courtesy rather than aggressiveness by mentioning that you know he or she is busy. You hope to schedule a mutually convenient time for a brief meeting to discuss your questions and career plans. Most people will be flattered by such a request and happy to talk with you about their work — if they have time and are interested in you.

CLOSINGS: In closing the letter, mention that you will call the person to see if an appointment can be arranged. Be specific by stating the time and day you will call — for example, Thursday at 2:00 p.m. You must take the initiative in this manner to followup the letter with a definite contact time. If you don't, you cannot expect to hear from the person. It is *your* responsibility to make the telephone call to schedule a meeting.

ENCLOSURES: Do *not* enclose your resume with this approach letter. You should take your resume to the interview and present it as a topic of discussion near the end of your meeting. If you send it with the approach letter, you communicate a mixed and contradictory message. Remember your purpose for this interview: to gather information and advice. You are not — and never should be — asking for a job. A resume in a letter appears to be an application or a request for a job.

Most people will meet with you, assuming you are sincere in your approach. If the person tries to put you off when you telephone for an appointment, clearly state your purpose and emphasize that you are not looking for a job with this person — only information and advice. If the person insists on putting you off, make the best of the situation: write a nice thank-you letter in which you again state your intended purpose; mention your disappointment in not being able to learn from the person's experience; and ask to be remembered for future reference. Enclose your resume with this letter.

While you are ostensibly seeking information and advice, treat this meeting as an important preliminary interview. You need to communicate your qualifications — that you are competent, intelligent, honest, and likeable. These are the same qualities you should communicate in a formal job interview. Hence, follow the same advice given for conducting a formal interview and dressing appropriately for face-to-face meetings (Chapter Eleven).

CONDUCT THE INTERVIEW WELL

An informational interview will be relatively unstructured compared to a formal interview. Since you want the interviewer to advise you, you reverse roles by asking questions which should give you useful information. You, in effect, become the interviewer. You should structure this interview with a particular sequence of questions. Most questions should be open-ended, requiring the individual to give specific answers based upon his or her experience.

The structure and dialogue for the informational interview might go something like this. You plan to take no more than 45 minutes for this interview. The first three to five minutes will be devoted to small talk — the weather, traffic, the office, mutual acquaintances, or an interesting or humorous observation. Since these are the most critical moments in the interview, be especially careful how you communicate verbally and nonverbally. Begin your interview by stating your appreciation for the individual's time:

> *Thank you again for taking time to see me today. I appreciate your willingness to speak with me about my career plans. It is a subject which is very important to me at this juncture of my life.*

Your next comment should be a statement reiterating your purpose as stated in your letter:

> *I am in the process of exploring several job and career alternatives. I know what I do well and enjoy doing. But before I make any decisions in this regard, I am trying to benefit from the counsel of individuals, such as you, who have a great deal of experience in the area of _____ . I am particularly interested in learning more about opportunities, necessary skills, responsibilities, advantages, disadvantages, and the future outlook for this field.*

This statement normally will get a positive reaction from the individual who may want to know more about what it is you want to do. Be sure to clearly communicate your job objective. If you can't, you may communicate that you are lost, indecisive, or uncertain about yourself. The person may feel you are wasting his or her time.

Your next line of questioning should focus on "how" and "what" questions centering on (1) specific jobs and (2) the job search process. Begin by asking about various aspects of specific jobs:

- Duties and responsibilities.
- Knowledge, skills, and abilities required.

- Work environment relating to fellow employees, work flows, deadlines, stress, initiative.

- Advantages and disadvantages.

- Advancement opportunities and outlook.

- Salary ranges.

Your informer will probably take a great deal of time talking about his or her experience in each area. Be a good listener, but make sure you move along with the questions.

Your next line of questioning should focus on your job search activities. You need as much information as possible on how to:

- Acquire the necessary skills.

- Best find a job in this field.

- Overcome any objections employers may have to your background.

- Uncover job vacancies which may be advertised.

- Develop job leads.

- Approach prospective employers.

Your final line of questioning should focus on your resume. Do not show your resume until you focus on this last set of questions. The purpose of these questions is to: (1) get the individual to read your resume in-depth, (2) acquire useful advice on how to strengthen it, (3) refer you to prospective employers, and (4) be remembered. With the resume in front of you and your interviewee, ask the following questions:

RESUME REVIEW QUESTIONS

- *Is this an appropriate type of resume for the jobs I have outlined?*

- *If an employer received this resume in the mail, how do you think he or she would react to it?*

- *What do you see as possible weaknesses or areas that need to be improved?*

What should I do with this resume? Shotgun it to hundreds of employers with a cover letter? Use resume letters instead?

> • *What about the length, paper quality and color, layout, and typing? Are they appropriate?*
>
> • *How might I best improve the form and content of the resume?*

You should receive useful advice on how to strengthen both the content and use of your resume. Most important, these questions force the individual to **read** your resume which, in turn, may be **remembered** for future reference.

Your last question is especially important in this interview. You want to be both **remembered** and **referred**. Some variation of the following question should help:

> *Thanks very much for all your assistance. I have learned a great deal today. Your advice will certainly help me give my job search better direction. I would like to ask one more favor. By conducting research on various jobs, I am trying to benefit from the counsel of several people. Do you know two or three other people who might be willing to meet with me, as you have today?*

Just before you leave, ask to be **remembered** for future reference:

> *While I know you may not know of a job opening at present for someone with my qualifications, I would appreciate it if you could keep me in mind if you learn of any openings. Please feel free to pass my name on to anyone you feel might be interested in my qualifications.*

Send a nice thank-you letter within 48 hours of completing this informational interview. Following the example in Appendix B, express your genuine gratitude for the individual's time and advice. Reiterate your interests, and ask to be remembered and referred to others.

Follow-up on any useful advice you receive, particularly referrals. Approach referrals in the same manner you approached the person who gave you the referral. Write a letter requesting a meeting. Begin the letter by mentioning that *"Mr./Ms. _____ suggested that I contact you concerning my research on careers in_____"*.

If you continue prospecting, networking, and conducting informational interviews, soon you will be busy conducting interviews and receiving job offers. While 100 informational interviews over a two-month period should lead to several formal job interviews and offers, the pay-offs are uncertain because job vacancies are unpredictable. We know cases where the first referral turned into a formal interview and job offer. More typical cases require constant prospecting, networking, and informational interviewing activities. The telephone call or letter inviting you to a job interview can come at any time. While the timing may be unpredictable, your persistent job search activities will be largely responsible for the final outcome.

TELEPHONE FOR JOB LEADS

Telephone communication plays a role in prospecting, networking, and informational interviewing activities. However, controversy centers around how and when to use the telephone for generating job leads and scheduling interviews. Some people recommend writing a letter and waiting for a written or telephone reply. Others suggest writing a letter and following it with a telephone call. Still others argue you should use the telephone exclusively rather than write letters.

How you use the telephone will indicate what type of job search you are conducting. Exclusive reliance on the telephone is a technique used by highly formalized job clubs which operate phone banks for generating job leads. Using the Yellow Pages as the guide to employers, a job club member may call as many as 50 employers a day to schedule job interviews. A rather aggressive yet typical telephone dialogue goes something like this:

TELEPHONE DIALOGUE

"Hello, my name is Jim Baker. I would like to speak to the head of the training department. By the way, what is the name of the training director?"

"You want to talk to Ms. Stevens. Her number is 723-8191 or I can connect you directly."

"Hello, Ms. Stevens. My name is Jim Baker. I have several years of training experience as both a trainer and developer

> *of training materials. I would like to meet with you to discuss possible openings in your department for someone with my qualifications. Would it be possible to see you on Friday at 2:00 p.m.?"*

Not surprising, this telephone approach generates many "nos." If you have a hard time handling rejections, this telephone approach will help you confront your anxieties. The principle behind this approach is *probability*: for every 25 telephone "nos" you receive, you will probably get one or two "yeses." Success is just 25 telephone calls away! If you start calling prospective employers at 9:00 a.m. and finish your 25 calls by 12:00 noon, you should generate at least one or two interviews. That's not bad for three hours of job search work. It beats a direct-mail approach.

The telephone is more efficient than writing letters. However, its effectiveness is questionable. When you use the telephone in this manner, you are basically asking for a job. You are asking the employer: *"Do you have a job for me?"* There is nothing subtle or particularly professional about this approach. It is effective in uncovering particular types of job leads for particular types of individuals. If you need any job in a hurry, this is one of the most efficient ways of finding employment. It sure beats standing in line at the state employment office! However, if you are more concerned with finding a job that is right for you — a job you do well and enjoy doing, one that is fit for you — this telephone approach may be inappropriate.

You must use your own judgment in determining when and how to use the telephone in your job search. There are appropriate times and methods for using the telephone, and these should relate to your job search goals and needs. We prefer the more conventional approach of writing a letter followed by a telephone call. While you take the initiative in scheduling an appointment, you do not put the individual on the spot by asking for a job. You are only seeking information and advice. This low-keyed approach results in numerous acceptances and has a higher probability of paying off with interviews than the aggressive telephone request. You should be trying to uncover jobs that are right for you rather than any job that happens to pop up from a telephoning blitz.

CONSIDER USING JOB CLUBS AND SUPPORT GROUPS

The techniques we outlined thus far are designed for individuals conducting a self-directed job search. Job clubs and support groups are two important alternatives to these techniques.

Job clubs are designed to provide a group structure and support system to individuals seeking employment. These groups consist of about 12 individuals who are led by a trained counselor and supported with telephones, copying machines, and a resource center.

Highly formalized job clubs, such as the 40-Plus Club, organize job search activities for both the advertised and hidden job markets. As outlined by Azrin and Besalel in their book *Job Club Counselor's Manual*, job club activities include:

_____ JOB CLUB ACTIVITIES _____

- Signing commitment agreements to achieve specific job search goals and targets.
- Contacting friends, relatives, and acquaintances for job leads.
- Completing activity forms.
- Using telephones, typewriters, photocopy machines, postage, and other supplies and equipment.
- Meeting with fellow participants to discuss job search progress.
- Telephoning to uncover job leads.
- Researching newspapers, telephone books, and directories.
- Developing research, telephone, interview, and social skills.
- Writing letters and resumes.
- Responding to want ads.
- Completing employment applications.

In other words, the job club formalizes many of the prospecting, networking, and informational interviewing activities within a group context and interjects the role of the telephone as the key communication device for developing and expanding networks.

Job clubs place excessive reliance on using the telephone for uncovering job leads. Members call prospective employers and ask about job openings. The Yellow Pages become the job hunting bible. During a two-week period, a job club member might spend most of his or her mornings telephoning for job leads and scheduling interviews. Afternoons are normally devoted to job interviewing.

Job clubs have limitations for obvious reasons. Job club methods tend to be designed for the hardcore unemployed or for individuals who need a job — any job — quickly. Individuals try to fit into available vacancies; their objectives and skills are of secondary concern. We recommend conducting your own job search or forming a support group which adapts some job club methods to our central concept of *finding a job fit for you* — one appropriate to your objective and in line with your particular mix of skills, abilities, and interests.

Support groups are a useful alternative to job clubs. They have one major advantage: they may cut your job search time in half. Forming or joining one of these groups can help direct as well as enhance your individual job search activities.

Your support group should consist of three or more individuals who are job hunting. Try to schedule regular meetings with specific purposes in mind. While the group may be highly social, especially if it involves close friends, it also should be *task-oriented*. Meet at least once a week and include your spouse. At each meeting *set performance goals* for the week. For example, your goal can be to make 20 new contacts and conduct five informational interviews. The contacts can be made by telephone, letter, or in person. Share your experiences and job information with each other. *Critique each other's progress*, make suggestions for improving the job search, and develop new strategies together. By doing this, you will be gaining valuable information and feedback which is normally difficult to gain on one's own. This group should provide important psychological supports to help you through your job search. After all, job hunting can be a lonely, frustrating, and exasperating experience. By sharing your experiences with others, you will find you are not alone. You will quickly learn that rejections are part of the game. The group will encourage you, and you will feel good about helping others achieve their goals. Try building small incentives into the group, such as the individual who receives the most job interviews for the month must be treated to dinner by other members of the group.

REMEMBER YOU'RE NOT ALONE!

Whatever strategy you choose, remember that millions of other people are going through the same experience of looking for a job. Most people will go about it haphazardly. You have the opportunity to put your best foot forward by developing your own job search campaign as well as joining others in forming a job search network. Putting your best foot forward requires you to prospect, network, and conduct informational and referral interviews on a regular basis. This requires a great deal of work, moreso than sitting behind a desk writing letters or telephoning in response to job listings in newspapers. It also is one of the most rewarding personal experiences you will encounter. You will uncover a world of concerned people who understand your needs and want to help you be successful. In the end, you may discover that finding a job may be more enjoyable than doing a job!

Chapter Eleven

INTERVIEW FOR JOB OFFERS

Nearly 95 percent of all organizations require job interviews prior to hiring employees. In fact, employers consider an effective interview to be the most important hiring criteria — outranking grade point average, related work experience, and recommendations.

While resumes are designed to get interviews, interviews are supposed to result in job offers. If you want to receive job offers, you simply must develop effective interview skills. The more interviews you conduct, the higher the probability you will receive job offers.

This chapter outlines the basic interview skills you should acquire prior to meeting prospective employers. These involve written, telephone, and face-to-face verbal and nonverbal communication. A more extended treatment of this subject is found in our other book, *Interview for Success*.

PREPARE FOR STRESS

The job interview is the most important yet stressful step to getting a job. While your resume and letters got you the interview, the interview is where you must sell yourself in order to receive a job offer. Knowing the stakes are high, most people face interviews with dry throats and sweaty palms; it is a time of great stress. You will be on stage. How well you perform may determine your career future.

But how do you best prepare for the job interview? Unfortunately, you will receive a great deal of conflicting advice on how to conduct an effective job interview. "Experts" will tell you everything from how you should shake hands to when you should visit the restroom. Such advice is based on a combination of folklore, fads, common sense, experience, and research. You need to cut through this advice and get to what is most useful for you.

PLAY ROLES

Most people view the job interview from one of two perspectives. The first perspective advises you to play a *role*. Your role is that of the interviewee who is seeking a job by interacting with an interviewer. Hence, you need to identify the expectations of the interviewer and adjust your behavior accordingly. Your task is to manage the interview encounter to your advantage by behaving in certain prescribed manners.

This interviewer-interviewee perspective is the predominate view of most career counselors. Having somehow discovered the expectations of interviewers, they advise you on how you can best persuade the interviewer to give you a job offer. The College Placement Council, (Rogers, *Getting Hired*), for example, identifies sixteen traits employers expect in candidates:

EXPECTATIONS OF EMPLOYERS

1. **Ability to Communicate**. Do you have the ability to organize your thoughts and ideas effectively? Can you express them clearly when speaking or writing? Can you present your ideas to others in a persuasive way?

2. **Intelligence**. Do you have the ability to understand the assignment? Learn the details of operation? Contribute original ideas to your work?

3. **Self-Confidence**. Do you demonstrate a sense of maturity that enables you to deal positively and effectively with situations and people?

4. **Willingness to Accept Responsibility**. Are you someone who recognizes what needs to be done and is

willing to do it?

5. **Initiative.** Do you have the ability to identify the purpose for work and to take action?

6. **Leadership.** Can you guide and direct others to obtain the recognized objectives?

7. **Energy Level.** Do you demonstrate a forcefulness and capacity to make things move ahead? Can you maintain your work effort at an above-average rate?

8. **Imagination.** Can you confront and deal with problems that may not have standard solutions?

9. **Flexibility.** Are you capable of changing and being receptive to new situations and ideas?

10. **Interpersonal Skills.** Can you bring out the best efforts of individuals so they become effective, enthusiastic members of a team?

11. **Self-Knowledge.** Can you realistically assess your own capabilities? See yourself as others see you? Clearly recognize your strengths and weaknesses?

12. **Ability to Handle Conflict.** Can you successfully contend with stress situations and antagonism?

13. **Competitiveness.** Do you have the capacity to compete with others and the willingness to be measured by your performance in relation to that of others?

14. **Goal Achievement.** Do you have the ability to identify and work toward specific goals? Do such goals challenge your abilities?

15. **Vocational Skills.** Do you possess the positive combination of education and skills required for the position you are seeking?

16. **Direction.** Have you defined your basic personal needs? Have you determined what type of position will satisfy your knowledge, skills and goals?

When applying this role perspective, many writers view the interviewer as particularly sensitive to the "laws" of verbal and nonverbal communication. Some interviewers appear naive; they can be manipulated by clever interviewers who know how to meet their expectations.

This role perspective is responsible for most interview success formulas and checklists of "dos" and "don'ts." Komar in *The Interview Game*, for example, tells you the key to successful interviewing is his formula of "presence":

PRESENCE = *grooming and clothing +*
nonverbal communication

According to this formula, *how* you communicate is an important part of *what* you communicate. You should package your image more than your job-related competencies; form outranks content.

Other experts such as Lathrop in *Who's Hiring Who*, include some content with their emphasis on form. Accordingly, your interview behavior should include:

- proper attire

- good grooming

- a firm handshake

- the appearance of control and confidence

- smiling and displaying appropriate humor

- showing interest in the employer and listening attentively

- being positive about past performance

- empathizing with the employer and appearing willing to help him or her

- communicating solid ideas

- taking control if the employer has difficulty interviewing

Furthermore, you should prepare for the job interview by doing these things:

- Research the organization and the interviewer ahead of time.

- Think about what it is you want to contribute to the interviewer and his or her organization, such as increase quality and productivity. Be prepared to communicate this information in the interview.

- Learn to ask intelligent questions about job duties and personal qualities desired in employees. Be prepared to demonstrate how you meet or exceed the employer's expectations.

- Avoid questions about pay, vacations, and other benefits until later.

- Be prepared to ask questions and discuss problems facing the interviewer's employees in order to stress your qualifications in relation to the problems.

- Be well groomed. Wear attire appropriate to the job you will be interviewing for. Avoid faddish clothing and hair styles as well as heavy perfumes.

- Take to the interview extra copies of your resume, a list of references, and a sample of your work if design or writing skills are required.

- Confirm your appointment time and arrive five minutes early.

- Communicate energy, self-confidence, sincerity, and friendliness. Smile, have a firm hand shake, be relaxed, and maintain eye contact.

Bolles in *What Color Is Your Parachute* agrees with this advice, but he goes one step further. He advises you to identify employers' problems and suggest solutions to them. While this novel approach makes sense, it is somewhat presumptuous, especially when you discover the so-called problem is the employer's pet project!

Most of this interview advice can be condensed into a handy list of "dos" and "don'ts," many of which remind you of Grandma's admonitions! Stanat in *Job Hunting Secrets & Tactics* provides one of the most comprehensive such checklists:

EFFECTIVE INTERVIEW RULES

"DOS"

____ *Do* have attractive hands — clean and nails trimmed.
____ *Do* comb your hair and wear it in a conservative style.
____ *Do* use a *moderate* amount of perfume or cologne.

____ *Do* use the restroom before the interview.

____ *Do* get a good night's sleep.

____ *Do* maintain eye contact since interviewers place a great deal of emphasis on it.

____ *Do* appear enthusiastic. Use gestures but make them smooth.

____ *Do* smile.

____ *Do* learn the name of the interviewer and use it occasionally during the interview.

____ *Do* take enough money with you, just in case you have an emergency of some kind.

____ *Do* research the organization ahead of time. Observe the dress modes and working environment.

____ *Do* take notes during the interview since the interviewer will be doing the same. Jot down some of your questions before the interview.

____ *Do* defer to the interviewer in setting the interview pace.

____ *Do* let the interviewer close the interview.

____ *Do* inquire about when you might expect to hear from the interviewer next.

"DON'TS"

____ *Don't* be late to the interview.

____ *Don't* wear an overcoat, topcoat, or rubber boots into an interview — you look anxious to leave.

____ *Don't* sit down or dash to your chair until the interviewer gives some indication to be seated; otherwise, you look forward.

____ *Don't* have a mouthful of anything except your teeth.

____ *Don't* lean on the interviewer's desk. Sit erect in your chair.

____ *Don't* wear dark glasses.

____ *Don't* carry a large handbag.

____ *Don't* have extremely long fingernails.

____ *Don't* demonstrate your nervousness by tapping your fingers, swinging your leg, or playing with your hands.

____ *Don't* fidget with your clothes.

____ *Don't* pick up items on the interviewer's desk unless invited to do so.

____ *Don't* appear to eavesdrop on any phone calls the interviewer receives in your presence.

___ *Don't* stand if someone enters the office during the interview.

___ *Don't* read materials on the interviewer's desk.

___ *Don't* refer to the interviewer as "sir" or "Ma'am".

___ *Don't* use the interviewer's name too much.

___ *Don't* over-extend your jokes and humor.

___ *Don't* answer questions with one and two word remarks.

___ *Don't* dominate the conversation. Answer the questions without lingering.

___ *Don't* interrupt the interviewer.

___ *Don't* swear, even though the interviewer may.

___ *Don't* use slang.

___ *Don't* gush or be syrupy.

___ *Don't* punctuate your conversation with "you know."

___ *Don't* use the interviewer's first name.

___ *Don't* be preachy.

___ *Don't* mumble.

___ *Don't* interpret your resume unless asked to.

___ *Don't* try to impress the interviewer by bragging.

___ *Don't* lie.

___ *Don't* criticize your employer.

___ *Don't* get angry or irritated during the interview.

___ *Don't* answer questions you consider too personal – but explain your reason for doing so.

___ *Don't* glance at your watch.

___ *Don't* ask if you can have the job. Instead, indicate your interest in the job.

___ *Don't* mention salary in the initial interview.

Irish in *Go Hire Yourself an Employer* rounds out this list with a few of his own "dos" and "don'ts":

___ Women should take the initiative in extending the handshake when meeting the interviewer.

___ Don't smoke, chew gum, tobacco, or your fingernails.

___ Maintain eye contact, but don't stare at the interviewer. Occasionally glance off into another direction.

___ If the interviewer seems to run out of questions, ask him or her if you are giving them the information they want.

___ If a question sounds irrelevant, unprincipled, or unimportant, ask why the interviewer feels it's important.

_____ Don't be "cool" and laid-back in the interview, unless you want to let the interviewer know you are a con-artist.

Since John Molloy became a popular wardrobe and image consultant, "dress for success" has become another important "interview for success" role theme. Molloy tells you exactly what to wear in terms of style, color, and quality of clothes. Women, for example, should wear a navy blue or gray skirted suit, light make-up, and little jewelry. Men should wear a dark blue or gray suit and a good quality white or light blue shirt; they should shine their shoes and have no facial hair. This upper class look of success should put you in a good light with interviewers.

Still others are more sophisticated with color shades and combinations. For them, just what does Molloy mean when navy blues and grays come in hundreds of shades? Some shades of blue and gray are inappropriate for many people. And these image and color consultants disagree among themselves as to whether everyone fits into a standard set of seasonal colors (Jackson in *Color Me Beautiful*) or whether you possess a unique color spectrum (Lewis and Nicholson in *Color Wonderful*). The increasing sophistication of the image and color consultants appears to suggest that the basics Molloy reports should be taken a step further and applied with an understanding of one's own personal body colors.

BE HONEST AND INSIGHTFUL

Contrasting with the role perspective is another perspective perhaps best termed "just be yourself." It stresses the importance of being honest and straightforward when interviewing for a position. Don't try to be something you are not because you will be discovered in the end. Therefore, just be your natural self in the interview. Playing a role is seen as being less than honest.

Both perspectives will pose problems for you. Learning to play the role of interviewee assumes we know the expectations of interviewers and that those expectations are similar for all interviewers. Furthermore, it assumes it is best to *meet* the expectations of others. The problem is twofold. Since interviewers differ, so do expectations. Some interviewers know how to interview effectively whereas others do not. As for meeting expectations, there is no evidence you should do this. It is probably better for you to *exceed* in a positive manner the expectations of the interviewer. For example, without being threatening, you want to communicate to the interviewer that you will be more productive than he or she originally anticipated. This will put you in a better position relative to other candidates who are trying to meet the interviewer's expectations.

The "just be yourself" perspective can pose difficulties too. Honest, frank, and straightforward people sometimes are inconsiderate, insensitive, and unprofessional with others. While employers want interviewees to be honest, they also want them to observe social graces, be considerate and sensitive to others, and play a professional role. Therefore, just being yourself is not as readily valued by employers as one might think.

In the end, there are few hard and fast rules in the interview game. You should take much of the advice on how to interview with reservations. Our approach is to combine the "role" and "just be yourself" perspectives into a useful set of interviewing prescriptions. Using a contingency approach, we believe it is best to *know your situation and behave accordingly*. You need to develop your own insights and prescriptions based upon your unique experiences. This means you may have to create your own "dos" and "don'ts" as you become more knowledgeable about your own job search situation.

EXCHANGE CRITICAL INFORMATION

An interview is a two-way communication exchange between an interviewer and an interviewee. It involves both verbal and nonverbal communication. While we tend to concentrate on the content of what we say, research shows that approximately 65 percent of most communication is nonverbal. Furthermore, we tend to give more credibility to nonverbal than to verbal messages. Regardless of what you say, how you sit, stand, use your hands, move your head and eyes, and listen will communicate both positive and negative messages.

Job interviews entail various communication mediums and situations. You will write job interview letters, schedule interviews over the telephone, be interviewed by telephone, and encounter one-on-one as well as panel and group interviews. Each situation requires a different set of communication behaviors. For example, while telephone communication is efficient, it may be ineffective for interview purposes. Only certain types of information can be effectively communicated over the telephone because this medium limits your nonverbal behavior. Honesty, intelligence, and likeability — three of the most important values you want to communicate to employers — are primarily communicated nonverbally. Therefore, you should be very careful of telephone interviews — whether giving or receiving them.

Job interviews have different purposes and can be negative in many ways. From the perspective of the applicant, the purpose of most initial job interviews is to get a second interview, and the purpose of the second interview is to get a job offer. But from the perspective of employers, the purpose of the interview is to eliminate you from a second interview or job offer. The interviewer wants to know why he or she should *not* hire you. Thus, the interviewer has a negative goal — to identify your weaknesses in order to eliminate you from further consideration. These differing purposes create an adversarial relationship and contribute to a great deal of interviewing stress for both the applicant and the interviewer.

Since the interviewer wants to identify your weaknesses, you must counter by *communicating your strengths* to lessen the interviewer's fear of hiring you. After all, you are a risk which may cost the organization $35,000 or more a year. If the interviewer shows poor judgement, he or she may be threatened with a job loss. Your job is to help the interviewer overcome negative expectations by stressing your positives and by raising expectations.

PREPARE TO ANSWER QUESTIONS

Assume your networking has paid off with an invitation to interview with a company. What do you do next? Prepare for the interview as if it were a $1,000,000 prize. After all, this company may give you that much in income over the next 15 to 20 years.

The invitation to interview will most likely come by telephone. It may consist of a telephone interview or a request to meet for an interview at a certain time. The telephone interview is used frequently because employers may want to shorten their list of candidates from 10 to 3. By calling each candidate by telephone, the employer can make quick decisions on marginal candidates or update the job status of each candidate. When you get such a telephone call, you have no time to prepare. You may be dripping wet from just getting out of the shower or you may have a splitting headache. It always seems to come at the wrong time. Whatever your situation, put your best foot forward based upon your thorough preparation for an interview. We will examine this special case of the telephone interview shortly.

Once you have confirmed a job interview time and place, you should do as much research on the organization and employer as possible as well as learn to lessen your anxiety and stress levels by practicing the interview situation. *Preparation and practice* are the keys to doing your best.

During the interview, you want to impress upon the interviewer your knowledge of his or her organization by asking intelligent questions and giving intelligent answers. Your library and networking research (Chapters Nine and Ten) should yield useful information on the organization and employer. Be sure you know something about the organization. Talk to people who know about the employer and the organization. This can include the competition, the chamber of commerce, the Better Business Bureau, suppliers, clients, and present or former employees. Your research will establish a common ground of information for conducting the interview.

You should mentally address as well as do a "dry run" of the interview with your spouse or friend. Most of the questions will relate to your educational background, work experience, career goals, personality, and other concerns. The most frequently asked questions include:

```
┌──────────── QUESTIONS FREQUENTLY ASKED ────────────┐
                    BY INTERVIEWERS
```

YOUR EDUCATION

- *Describe your educational background.*
- *Why did you attend _____ University (or College)?*
- *Why did you major in _____ ?*
- *What was your grade point average?*
- *What subjects did you enjoy the most? The least? Why?*
- *What leadership positions did you hold?*
- *How did you finance your education?*
- *If you started all over, what would you change about your education?*
- *Why were your grades so low? So high?*
- *Did you do the best you could in school? If not, why not?*

YOUR WORK EXPERIENCE

- *What were your major achievements in each of your past jobs?*
- *Why did you change jobs before?*
- *What is your typical workday like?*
- *What functions do you enjoy doing the most?*
- *What did you like about your boss? Dislike?*
- *Which job did you enjoy the most? Why? Which job did you enjoy the least? Why?*
- *Have you ever been fired? Why?*

YOUR CAREER GOALS

- *Why do you want to join our organization?*
- *Why do you think you are qualified for this position?*
- *Why are you looking for another job?*
- *Why do you want to make a career change?*
- *What ideally would you like to do?*
- *Why should we want to hire you?*
- *How would you improve our operations?*
- *What is the lowest pay you will take?*
- *How much do you think you are worth for this job?*
- *What do you want to be doing five years from now?*
- *How much do you want to be making five years from now?*
- *What are your short-range and long-range career goals?*
- *If you could choose your job and organization, where would you go?*
- *What other types of jobs are you considering? Other companies?*
- *When will you be ready to begin work?*
- *How do you feel about relocating, traveling, working overtime, and spending weekends in the office?*
- *What attracted you to our company?*

YOUR PERSONALITY
AND OTHER CONSIDERATIONS

- *Tell me about yourself.*
- *Where are your major weaknesses? Your major strengths?*
- *What causes you to lose your temper?*
- *What do you do in your spare time? Any hobbies?*
- *What types of books do you read?*
- *What role does your family play in your career?*
- *How well do you work under pressure? In meeting deadlines?*
- *Tell me about your management philosophy.*
- *How much initiative do you take?*
- *What types of people do you prefer working with?*
- *How _____ (creative, analytical, tactful, etc.) are you?*
- *If you could change your life, what would you do differently?*
- *Who are your references?*

Your answers to each question should be positive and emphasize your **strengths**. Remember, the interviewer wants to know about your **weaknesses**. For example, if you are asked *"What are your weaknesses?"*, you can turn this potential negative question into a positive by answering something like this:

> *"I sometimes get so involved with my work that I neglect my family as well as forget to complete work around the house. I guess I'm somewhat of a workaholic."*

What employer could hold this negative against you? You have taken a negative and raised the expectations of the employer by basically saying you are a hard and persistent worker; the organization will get more for its money than expected.

Other questions are illegal, but some employers ask them nontheless. Consider how you would respond to these:

ILLEGAL QUESTIONS

- *Are you married, divorced, separated or single?*
- *How old are you?*
- *Do you go to church regularly?*
- *Do you have many debts?*
- *Do you own or rent your home?*
- *What social and political organizations do you belong to?*
- *What does your spouse think about your career?*
- *Are you living with anyone?*
- *Are you practicing birth control?*
- *Were you ever arrested?*
- *How much insurance do you have?*
- *How much do you weigh?*
- *How tall are you?*

Don't get upset and say *"That's an illegal question and I refuse to answer it!"* While you may be perfectly right in saying so, this response lacks tact, which may be what the employer is looking for. For example, if you are divorced and the interviewer asks about your divorce, you might respond with *"Does a divorce have a direct bearing on the responsibilities of _____?"* Some employers may ask such questions just to see how you answer or react under stress.

For example, if an interviewer asks if you are on the pill, he may want to see if you will blow your top, become embarrassed, or keep your cool. We recommend keeping your cool by responding with fact and humor:

> *"Yes, I take three pills a day — vitamins A, B, and C, and they make me especially fit for this job!"*

The interviewer will get the message, and you will have indicated that you can handle stressful communication. Others may ask such questions out of ignorance of the law.

ASK APPROPRIATE QUESTIONS

Interviewers expect candidates to ask intelligent questions concerning the organization and the nature of the work. Moreover, you need information and should indicate your interest in the employer by asking questions. Consider asking some of these questions if they haven't been answered early in the interview:

QUESTIONS YOU SHOULD ASK

- *Tell me about the duties and responsibilities of this job.*
- *How does this position relate to other positions within this organization?*
- *How long has this position been in the organization?*
- *What would be the ideal type of person for this position? Skills? Personality? Working style? Background?*
- *Can you tell me about the people who have been in this position before? Backgrounds? Promotions? Terminations?*
- *Who would I be working with in this position?*
- *Tell me something about these people? Strengths? Weaknesses? Performance expectations?*
- *What am I expected to accomplish during the first year?*
- *How will I be evaluated?*
- *Are promotions and raises tied to performance criteria?*
- *Tell me how this operates.*
- *What is the normal salary range for such a position?*
- *Based on your experience, what type of problems would someone new in this position likely encounter?*
- *I'm interested in your career with this organization.*

> *When did you start? What are your plans for the future?*
> - *I would like to know how people get promoted and advance in this organization.*
> - *What is particularly unique about working in this organization?*
> - *Can you explain the various benefits employees receive?*
> - *What does the future look like for this organization?*

You may want to write these questions on a 3 x 5 card and take them with you to the interview. While it is best to memorize these questions, you may want to refer to your list when the interviewer asks you if you have any questions. You might do this by saying: *"Yes, I jotted down a few questions which I want to make sure I ask you before leaving."* Then pull out your card and refer to the questions.

COMMUNICATE NONVERBALLY

The interview is an image management activity. Interviewers normally make a positive or negative decision based upon the impression you make during the first four or five minutes of the interview. The major factors influencing this decision are your nonverbal cues communicated at the very beginning of the interview. Therefore, what you wear, how you look, the way you shake hands, how you smell, whether you are interested and enthusiastic, where and how you sit, and how you initiate the small talk are extremely important to the interviewer's decision. These factors may be more important than your answers to the interview questions. Your answers will tend to either reinforce or alter the initial impression.

While it may seem unfair for employers to make such snap decisions, it happens nonetheless. Accept it as an important reality of the job search, and learn to adjust your behavior to your best advantage. Remember, those first five minutes may be the most critical moments in your job search and for your future job or career. Put your best foot forward with the most positive image you can generate.

DRESS APPROPRIATELY

Appearance is the first thing you communicate to others. Before you have a chance to speak, others notice how you dress and accordingly draw certain conclusions about your personality and competence. Indeed, research shows that appearance makes the greatest difference when an evaluator has little information about the other person. This is precisely the situation you find yourself in at the start of the interview.

Many people object to having their capabilities evaluated on the basis of their appearance and manner of dress. *"But that is not fair,"* they argue. *"People should be hired on the basis of their ability to do the job — not on how they look."* But debating the lack of merit or complaining about the unfairness of such behavior does not alter reality. Like it or not, people do make initial judgments about others based on their appearance. Since you cannot alter this fact, and bemoaning it will get you nowhere, it is best to learn to use it to your advantage. If you learn to effectively manage your image, you can convey marvelous messages regarding your authority, credibility, and competence.

Some estimates indicate that as much as 65 percent of the hiring decision may be based on the nonverbal aspects of the interview. Employers sometimes refer to this phenomenon with such terms as "chemistry," "body warmth," or that "gut feeling" the individual is right for the job. This correlates with findings of communication studies that approximately 65 percent of a message is communicated nonverbally. The remaining 35 percent is communicated verbally.

Know the Rules

Knowing how to dress appropriately for the interview requires knowing important rules of the game. Like it or not, employers play by these rules. Once you know the rules, you at least can make a conscious choice whether or not you want to play. If you decide to play, you will stand a better chance of winning by using the often unwritten rules to your advantage.

Much has been written on how to dress professionally, especially since John Molloy first wrote his books on dress for success in the 1970s. While this approach has been criticized for promoting a "cookie cutter" or "carbon copy" image, it is still valid for most interview situations. The degree to which employers adhere to these rules, however, will depend on particular individuals and situations. Your job is to know when, where, and to what extent the rules apply to you. When in doubt, follow our general advice on looking professional.

Knowing and playing by the rules does not imply incompetent people get jobs simply by dressing the part. Rather, it implies that qualified and competent job applicants can **gain an extra edge** over a field of other qualified, competent individuals by dressing to convey positive professional images.

Know Your Colors

Much of the general advice on how to dress for success is sound. However, there is a major flaw in most of the advice you encounter. Researchers on the subject have looked at how people in positions of power view certain colors for professional attire. Few have gone beyond this to note that colors do different things on different people. Various shades or clarities of a color or combinations of contrast between light and dark colors when worn together may be unenhancing to some individuals and actually diminish that person's "power look."

For example, the combination of a white shirt or blouse paired with a navy suit — one of the success and power looks promoted by many — will be enhancing both to the appearance and the image of power on some individuals, but will be unenhancing and actually overpower the appearance of others. Or suppose you take the advice that a medium to charcoal gray suit is a good color in the professional world. It is, but the advice to wear medium to charcoal gray only recognizes differences of light to dark. In that medium to charcoal range we could pick scores of shades of gray from very blue grays to taupe grays. The wrong gray shade on individuals can make them look unattractive, unhealthy, and even older than their age. Who wants to hire someone who appears to be in poor health?

If we combine the results of research done by John Molloy for his **Dress for Success** and **The Woman's Dress for Success Book** on how colors relate to one's power look and that done by JoAnne Nicholson and Judy Lewis-Crum explained in their book **Color Wonderful** on how colors relate to us as unique individuals, we can achieve a win-win situation. You can retain your individuality and look your most enhanced while, at the same time, achieving a look of success, power, and competence.

Present Your Winning Image

The key to effective dressing is to know how to relate the clothing you put on your body to your own natural coloring. Let's pose a few questions to start you thinking about color in what may be some new ways. Ask yourself these questions:

- Can you wear black and white together and look good, or does that much contrast wear you?

- Can you wear navy and white together and retain your "power look" or does that much contrast actually diminish your look of power and authority?

- Can you wear a pure white or is a slightly cream toned white more flattering?

- Do you look better in clear or toned down shades of colors?

The answers to these questions vary with each individual and their own natural coloring. So it is important to know what the appropriate answer is for you.

Into which category does your coloring fit? Let's find out where you belong in terms of color type:

IDENTIFYING YOUR COLOR TYPE

- **Contrast coloring:** If you are a contrast color type, you have a definite dark-light appearance. You have very dark brown or black hair and light to medium ivory or olive toned skin. Black men and women in this category will have clear light to dark skin tones and dark hair.

- **Light-bright coloring:** If you are of this color type, you have golden tones in your skin and golden tones in your blond or light to medium brown hair. You probably had blond or light brown hair as children. Black men and women in this category will have clear golden skin in their face and dark hair.

- **Muted coloring:** If you are a muted color type, you have a definite brown-on-brown or red-on-brown appearance. Your skin tone is an ivory-beige, brown-beige, or golden-beige tone — that is, you have a beige skin with a golden-brown cast. Your hair could be red or light to dark brown with camel, bronze, or red highlights. Black men and women in this category will have golden or brown skin tones and dark hair.

- **Gentle coloring:** If you are of this color type, you have a soft, gentle looking appearance. Your skin tone is a light ivory or pink-beige tone and your hair is ash blond

> or ash brown. You probably had blond or ash brown hair as a child. Black men and women in this category will have pink tones in their skin and dark hair.

Some individuals may be a combination of two color types. If your skin tone falls in one category and your hair color in another, you are a combination color type.

These color types will be referred to in the next two sections when guidelines are given for effectively combining shirts, suits, and ties for men, and skirted suits, blouses, and accessories for women to both enhance and maximize each individual's professional look.

However, if you are uncertain which hair or skin tone is yours and are hence undecided as to which color type category you belong to, you may wish to contact Color 1 Associates by calling their toll-free number: 1-800-523-8496. They can refer you to the Color 1 consultant nearest you. In addition, the *Color Wonderful* book includes a listing of professionally trained associates located nearest you.

Color 1 provides you with an individualized color chart that allows you to wear every color in the spectrum, but in your best *shade* and *clarity* as well as written material telling you how you can combine your colors for the best amounts of contrast for your natural coloring (color type).

The color chart is an excellent one-time investment considering the costs of buying the wrong colored suit, shirt, or blouse. It will more than pay for itself if it contributes to an effective interview as you wear your suit in your best shade and put your clothing together to work with, rather than against, your natural coloring. It can help you convey positive images during those crucial initial minutes of the interview — as well as over a life-time.

Male Personalized Power Dressing

John Molloy has conducted extensive research on how individuals can dress effectively. Aimed at individuals already working in professional positions who want to communicate a success image, his advice is just as relevant for someone interviewing for a job.

Except for some blue collar jobs, basic attire for men interviewing for a position is *a suit*. Let's look at appropriate suits in terms of color, fabric, and style. The suit color can make a difference in creating an image of authority and competence. In general, blue, gray, camel, or beige are proper colors for men's suits. Usually the darker the shade, the greater amount of authority it conveys to the wearer. Given your situation (the interview) and your audience (the interviewer), you should aim at conveying enough authority to command attention and a positive regard, but not so much as to threaten the interviewer. Hence, the **medium to charcoal gray or navy blue** would be good suit colors. Black, a basic funeral or formal attire, can threaten the interviewer by conveying too much authority.

When selcting your gray, navy, camel, or beige suit, choose a shade that is enhancing to you. Should you wear a blue-gray, a taupe-gray, or a shade in-between? Do you look better in a somewhat bright navy or a more toned-down navy; a blue navy or a black navy; a navy with a purple or a yellow base to it?

In general, most people will look better in somewhat blue grays than in grays that are closer to the taupe side of the spectrum. Most people will be enhanced by a navy that is not too bright or contain so much black that it is difficult to distinguish whether the color is navy or black. When selecting a beige or a camel, select a tone that complements your skin color. If your skin has pink tones, avoid beiges and camels that contain gold hues and select pink based beiges/camels that enhance your skin color. Similarly, those of you who have gold/olive tones to your skin should avoid the pink based camel and beiges.

Should your camels or beiges be pink-toned, ivory-toned or golden-toned? If you are unsure, get the name of the Color 1 Associate nearest you and schedule an appointment. If you are going to spend a lot of money on a suit — and if you buy a good, well-made suit you are going to spend a lot of money — buy a suit that will work for you.

Your suit(s) should be made of a **natural fiber**. A good blend of a natural fiber with some synthetic is acceptable as long as it has the "look" of the natural fiber. The very best suit fabrics are wool, wool blends, or fabrics that look like them. Even for the warmer summer months, men can find summer weight wool suits that are comfortable and look marvelous. They are your best buy. For really hot climates, linen, or a fabric that looks like linen tests well. Normally a linen will have to be blended with another fiber, often a synthetic, in order to retain a pressed, neat look. The major disadvantage of pure linen is that it wrinkles. Avoid 100 percent polyester materials, or anything that looks like it — especially double-knits — like the plague! It is a definite negative for your look of competence, power, and success.

The style of your suit should be **classic**. It should be well-tailored and well-styled. Avoid suits that appear "trendy" unless you are applying for a job in a field such as arts or perhaps advertising. A conservative suit that has a timeless classic styling and also looks up-to-date will serve you best not only for the interview, but it will give you several years wear once you land the job.

Select a shirt color that is lighter than the color of your suit. John Molloy's book on appearance and dress for me, *Dress For Success*, goes into great detail on shirts, ties, and practically everything you might wear or carry with you. We recommend Molloy's book over others because it is based on research rather than personal opinion and promotional fads.

However, you must take Molloy's advice one step beyond where he takes you: keep in mind *your color type*. If you have contrast or light-bright coloring, you will look great wearing your shade of white in a shirt with your navy blue shade in a suit. But if you have muted or gentle coloring, this is too much contrast for you. For muted or gentle coloring, the combination of navy and white will visually overpower you and you will not look your most enhanced.

If you are a muted or gentle color type, the look that gives you the greatest power look and yet does not overpower you will be a suit in your most flattering shade of gray worn with a shirt in your shade of white. You can expect your white to be less of a "pure" white (a bit more creamy) than the white a contrast or a light-bright would wear. When you wear a navy suit, pair it with a blue shirt rather than a white one. This combines your colors in a level of contrast effective for your coloring.

Female Personalized Power Dressing

Few men would consider wearing anything other than a suit to a job interview — especially an interview for a managerial or professional position. Women are often less certain what is appropriate. As a result of research conducted by John Molloy and others, the verdict is now in. A skirted suit is the definite choice for the interview. This attire allows a woman to best convey images of professionalism, authority, and competence. Wearing a skirted suit can initially help a woman overcome negative stereotypes that some men still hold toward women in managerial and other professional positions.

Let's survey appropriate suits in terms of color, fabric, and style. As in the case of men's suits, the color of your suit can help create an image of authority and competence. The suit colors that make the strongest positive statements for you are your shade of gray in a medium to charcoal depth or your shade of blue in a medium to navy depth of color. Other dark shades, such as maroon, test well as does camel. Avoid black, which can convey so much authority; many interviewers find it threatening. Also, avoid solid brown. British looking tweeds and small plaids or herringbone designs in brown are acceptable, but a solid dark brown suit does not score well in most geographical areas.

When selecting your gray, navy, camel, or any other colored suit, follow the same rules we outlined for men: choose a shade that is enhancing to you. If you are uncertain which shades are best for you, contact a Color 1 Associate for advice.

Similar to men's suits, your suit should be made of a *natural fiber* or have the "look" of a natural fiber. The very best winter-weight suit fabrics are wool or wool blends. For the warmer climates or the summer months, women will find few, if any, summer weight wool suits made for them. Hence linen, blended with a synthetic so it will not look as if it needs constant pressing, is your first choice. Other fabrics, such as polyester blended with rayon, in clothing of good quality often has the definite look of linen but without the hassels of caring for real linen. But the key word here is *quality*. A cheap polyester/rayon fabric will look just that. Avoid 100 percent polyester material, or anything that looks like it — especially double-knits.

Your suit style should be *classic*. Following similar rules as for men, women's suits should be well-tailored, well-styled, and avoid a "trendy" look unless appropriate for certain occupations. A conservative, classic suit will last for years and is an excellent investment. Indeed, you can afford to buy good quality clothing if you know you will get a lot of use from the item. When deciding on your professional wardrobe, always buy clothes to last and buy quality.

Quality also means buying *silk blouses* if you can afford them. Keep in mind not only the price of the blouse itself, but the cleaning bill. There are many polyester blouse fabrics that have the look and feel of silk — this is an exception to the "no polyester" rule. Silk or a polyester that has the look and feel of silk are the fabrics for blouses to go with your wool suits. Cotton blouses should generally not be paired with a wool suit. Choose your blouses in your most flattering shades and clarity of color. John Molloy's book on appearance and dress for women, *The Woman's Dress for Success Book*, goes into great detail on the blouse styles that test best as well as expands on suit colors. It includes information on almost anything you might wear or carry with you to the interview or on the job.

But remember, as in the case of men, you must take Molloy's advice one step further: keep in mind *your color type*. Contrast or light-bright coloring types look great wearing their shade of white in a blouse with their navy blue shade in a suit. Muted and gentle color types will find this to be too much contrast and thus overpower their natural coloring. Such a color combination actually diminishes their power look.

If you are a muted or gentle color type, why not try your coral red shade blouse with your navy suit or wear your shade of white with your gray shade suit. Once you are aware of your color type and how to best enhance it while retaining visual authority, you will find many new and flattering combinations.

Give your outfit a more "finished and polished" look by *accessorizing* it effectively. Collect silk scarves and necklaces of semiprecious stones in your suit colors. Wear scarves and necklaces with your suits and blouses in such a way that they repeat the color of the suit. For example, a woman wearing a navy suit and a red silk blouse could accent the look by wearing a necklace of navy sodalite beads or a silk scarf that has navy as a predominate color. The *Color Wonderful* book includes a great deal of information to help you accessorize your look geared to your color type.

The most appropriate shoe to wear with a business suit is a *classic pump* — closed heel and toe and little or no decoration. Not only does this shoe stand by itself as creating the most professional look, it also teams best with a business suit and is flattering at the same time. A sling-back shoe (heel open with a strap across the heel) can be worn with a suit, but will slightly diminish the wearer's professional look. Avoid shoes with both the heel and toe open as well as any sandal look. They can be beautiful shoes, but save them for evening wear. We have observed many women arriving for job interviews wearing suits, but ruining their professional image by wearing strappy sandal shoes. In general, wear shoes as dark or darker than your skirt. If not, you may draw the other person's eyes to your feet when, instead, you want them to focus on your face and on what you are saying.

You may choose to carry a *purse or an attache case*, but not both at the same time. It is difficult not to look clumsy trying to handle both a purse and an attache case, and it is likely to diminish your power look as well. One way to carry both is to keep a slim purse with essentials such as lipstick, mirror, and money inside the attache case. If you need to go out to lunch, or any place where you choose not to carry the attache case, just pull out your purse and you're off.

Buy Quality Apparel

Aside from information on what articles of apparel to wear, a word on the quality of what you purchase is in order. *Buy the best you can afford.* If you are not gainfully employed, this may seem like impractical advice. But it still remains your best advice. Two really good suits with a variety of shirts or blouses will look better from the first day you own them than four suits of inferior quality — and will out last them as well. To buy quality rather than quantity is a good habit to form.

Stretch your money by shopping sales or good discount outlets if you wish. But remember, it isn't a bargain if it isn't right for you. A suit that never quite fits or isn't exactly your best shade is not a bargain no matter how many times it has been marked down. John Molloy's books have useful hints on how to overcome a middle-class background and learn to buy good quality clothing at reasonable prices.

In addition to buying natural fibers in clothing whenever possible, *invest in real leather* for shoes, attache case, and handbag — if you carry one. Leather conveys a professional look and will out last the cheap looking imitations you might buy. In the end, we get what we pay for.

REMEMBER FIRST IMPRESSIONS

As noted previously, interviewers admit that impressions formed during the first five minutes of the interview are seldom changed during the remainder of the interview. In at least 75% of the cases, the basic outcome of the interview has already been determined during those first few minutes!

If we ask, *"How can that be? How can anyone possibly make an important, objective, and informed decision in such a short period of time,"* the answer is, *"they probably can't."* Nonetheless, they often decide in this manner. Employers concentrate on nonverbal cues because very little verbal information — other than "small talk" — has been exchanged in the initial stages of the interview.

APPEAR LIKEABLE

Remember, most people invited to an employment interview have already been "screened in." They supposedly possess the basic qualifications for the job, such as education and work experience. At this point employers will look for several qualities in the candidates, such as honesty, credibility, intelligence, competence, enthusiasm, spontaneity, friendliness, and likeability. Much of the message communicating these qualities will be conveyed through your dress as well as through other nonverbal behaviors.

In the end, employers hire people they *like* and who will interact well on an interpersonal basis with the rest of the staff. Therefore, you should communicate that you are a likeable candidate who can get along well with others. You can communicate these messages by engaging in several nonverbal behaviors. Four of the most important ones include:

IMPORTANT NONVERBAL BEHAVIORS

1. **Sit with a very slight forward lean toward the interviewer.** It should be so slight as to be almost imperceptible. If not overdone and obvious, it communicates your interest in what the interviewer is saying.

2. **Make eye contact frequently, but don't overdo it.** Good eye contact establishes better rapport with the interviewer. You will be perceived as more trustworthy if you will look at the interviewer as you ask and answer questions. To say someone has "shifty eyes" or cannot "look us in the eye" is to imply they may not be completely honest. To have a direct, though moderate eye gaze, conveys interest, as well as trustworthiness.

3. **A moderate amount of smiling will also help reinforce your positive image.** You should smile enough to convey your positive attitude, but not so much that you will not be taken seriously. Some people naturally smile often and others hardly ever smile. Monitor your behavior or ask a friend to give you honest feedback.

4. **Try to convey interest and enthusiasm through your vocal inflections.** Your tone of voice can say a lot about you and how interested you are in the interviewer and organization.

COMMUNICATE CLASS

A study reported by John Molloy in *Live For Success* indicated that 25% of personnel officers would not hire anyone with a wet handshake for an important position. If your hands tend to perspire when you are nervous, try using some talcum powder before leaving for the interview or wipe your hands on your handkerchief just before entering the outer office.

The way you stand, sit and walk — essentially how you carry yourself — has a bearing on how others perceive you. Molloy is convinced that the "look" that impresses interviewers the most is the upper middle class carriage — the look of class.

Even if your background is not upper middle class, as a youth you were probably told by someone in your family to improve how you stand, sit, and walk. Comments such as: *"Keep your shoulders back"* or *"Keep your head erect"* were good pieces of advice. If you did not pay much heed to them then, it would be to your advantage to do so now. The image of class includes these behaviors:

PRESENTING AN IMAGE OF CLASS

- Keep your shoulders back.
- Keep your head erect.
- Avoid folding your arms across your chest.
- Avoid sitting or standing with arms or legs far apart or what could be described as an "open" position.
- Use gestures that enhance your verbal message.
- Nod your head affirmatively at appropriate times — but do not overdo it.
- Project your voice loudly enough to be heard by the interviewer.
- Articulate clearly — do not mumble.
- Use pauses for emphasis.
- Watch your pace — avoid talking too fast or too slow.
- Many people talk fast when they are nervous.
- Know yourself and try to regulate your pace accordingly.

CHANGE YOUR BEHAVIOR

Each of us has learned behaviors we reinforce daily. Many of these behaviors generate positive responses from others; but some of them are bad habits we should break. We can change our behaviors if we are strongly **motivated** to do so. But it is easy to slip back into the old patterns if we are not careful.

If you feel you need to break certain habits and learn new behaviors, you can make the changes. You must first be aware of the undesirable behavior you wish to replace as well as the desirable behavior you wish to acquire. Second, you must be aware of the undesirable behavior whenever it takes place. For this you may need to enlist the aid of your spouse or good friend; ask them to: *"Please observe me and inform me whenever I am doing* _____ *."* After a while you will develop greater awareness of the particular behavior.

Once we are conscious of our behavior, gradually we will become alert to our behavior early enough to alter the behavior. Given even more time of diligent awareness, the new behavior replaces the old one and eventually becomes as natural as the undesirable behavior once was.

Conducting effective interviews and getting a job that is right for you are significant reasons to motivate you to change some of your behaviors. If you think a behavior may be holding you back, try changing it now. The more time you give yourself, the more likely the change will become permanent and the less likely you will slip back into your former behavior.

LISTEN EFFECTIVELY

Listening is a learned skill. We learned to listen before we began our formal education — in fact, probably before we can even remember. However, we tend to believe listening is something we acquire automatically. While we can probably remember learning to play the piano, play baseball, or to type, we usually can't recall learning to listen.

Being a good listener takes effort. You can't lean back in your chair and listen passively and listen well. Listening requires active involvement. Good listening will produce several important outcomes. You will have the information needed to help you ask better questions, respond to questions more effectively, and eventually to make a decision as to whether this is a job that is really fit for you. In order to do this, you should:

GOOD LISTENING BEHAVIORS

1. **Focus your attention on the interviewer and what he or she is saying**. Don't let your mind wander to such things as: the strange or good looking appearance of the interviewer, the photographs on the desk, your fears about not getting the job offer, or your plans for that evening or the weekend. We can listen and compre-

hend information about four times faster than the speaker can talk. Don't use that extra time to let your mind wander, but rather to concentrate on the other person's message.

2. **Look beyond the personal appearance or mannerisms of the interviewer or any irritating words or ideas as you listen for content**. Don't let certain annoying words, ideas or mannerisms of the interviewer so prejudice you that you can't listen objectively to what is being said.

3. **Try to listen for information and withhold evaluation of the message until later**. This may be difficult to do, but it can make an important difference in what you get from the message. As we evaluate, our thoughts are on our reaction to the message, and thus we miss part of what the other person is saying.

4. **Give positive nonverbal feedback to the interviewer.** Nod in agreement occasionally if you agree, and smile occasionally if appropriate. Most everyone likes to receive positive responses from others. Since most people interpret no response as a negative response, avoid an expressionless face. Your feedback is also likely to be interpreted as a sign of interest on your part.

If you try to concentrate on what is being said rather than how you are doing, you will most likely create a good impression on the interviewer. Being other-directed with your nonverbal communication will make you seem more likeable and competent than many other candidates who remain self concerned and nervous throughout the interview.

CLOSE THE INTERVIEW

Be prepared to end the interview. Many people don't know when or how to close interviews. They go on and on until someone breaks an uneasy moment of silence with an indication that it is time to go.

Interviewers normally will initiate the close by standing, shaking hands, and thanking you for coming to the interview. Don't end by saying "Goodbye and thank you." You should **summarize the interview** in terms of your interests, strengths, and goals. Briefly restate your qualifications and continuing interest in working with the employer. At this point it is proper to ask the interviewer about selection plans: *"When do you anticipate making your final decision?"* Follow this question with your final one: *"May I call you next week to inquire about my status?"* By taking the initiative in this manner, the employer will be prompted to clarify your status soon, and you will have an opportunity to talk to her further.

Many interviewers will ask you for a list of references. Be sure to prepare such a list prior to the interview. Include the names, addresses, and phone numbers of four individuals who will give you positive professional and personal recommendations.

MANAGE TELEPHONE INTERVIEWS

Few people are effective telephone communicators. Several channels of nonverbal communication, such as eye contact, facial expression, and gestures, are absent in telephone conversations. People who may be dynamic in face-to-face situations may be dull and boring over the telephone. Since critical communication relating to the interview will take place over the telephone, pay particular attention to how you handle your telephone communication.

Two potential telephone interview situations may arise at any time. First, you may request an interview by calling an employer. Second, the employer may call you and conduct a screening interview over the phone. While the rules for both types of telephone conversations vary, certain principles should be followed.

When you telephone to request an interview, always know the name of the person you wish to contact. If you don't know the person's name, you can easily get the name by making two phone calls: one to the receptionist or secretary and another to the person you want to speak to. When calling the receptionist or secretary, just ask for the name of the person you wish to contact: *"Who is the head of the _____ office?"* Your second call should be directly to the person you wish to contact.

Most often your telephone calls will go through a secretary. The easiest way to avoid being screened out is to sound like you know the person or he or she is expecting your call. Do not ask: *"May I speak with Mr. Casey?"* This question often results in being screened out; a secretary next asks who you are and the nature of your business. Instead, try a more direct and authoritative statement for openers: *"This is Mary Allen calling for David Casey."* A surprising number of secretaries will put you directly through to the individual without asking you a series of screening questions.

Should the secretary want more information about the nature of your call, say you wish to make an appointment to see the person about some business. If the secretary persists in trying to identify what exactly you want, say it's "personal business." If this line of questioning fails to get you through, try to call at odd times, such as one half hour before the office opens and a half hour after it closes. Many managers arrive early and leave late — times when no one else is around to answer the telephone.

Telephone introductions are easier if you are following-up on a letter you sent earlier. You might begin by saying,

> *"Hello, this is Mary Allen. I'm calling in regards to the letter I sent you last week. I mentioned I would call you today to see if we could meet briefly. You may recall my interests and experience in training and development. I would like to meet with you briefly to discuss. . ."*

However, if this is a "cold turkey" request-for-interview call, you may have difficulty scheduling an interview. Many employers will not invite you to a job interview based on this aggressive approach. Be straightforward, assertive, and hope for the best. Try to avoid the "give-me-a-job" mentality often associated with such calls. Use one of these opening statements to ease the aggressiveness of this call:

> *"I heard about the innovative work you are doing in technical training. . ."*

> *"I've always wanted to learn more about opportunities with your organization. Would it be possible for us to get together briefly to discuss your training needs?"*

> *"I was told you might know someone who would be interested in my background: 10 years of increasingly responsible training and development experience. . ."*

It is best to write down these opening statements and refer to them in your conversation. Avoid a lengthy phone conversation. You do not want to turn this into a job interview. Your goal is to schedule a face-to-face interview. If the individual asks you interview-type questions, stress your strengths and specify an interview time.

Keep in mind that your telephone voice will be a slightly higher pitch than your normal voice. Therefore, lower your pitch and speak in a moderate volume and rate. If you vary your volume, rate, and pitch for emphasis, you will sound relatively enthusiastic and interesting over the phone.

The second type of telephone encounter, as we noted earlier, is the unexpected call from the employer who is attempting to eliminate several finalists by conducting a telephone screening interview. If you receive such a call, be prepared for questions probing both your strengths and weaknesses. Although this may be a stressful situation for you, try to sound as enthusiastic, interested, and positive as possible. Stress your strengths and try to arrange a formal interview. Keep your list of questions near the telephone so you also can interview the employer. In closing this interview, try to arrange an interview:

> *"I would appreciate an opportunity to meet with you to further discuss how my skills might best meet your needs. Would it be possible for us to meet briefly sometime in the next few days?"*

Many interviewers will probe salary questions with you over the phone. They want to know if you are within a realistic range for further consideration. While it is always best to keep this question to the end of the final interview, be prepared to answer it over the telephone. Based on your research, you should already know the salary range for the position. You should either respond with *"I'm open to discussions on this question,"* or state your range which also includes part of the employer's range as common ground for negotiations. Use this question as the basis for requesting an interview. Mention that you need more information on the position. Out of fairness to the employer, he or she needs to know more about you and your value. A job interview would be most appropriate at this time.

You can prepare for these telephone conversations. Role play them with a friend. Tape-record various conversation scenarios, but do not look at each other during these conversations. Have someone else critique the tape and discuss how you might improve your telephone answers and questions.

HANDLE OBJECTIONS WITH EASE

Interviewers must have a healthy scepticism of job candidates. They expect people to exaggerate their competencies and overstate what they will do for the employer. They sometimes encounter dishonest applicants, and many people they hire fail to meet their expectations. Being realists who have made poor hiring decisions before, they want to know why they should *not* hire you. Although they do not always ask you these questions, they think about them nonetheless:

- *Why should I hire you?*
- *What do you really want?*
- *What can you really do for me?*
- *What are your weaknesses?*
- *What problems will I have with you?*

Underlying these questions are specific employers' objections to hiring you:

- *You're not as good as you say you are; you probably hyped your resume or lied about yourself.*
- *All you want is a job and security.*
- *You have weaknesses like the rest of us. Is it alcohol, sex, drugs, finances, shiftlessness, petty politics?*
- *You'll probably want my job in another 5 months.*
- *You won't stay long with us.*

Employers raise such suspicions and objections because it is difficult to trust strangers in the employment game and they may have been "burned" before. Indeed, there is an alarming rise in the number of individuals lying on their resumes or falsifying their credentials.

How can you best handle employers' objections? You must first recognize their biases and stereotypes and then *raise* their expectations. You do this by stressing your strengths and avoiding your weaknesses. You must be impeccably honest in doing so. Take, for example, the question *"Why are you leaving your present job?"* If you have been fired and you are depressed, you might blurt out all your problems:

> *"I had a great job, but my crazy boss began cutting back on personnel because of budgetary problems. I got the axe along with three others."*

You might be admired for your frankness, but this answer is too negative; it reveals the wrong motivations for seeking a job. Essentially you are saying you are unemployed and bitter because you were fired. A better answer would be:

> *"My position was abolished because of budget reductions. However, I see this as a new opportunity for me to use the skills I acquired during the past 10 years to improve profits. Having worked regularly with people in your field, I'm now anxious to use my experience to contribute to a growing organization."*

Let's try another question reflecting objections to hiring you. The interviewer asks:

> *"Your background bothers me somewhat. You've been with this organization for 10 years. You know, its different working in our organization. Why should I hire you?"*

One positive way to respond to this probing question is to clearly communicate your understanding of the objection and then give evidence that you have resolved this issue in a positive manner:

> *"I understand your hesitation in hiring someone with my background. I would too, if I were you. Yes, many people don't do well in different occupational settings. But I don't believe I have that problem. I'm used to working with people. I work until the job gets done, which often means long hours and on weekends. I'm very concerned with achieving results. But most important, I've done a great deal of thinking about my goals. I've researched your organization as well as many others. From what I have learned, this is exactly what I want to do, and your organization is the one I'm most interested in joining. I know I will do a good job as I have always done in the past."*

Always try to avoid confessing weaknesses, negatives, or lack of experience. You want to communicate your strengths and positives loud and clear to the interviewer. *Be honest, but not stupid!*

BE SURE TO FOLLOW-UP

Once you have been interviewed, be sure to follow through to get nearer to the job offer. One of the best follow-up methods is the thank-you letter. An example is included in Appendix C. After talking to the employer over the telephone or in a face-to-face interview, send a thank-you letter. This letter should be typed on good quality bond paper. In this letter express your gratitude for the opportunity to interview. Re-state your interest in the position and highlight any particularly noteworthy points made in your conversation or anything you wish to further clarify. Close the letter by mentioning that you will call in a few days to inquire about the employer's decision. When you do this, the employer should remember you as a thoughtful person.

If you call and the employer has not yet made a decision, follow through with another phone call in a few days. Send any additional information to the employer which may enhance your application. You might also want to ask one of your references to call the employer to further recommend you for the position. However, don't engage in overkill by making a pest of yourself. You want to tactfully communicate two things to the employer at this point: (1) you are interested in the job, and (2) you will do a good job.

PROJECT A POSITIVE IMAGE

Most employers quickly assess candidates' strengths and weaknesses based upon resumes and letters. If your resume and letter pass the 30 second test, you move on to the telephone interview. If you sufficiently impress the employer in the 10 minute telephone interview, you move on to the formal interview stage. At each step you must manage your image in order to make a positive impression. How you communicate your "qualifications" is as important as your job-related qualifications.

The interview is an image management activity. For example, interviewers normally make a positive or negative decision based upon the impression you make during the first 4 or 5 minutes of the interview. The major factors influencing this decision are your nonverbal cues communicated at the very beginning of the interview.

Therefore, what you wear, how you look, the way you shake hands, how you smell, whether you are interested and enthusiastic, where and how you sit, and how you initiate the small talk are extremely important to the interviewer's decision; these factors may be more important than your answers to the interview questions. Your answers will tend to either reinforce or alter the initial impression.

While it may seem unfair for employers to make such snap decisions, it happens nonetheless. Accept it as an important reality of the job search, and learn to adjust your behavior to your best advantage. Remember those first five minutes may be the most critical moments in your job search and for your future job or career. Put your best foot forward with the most positive image you can generate.

Chapter Twelve

NEGOTIATE SALARY, BENEFITS, AND YOUR FUTURE

Throughout your job search you need to seriously consider several questions about your money value and future income. What, for example, are you worth? How much should you be paid for your work? How will you demonstrate your value to an employer? What dollar value will the employer assign to you? What salary are you willing to accept?

You think you are worth a lot. After impressing upon the employer that you are the right person for the job, the bottom line becomes money — your talent and labor in exchange for the employer's cash and benefits. How, then, are you going to deal with these questions in order to get more than the employer may initially be willing to offer?

APPROACH SALARIES AS NEGOTIABLE

The salary question is awkward for many applicants who are reluctant to talk about money. They think one must take what is offered because salaries are set by employers. Such thinking is unfortunate, because it means many people are paid less than what they could be getting if they knew some basic techniques for negotiating salaries. Most people are probably underpaid by $2,000 or more because they don't use such techniques.

Salary is seldom predetermined. Most employers have some flexibility to **negotiate** salary. While they do not try to exploit applicants, neither do they want to pay applicants more than what they are willing to accept.

Salaries are usually assigned to positions or jobs rather than to individuals. But not everyone is of equal value in performing the job; some are more productive than others. Since individual performance differs, you should attempt to establish *your* value in the eyes of the employer rather than accept a salary figure for the job. The art of salary negotiation will help you do this.

LOOK TO YOUR FINANCIAL FUTURE

We all have financial needs which our salary helps to meet. But salary has other significance too. It is an indicator of our worth to others. It also influences our future income. Therefore, it should be treated as one of the most serious considerations in the job interview.

The salary you receive today will influence your future earnings. Yearly salary increments will be figured as a percentage of your base salary. When changing jobs, expect employers to offer you a salary similar to the one you earned in your last job. Once they learn what you made in your previous job, they will probably offer you no more than a 10% to 15% increase, regardless of your productivity. If you hope to improve your income in the long run, then you must be willing to negotiate your salary from a position of strength.

PREPARE FOR THE SALARY QUESTION

You should be well prepared to deal with the question of salary anytime during your job search but especially during the job interview. Based on your library research (Chapter Nine) as well as salary information gained from your networking activities (Chapter Ten), you should know the approximate salary range for the position you are seeking. If you fail to gather this salary information prior to the screening or job interview, you may do yourself a disservice by accepting too low a figure or pricing yourself out of consideration. It is always best to be informed so you will be in better control to negotiate salary and benefits.

KEEP SALARY ISSUES TO THE VERY END

The question of salary may be raised anytime during the job search. Employers may want you to state a salary expectation figure on an application form, in a cover letter, or over the telephone. Most frequently, however, employers will talk about salary during the employment interview. If at all possible, keep the salary question open until the very last. Even with application forms, cover letters, and telephone screening interviews, try to delay the discussion of salary by stating *"open"* or *"negotiable."* After all, the ultimate purpose of your job search activities is to **demonstrate your value to employers**. You should not attempt to translate your value into dollar figures until you have had a chance to convince the employer of your worth. This is best done near the end of the job interview.

Although employers will have a salary figure or range in mind when they interview you, they still want to know your salary expectations. How much will you cost them? Will it be more or less than the job is worth? Employers preferably want to hire individuals for the least amount possible. You, on the other hand, want to be hired for as much as possible. Obviously, there is room for disagreement and unhappiness as well as negotiation and compromise.

One easy way employers screen you in or out of consideration is to raise the salary question early in the interview. A standard question is *"What are your salary requirements?"* When asked, don't answer with a specific dollar figure. You should aim at establishing your **value** in the eyes of the employer prior to talking about a figure. If you give the employer a salary figure at this stage, you are likely to lock yourself into it, regardless of how much you impress the employer or what you find out about the duties of the job. Therefore, salary should be the last major item you discuss with the employer.

You should never ask about salary prior to being offered the job, even though it is one of your major concerns. Try to let the employer initiate the salary question. And when he or she does, take your time. Don't appear too anxious. While you may know — based on your previous research — approximately what the employer will offer, try to get the employer to state a figure first. If you do this, you will be in a stronger negotiating position.

HANDLE THE SALARY QUESTION WITH TACT

When the salary question arises, assuming you cannot or do not want to put it off until later, your first step should be to clearly **summarize the job responsibilities/duties as you understand them**. At this point you are attempting to do two things:

1. Seek clarification from the interviewer as to the actual
    job and all it involves.

2. Emphasize the level of skills required in the most positive
    way. In other words, you emphasize the value and worth
    of this position to the organization and subtly this may
    help support the actual salary figure that the interviewer
    or you later provide.

You might do this, for example, by saying,

> *As I understand it, I would report directly to the vice-*
> *president in charge of marketing and I would have*
> *full authority for marketing decisions that involved*
> *expenditures of up to $50,000. I would have a staff*
> *of five people — a secretary, two copywriters, and*
> *two marketing assistants.*

Such a summary statement establishes for both you and the interviewer that (1) this position reports to the highest levels of authority;
(2) this position is responsible for decision-making involving fairly
large sums of money; and (3) this position involves supervision of
staff.

Although you may not explicitly draw the connection, you are
emphasizing the value of this position to the organization. This
position should be worth a lot more than one in which the hiree will
report to the marketing manager, be required to get approval for all
expenditures over $100, and has no staff — just access to the secre-
tarial pool! By doing this you will focus the salary question (that you
have not yet responded to) around the exact work you must perform on the job in exchange for salary and benefits. You have also
seized the opportunity to focus on the value of the person who will
be selected to fill this vacancy.

Your conversation might go something like this. The employer
poses the question:

> *What are your salary requirements?*

Your first response should be to summarize the responsibilities of
the position:

> *Let me see if I understand all that is involved with*
> *this position and job. I would be expected to _____*
> _____ *Have I covered*

> *everything or are there some other responsibilities I
> should know about?*

This response focuses the salary question around the value of the position in relation to you. After the interviewer responds to your final question, answer the initial salary expectation question in this manner:

> *What is the normal range in your company for a
> position such as this?*

This question establishes the value as well as the range for the ***position or job*** — two important pieces of information you need before proceeding further into the salary negotiation stage. The employer normally will give you the requested salary range. Once he or she does, depending on how you feel about the figure, you can follow up with one more question:

> *What would be the normal salary range for someone
> with my qualifications?*

This question further establishes the value for the ***individual*** versus the position. This line of questioning will yield the salary expectations of the employer without revealing your desired salary figure or range. It also will indicate whether the employer distinguishes between individuals and positions when establishing salary figures.

REACH COMMON GROUND AND AGREEMENT

After finding out what the employer is prepared to offer, you have several choices. First, you can indicate that his or her figure is acceptable to you and thus conclude your final interview. Second, you can haggle for more money in the hope of reaching an acceptable compromise. Third, you can delay final action by asking for more time to consider the figure. Finally, you can tell the employer the figure is unacceptable and leave.

The first and the last options indicate you are either too eager or playing hard-to-get. We recommend the second and third options. If you decide to reach agreement on salary in this interview, haggle in a professional manner. You can do this best by establishing a salary range from which to bargain in relation to the employer's salary range. For example, if the employer indicates that he or she is prepared to offer $25,000 to $30,000, you should establish common ground for negotiation by placing your salary range into the employer's range. Your response to the employer's $25,000 to $30,000 range might be:

> *Yes, that does come near what I was expecting. I was thinking more in terms of $28,000 to $34,000.*

You in effect, **place the top of the employer's range into the bottom of your range**. At this point you should be able to negotiate a salary of $30,000 to $32,000, depending on how much flexibility the employer has with salaries. Most employers have more flexibility than they are willing to admit.

Once you have placed your expectations at the top of the employer's salary range, you need to **emphasize your value with supports**, such as examples, illustrations, descriptions, definitions, statistics, comparisons, or testimonials. It is not enough to simply state you were "thinking" in a certain range; you must state **why** you believe you are worth what you want. Using statistics and comparisons as your supports, you might say, for example,

> *The salary surveys I have read indicate that for the position of _____ in this industry and region the salary is between $28,000 and $35,000. Since, as we have discussed, I have extensive experience in all the areas you outlined, I would not need training in the job duties themselves — just a brief orientation to the operating procedures you use here at _____ I'm sure I could be up and running in this job within a week or two. Taking everything in consideration — especially my skills and experience and what I see as my future contributions here — I really feel a salary of $34,000 is fair compensation. Is this possible here at _____?*

Another option is to **ask the employer for time** to think about the salary offer. You want to sleep on it for a day or two. A common professional courtesy is to give you at least 48 hours to consider an offer. During this time, you may want to carefully examine the job. Is it worth what you are being offered? Can you do better? What are other employers offering for comparable positions? If one or two other employers are considering you for a job, let this employer know his or her job is not the only one under consideration. Let the employer know you may be in demand elsewhere. This should give you a better bargaining position. Contact the other employers and let them know you have a job offer and that you would like to have your application status with them clarified before you make any decisions with the other employer. Depending on how much flexibility an employer may have to accelerate a hiring decision, you may be able to go back to the first employer with another job offer. With a second job offer in hand, you should greatly enhance your bargaining position.

In both recommended options, you need to keep in mind that you should negotiate from a position of strength — not greed. Establish your value, learn what the employer is willing to pay, and negotiate in a professional manner. How you handle the salary negotiations will affect your future relations with the employer. In general, applicants who negotiate well will be treated well on the job.

TREAT BENEFITS AS STANDARD

Many employers will try to impress candidates with the benefits offered by the company. These might include retirement, bonuses, stock options, medical and life insurance, and cost of living adjustments. If the employer includes these benefits in the salary negotiations, do not be overly impressed. Most benefits are standard — they come with the job. When negotiating salary, it is best to talk about specific dollar figures.

On the other hand, if the salary offered by the employer does not meet your expectations, but you still want the job, you might try to negotiate for some benefits which are not considered standard. These might include longer paid vacations some flextime, and profit sharing.

OFFER A RENEGOTIATION OPTION

You should make sure your future salary reflects your value. One approach to doing this is to reach an agreement to renegotiate your salary at a later date, perhaps in another six to eight months. Use this technique especially when you feel the final salary offer is less than what you are worth, but you want to accept the job. Employers often will agree to this provision since they have nothing to lose and much to gain if you are as productive as you tell them.

However, be prepared to renegotiate in both directions — up and down. If the employer does not want to give you the salary figure you want, you can create good will by proposing to negotiate the higher salary figure down after six months, if your performance does not meet the employer's expectations. On the other hand, you may accept this lower figure with the provision that the two of you will negotiate your salary up after six months, if you exceed the employer's expectations. It is preferable to start out high and negotiate down rather than start low and negotiate up.

Renegotiation provisions stress one very important point: you want to be paid on the basis of your performance. You demonstrate your professionalism, self-confidence, and competence by negotiating in this manner. More important, you ensure that the question of your monetary value will not be closed in the future. As you negotiate the present, you also negotiate your future with this as well as other employers.

TAKE YOUR TIME BEFORE ACCEPTING

You should accept an offer only after reaching a salary agreement. If you jump at an offer, you may appear needy. Take time to consider your options. Remember, you are committing your time and effort in exchange for money and status. Is this the job you really want? Take some time to think about the offer before giving the employer a definite answer. But don't play hard-to-get and thereby create ill-will with your new employer. How you interview and negotiate your salary will influence how well you get along with your employer on the job.

While considering the offer, ask yourself several of the same questions you asked at the beginning of your job search:

- *What do I want to be doing five years from now?*
- *How will this job affect my personal life?*
- *Do I want to travel?*
- *Do I know enough about the employer and the future of this organization?*
- *Are there other jobs I'm considering which would better meet my goals?*

Accepting a job is serious business. If you make a mistake, you could be locked into a very unhappy situation for a long time.

If you receive one job offer while considering another, you will be able to compare relative advantages and disadvantages. You also will have some external leverage for negotiating salary and benefits. While you should not play games, let the employer know you have alternative job offers. This communicates that you are in demand, others also know your value, and the employer's price is not the only one in town. Use this leverage to negotiate your salary, benefits, and job responsibilities.

If you get a job offer but you are considering other employers, let the others know you have a job offer. Telephone them to inquire about your status as well as inform them of the job offer. Sometimes this will prompt employers to make a hiring decision sooner than anticipated. In addition, you will be informing them that you are in demand; they should seriously consider you before you get away!

Some job seekers play a bluffing game by telling employers they have alternative job offers even though they don't. Some candidates do this and get away with it. We don't recommend this approach. Not only is it dishonest, it will work to your disadvantage if the employer learns that you were lying. But more important, you should be selling yourself on the basis of your strengths rather than your deceit and greed. If you can't sell yourself by being honest, don't expect to get along well on the job. When you compromise your integrity, you demean your value to others and yourself.

Your job search is not over with the job offer and acceptance. You need to set the stage. Be thoughtful by sending your new employer a nice thank-you letter. As outlined in Appendix B, this is one of the most effective letters to write for getting your new job off on the right foot. The employer will remember you as a thoughtful individual whom he looks forward to working with.

The whole point of our job search methods is to clearly communicate to employers that you are competent and worthy of being paid top dollar. If you follow our advice, you should do very well with employers in interviews and in negotiating your salary as well as working on the job.

TRANSLATE YOUR VALUE
INTO PRODUCTIVITY FOR OTHERS

One final word of advice. Many applicants have unrealistic salary expectations and exaggerated notions of their worth to potential employers. Some occupational groups appear overpaid for the type of skills they use and the quality of the work they produce. In recent years several unions began renegotiating contracts in a new direction — downwards. Unions gave back salary increases and benefits won in previous years in order to maintain job security in the face of deepening recessions. Workers in many industries were not in a position to further increase their salaries. Many employers believed salaries had become extremely inflated in relation to profits. Such salaries, in turn, created even more inflated salary expectations among job hunters.

Given the declining power of unions, turbulent economic conditions, the increased prevalence of "give-back" schemes, and greater emphasis on productivity and performance in the workplace, many employers are reluctant to negotiate salaries upwards prior to seeing you perform in their organization. Especially in a tight job market, many employers feel they can maintain their ground on salary offers. After all, as more well qualified candidates glut the job market, many are willing to take lower salaries.

Given this situation, you may find it increasingly difficult to negotiate better salaries with employers. You will need to stress your value more than ever. For example, if you think you are worth $30,000, will you be productive enough to generate $200,000 of business for the company to justify that amount? If you can't translate your salary expectations into dollars and cents profits for the employer, perhaps you should not be negotiating at all!

PART III

CREATE YOUR OWN OPPORTUNITIES THROUGH ADVANCEMENT, RELOCATION, AND ENTREPRENEURSHIP

Chapter Thirteen

ADVANCE
YOUR CAREER

The career decisions you make today will affect your career development tomorrow. Indeed, throughout this book we have tried to prepare you for making critical career choices for today and tomorrow. While we cannot predict the future, we do know you will gain greater control over your future when you use our careering and re-careering methods.

After negotiating the job offer, shaking hands, and feeling great for having succeeded in getting a job that is right for you, what's next? How do you get started on the right foot and continue to advance your career? In this chapter we suggest how to best handle your job and career future after congratulating yourself on a job search well done.

TAKE MORE POSITIVE ACTIONS

If you managed your interviews and salary negotiations in a professional manner, your new employer should view you in a positive light. At this point you should do two things:

1. **Send your new employer a thank-you letter.**

   Mention your appreciation for the professional manner in which you were hired and how pleased you are to be joining the organization. Reaffirm your goals and your commitment to producing results. This letter should be well received. Employers seldom receive such thoughtful letters, and your reaffirmation helps ease the employer's fears of hiring an untested quantity.

2. **Send thank-you letters to those individuals who assisted you with your job search, especially those with whom you conducted informational and referral interviews.**

    Tell them of your new position, thank them for their assistance, and offer your assistance in the future. Not only is this a nice and thoughtful thing to do, it also is a wise thing to do for your future.

Always remember your networks. You work with people who can help you in many ways. Take good care of your networks by sending a thank-you letter and keeping in contact. In another few years you may be looking for another position. In addition, people in your network may later want to hire you away from your present employer. Since they know what you can do and they like you, they may want to keep you informed of new opportunities. While you will be developing new contacts and expanding your network in your new job, your former contacts should be remembered for future reference. An occasional letter, New Years card, or telephone call are thoughtful things to do.

BEWARE OF OFFICE POLITICS

After three months on the job, you should know who's who, who has clout, whom to avoid, and how to get things done in spite of people and their positions. In other words, you will become inducted into the *informal structure* of the organization. You should become aware of this structure and utilize it to your advantage.

While it goes without saying that you should *perform* in your job, you need more than just performance. You should understand the informal organization, develop new networks, and use them to advance your career. This means conducting an *internal career advancement campaign* as well as *an annual career check-up*.

Don't expect to advance by sitting around and doing your job, however good you may be. Power is distributed in organizations, and politics often is ubiquitous. Learn the power structure as well as how to *play positive politics*. For sound advice on this subject, see Andres

J. DuBrin's **Winning in Office Politics** (Van Nostrand Reinhold), and Marilyn Moat Kennedy's **Office Politics** (Follett).

After a while many organizations appear to be similar in terms of the quality and quantity of politics. Intensely interpersonal jobs are the most political. Indeed, people are normally fired because of politics – not incompetence. What do you do, for example, if you find yourself working for a tyrannical or incompetent boss or a jealous co-worker is out to get you?

CONDUCT AN ANNUAL CAREER CHECK-UP

We recommend an annual career check-up. Take out your resume and review it. Ask yourself several questions:

ANNUAL CAREER CHECK-UP QUESTIONS

- Am I achieving my objective?

- Has my objective changed?

- Is this job meeting my expectations?

- Am I doing what I'm good at and enjoy doing?

- Is this job worth keeping?

- How can I best achieve career satisfaction either on this job or in another job or career?

- What other opportunities elsewhere might be better than this job?

Individuals should increasingly ask these questions in the turbulent job market of today and tomorrow.

Perhaps changing jobs is not the best alternative for you. If you encounter difficulties with your job, you should first assess the nature of the problem. Perhaps the problem can be resolved by working with your present employer. Many employers prefer this approach. They are learning that increased job satisfaction translates into less job stress and absenteeism as well as more profits for the company. Progressive employers want happy workers because they are productive employees. They view job-keeping and job-revitalization as excellent investments in their futures.

USE JOB-KEEPING AND
ADVANCEMENT STRATEGIES

Assuming you enjoy your work, how can you best ensure keeping your job as well as advancing your career in the future? What job-keeping skills should you possess for the career environments of today and tomorrow? How can you best avoid becoming a victim of cutbacks, politics, and terminations?

As we noted in Chapter Eleven, most employers want their employees to perform according to certain expectations. Hecklinger and Curtin in *Training for Life* (Kendall/Hunt) further expand these expectations into thirteen basic job-keeping skills:

```
┌─────────────── CRITICAL JOB-KEEPING SKILLS ───────────────┐
```

1. *Ability to do the job well:* develop your know-how and competence.

2. *Initiative:* work on your own without constant direction.

3. *Dependability:* being there when you are needed.

4. *Reliability:* getting the job done.

5. *Efficiency:* being accurate and capable.

6. *Loyalty:* being faithful.

7. *Maturity:* handling problems well.

8. *Cheerfulness:* being pleasant to be with.

9. *Helpfulness:* willing to pitch in and help out.

10. *Unselfishness:* helping in a bind even though it is not your responsibility.

11. *Perseverance:* carrying on with a tedious project.

12. *Responsibility:* taking care of your duties.

13. *Creativity:* looking for new ways to solve your employer's problems.

While using these skills will not ensure job security, they will most likely enhance your security and potential for advancement.

A fourteenth job-keeping skill — managing your political environment — is one employers don't like to talk about. It may well be more important than all of the other job-keeping skills. Many people who get fired are victims of political assassinations rather than failures at meeting the bosses' job performance expectations or scoring well on the annual performance appraisal.

You must become politically sophisticated at the game of office politics in order to survive in many jobs. For example, what might happen if the boss you have a good working relationship with today is replaced tomorrow by someone you don't know or by someone you know but don't like? By no fault of your own — except having been associated with a particular mentor or patron — you may become a victim of the new bosses' house cleaning. Accordingly, you get a two-hour notice to clean out your desk and get out. Such political assassinations are common occurrences in the publishing, advertising, and other businesses.

Hecklinger and Curtin identify eight survival tactics that can be used to minimize the uncertainty and instability surrounding many jobs today:

EIGHT JOB SURVIVAL TACTICS

1. **Learn to read danger signals.** Beware of cutbacks, layoffs, and firings before they occur. Adjust to the danger signals by securing your job or by looking for another job.

2. **Document your achievements.** Keep a record of what you accomplish — problems you solve, contributions you make to improving productivity and profits.

3. **Expand your horizons.** Become more aware of other areas in the company and acquire skills for performing other jobs. The more skills you have, the more valuable you will be to the company.

4. **Prepare for your next job.** Seek more training through:

   - apprenticeships
   - community colleges
   - weekend colleges
   - private, trade, or technical schools

- home study through correspondence courses
- industrial training programs
- government training programs — U.S. Department of Agriculture
- military training
- cooperative education
- four-year college or university

5. **Promote yourself.** Talk about your accomplishments with co-workers and supervisors — but don't boast. Keep them informed of what you are doing; let them know you are available for promotion.

6. **Attach yourself to a mentor or sponsor.** Find someone in a position of influence and power whom you admire and who can help you acquire more responsibilities, skills, and advancement. Avoid currying favor.

7. **Continue informational interviewing.** Educate yourself as well as expand your interpersonal network of job contacts by regularly talking to people about their jobs and careers.

8. **Use your motivated skills.** Success tends to attract more success. Regularly use the skills you enjoy in different everyday settings.

The most important thing you can do now is to assess your present situation as well as identify what you want to do in the future with your career and life. You may conclude that your job is not worth keeping!

ASSESS AND CHANGE WHEN NECESSARY

We are not proposing disloyalty to employers or regular job-hopping. Instead, we believe in the great American principle of *"self-interest rightly understood"*; your first obligation is to yourself. No one owes you a job, and neither should you feel you owe someone your career. Jobs and careers should not be life sentences. Periodically assess your career health and feel free to make changes when necessary.

Since many jobs change for the worse, it may not be worth staying around for headaches and ulcers. If the organization does not meet your career expectations, use the same job search methods that got you into the organization. Be prepared to bail out for greener pastures by doing your job research and conducting informational and referral interviews. While the grass may not always be greener on the other side, many times it is; you will know by conducting another job search.

REVITALIZE YOUR JOB

Assuming you know how to survive on your job, what do you do if you experience burnout and high levels of job stress, or are just plain bored with your job? A job change, rather than resolving these problems, may lead to a repetition of the same patterns elsewhere. Techniques for changing the nature of your present job may prove to be your best option.

Most people will sometime experience what Kennedy (*Career Knockouts*, Follett) calls the "Killer Bs": blockage, boredom, and burnout. What can individuals do to make their jobs less stressful, more interesting, and more rewarding? One answer is found in techniques collectively referred to as "job-revitalization."

Job-revitalization involves changing work patterns. It requires you to take risks. Again, you need to evaluate your present situation, outline your career and life goals, and develop and implement a plan of action. A job-revitalization campaign may include meeting with your superior to develop an on-the-job career development plan. Set goals with your boss and discuss with him or her how you can best meet these goals on the job. If your boss is not familiar with career development and job-revitalization alternatives, suggest some of these options:

JOB-REVITALIZATION ALTERNATIVES

- Rotating jobs
- Redesigning your job
- Promotions
- Enlarging your job duties and responsibilities
- Sabbatical or leave of absence
- Part-time work

- Flextime scheduling
- Job sharing
- Retraining or educational programs
- Internship

Perhaps your supervisor can think of other options which would be acceptable to company policy as well as productive for both you and the organization.

More and more companies are recognizing the value of introducing career development programs and encouraging job-revitalization among their employees. They are learning it is more cost-effective to retain good employees by offering them new job options for career growth within the organization than to see them go. Such programs and policies are congruent with the productivity and profit goals of organizations. They are good management practices. As organizations in the 1990s stress greater productivity, they will place more emphasis on career development and job-revitalization.

PREPARE FOR CHANGE

You should prepare yourself for the job realities associated with a society that is undergoing major structural changes. This means avoiding organizations, careers, and jobs that are declining as well as knowing what you do well and enjoy doing. It also means regularly acquiring the necessary training and retraining to function in a turbulent job market. And it means using your career planning skills to effectively career and re-career in the decades ahead. If you do this, you should be well prepared to turn turbulence into new opportunities and to acquire new jobs which will become exciting and satisfying challenges.

Chapter Fourteen

RELOCATE TO THE RIGHT COMMUNITY

Relocation is an important job concern for millions of Americans each year. Indeed, one in every five families moves residences each year; approximately 6 million Americans move to another state. In many cases relocating also means changing jobs and life styles.

People relocate for many reasons. Some are forced to relocate because of a company policy that routinely moves personnel from one branch office to another or from headquarters to field offices, and vice versa. Others choose to relocate when their company closes in one community, consolidates its operations in another community, or opens a new office elsewhere. And still others choose to seek employment in communities that offer better job opportunities or more attractive life styles. For them, relocation becomes another strategy in their arsenal of job search techniques.

Whether you are forced to relocate due to company policies or you seek new opportunities in other communities, chances are you will relocate sometime during the 1990s. When you are faced with a relocation decision, you need to be prepared to deal with many new job, community, and life style issues.

247

RELOCATE TO
CAREER AND RE-CAREER

Where will you be working and living next year, five years, or 10 years from today? When you conduct a job search, you do so by targeting specific employers in particular communities. In most cases, individuals will conduct their job search in the same community in which they live. For other people, moving to another community is desirable for career and life style purposes. And for others, unemployment may be preferred to leaving their present community.

Whatever your choices, you should weigh the relative costs and benefits of relocating to a new community where job opportunities for someone with your skills may be plentiful. If you live in a declining community or one experiencing little economic growth, job and career opportunities for you may be very limited. You should consider whether it would be better for you to examine job opportunities in other communities which may offer greater long-term career advancement as well as more opportunities for careering and re-careering in the future.

In recent years economic development has shifted toward the West and Southwest and to selected metropolitan areas in the East and South. Millions of job seekers will continue to migrate to these areas throughout the 1990s in response to growing job opportunities. Perhaps you, too, will look toward these areas as you change jobs and careers in the future.

In this chapter we examine how to conduct both a long-distance and a community-based job search campaign. We include the case of Washington, D.C. to illustrate the importance of conducting community research as well as for identifying alternative job networks. Nowhere do we recommend that you pull up stakes and take to the road in search of new opportunities. Many people did so in the 1980s as they headed for the reputed promised lands of Houston and Denver. As the booming energy economies in these communities went bust by the mid-1980s, many of the people experienced a new round of unemployment. Don't ever take to the road until you have done your homework by researching communities, organizations, and individuals as well as created the necessary bridges for contacting employers in a new community. Most important, be sure you have the appropriate work-content skills for finding employment in specific communities.

TARGET COMMUNITIES

Many people are attached to their communities. Friends, relatives, churches, schools, businesses, and neighborhoods provide an important sense of identity which is difficult to leave for a community of strangers. Military and diplomatic personnel — the truly transient groups in society — may be the only ones accustomed to moving to new communities every few years.

The increased mobility of society is partly due to the nature of the job market. Many people voluntarily move to where job opportunities are most plentiful. Thus, Atlanta becomes a boom city with hundreds of additional cars entering the already congested freeways each week. The corporate structure of large businesses, with branches geographically spread throughout the national production and distribution system, requires the movement of key personnel from one location to another — much like military and diplomatic personnel.

When you begin your job search, you face two alternative community approaches. You can concentrate on a particular job, regardless of its geographic setting, or you can focus on one or two communities. The first approach, which we term *follow-the-job*, is widely used by migrant farm workers, cowboys, bank robbers, mercenaries, oil riggers, construction workers, newspaper reporters, college and university professors, and city managers. These people move to where the jobs are in their particular profession. Not surprising, many of these job seekers end up in boring communities.

If you follow-the-job, you will need to link into a geographically mobile communication system for identifying job opportunities. This often means subscribing to specialized trade publications, maintaining contacts with fellow professionals in other communities, or creatively advertising yourself to prospective employers through newspaper ads or letter blitzes.

On the other hand, you may want to *target a community*. This may mean remaining in your present community or locating a community you find especially attractive because of job opportunities, climate, recreation, or social and cultural environments. Regardless of rumored job opportunities, many people, for instance would not move to the "deep South" where the weather is hot and humid and the people display different linguistic, social, and cultural styles. The same is true for Southerners who are not particularly interested in moving to cold, dreary, and crime ridden northern cities. At the same time, Boston, Philadelphia, Washington, DC, San Francisco, St. Louis, Seattle, and Atlanta are reputed to be the new promised lands for many people. Oases of prosperity and centers for attractive urban life styles, these cities are on the community target list of many job seekers.

We recommend using this second approach of targeting specific communities. The follow-the-job approach is okay if you are young, adventuresome, or desperate; you find yourself in a geographically mobile profession; or your career takes precedence over all other aspects of your life. By targeting a community, your job search will be more manageable. Furthermore, moving to another community can be a liberating experience which will have a positive effect on both your professional and personal lives.

KNOW THE GROWING STATES AND COMMUNITIES

Frictional unemployment — the geographic separation of under-employed and unemployed individuals from high labor demand regions and communities — should present new options for you. Numerous job opportunities may be available if you are willing to relocate.

As noted in the chart on page 251, unemployment during the later half of the 1980s was unevenly distributed among the states. It was most pronounced in the States of West Virginia, Michigan, Alabama, Mississippi, and Louisiana. South Dakota, Nebraska, Connecticut, Massachusetts, and Arizona had the lowest unemployment rates. These patterns of unemployment will shift in the 1990s depending on the state of the economy. However, expect the large states of Florida, New York, Texas, and California to have above average employment rates.

Growing regions and communities are relatively predictable for the 1990s. Several metropolitan areas that experienced high population growth rates in the 1970s continued with similar growth rates in the 1980s:

- Los Angeles-Long Beach, San Francisco-Oakland, CA
- Washington, DC
- Baltimore, MD
- Dallas-Fort Worth, TX
- Houston, TX
- Minneapolis-St. Paul, MN
- Atlanta, GA
- Anaheim-Santa Ana-Garden Grove, CA
- San Diego, CA
- Denver-Boulder, CO

UNEMPLOYMENT IN THE STATES

	1,000's of PERSONS	PERCENTAGE
West Virginia	116	15.0%
Michigan	488	11.2%
Alabama	200	11.1%
Mississippi	116	10.8%
Louisiana	194	10.0%
Alaska	25	10.0%
Washington	194	9.5%
Ohio	481	9.4%
Oregon	125	9.4%
Kentucky	160	9.3%
Illinois	511	9.1%
Washington,DC	290	9.1%
Pennsylvania	499	9.1%
Arkansas	93	8.9%
Indiana	226	8.6%
Tennessee	190	8.6%
North Dakota	17	8.1%
Nevada	39	7.8%
California	972	7.8%
New Mexico	47	7.5%
Montana	30	7.4%
Wisconsin	176	7.3%
Missouri	172	7.2%
Idaho	33	7.2%
New York	584	7.2%
South Carolina	105	7.1%
Oklahoma	109	7.0%
Iowa	100	7.0%
North Carolina	205	6.7%
Utah	47	6.5%
Minnesota	141	6.3%
Florida	322	6.3%
Wyoming	16	6.3%
New Jersey	236	6.2%
Delaware	19	6.2%
New Hampshire	34	6.1%
Maine	34	6.1%
Georgia	166	6.0%
Texas	466	5.9%
Colorado	96	5.6%
Hawaii	27	5.6%
Maryland	121	5.4%
Rhode Island	26	5.3%
Vermont	14	5.2%
Kansas	63	5.2%
Virginia	143	5.0%
Arizona	71	5.0%
Massachusetts	145	4.8%
Connecticut	77	4.6%
Nebraska	35	4.4%
South Dakota	15	4.3%

- Seattle-Everett, WA
- Miami, FL
- Tampa-St. Petersburg, FL
- Riverside-San Bernardino-Ontario, CA
- Phoenix, AZ
- Portland, OR
- San Antonio, TX
- Fort Lauderdale-Hollywood, FL
- Salt Lake City-Ogden, UT

Disproportionately found in the West, Southwest, and Southeast, these communities along with a few in the Northeast and Midwest, should continue with high growth rates during the 1990s. Depending on the extent of another energy crisis in the 1990s, several communities in the energy rich Rocky Mountain states may once again become boom towns. Communities with large concentrations of high-tech and service industries will continue to expand both demographically and economically.

We foresee major population and economic growth in and around several large cities: Boston, Philadelphia, Pittsburgh, Raleigh-Durham, Atlanta, Tampa-St. Petersburg, St. Louis, Minneapolis-St. Paul, Dallas-Ft. Worth, San Antonio, Albuquerque, Denver, Phoenix, San Diego, Los Angeles, San Francisco, and Seattle. Population is likely to continue decreasing in New York, Chicago, Detroit, Newark, Cleveland, and Buffalo as more and more residents from these communities relocate to other parts of the country.

Even though the overall growth predictions point to the Southwest and West, these trends should not deter you from considering older cities in the Northeast and North Central regions. After all, 1-2 million new jobs are created nationwide each year. New jobs will continue to develop in cities such as Chicago, Philadelphia, and New York; these are still the best places to pursue careers in the growing fields of banking, publishing, and advertising. Several communities in the Midwest will rebound as they transform their local economies in the direction of new high-tech and service industries.

CONSIDER THE BEST PLACES TO START A NEW CAREER

If you are just finishing school and starting a new career, you should consider moving to a community that offers exceptionally good opportunities for people at your career stage. The *Places Rated Almanac* (Rand McNally) identifies 20 such communities with a population over 500,000. These communities score high in terms of low crime rates, good transportation facilities, a fine range of cultural activities, and promising economic opportunities:

```
━━━━━━━━━━ THE BEST METRO AREAS ━━━━━━━━
               FOR STARTING A CAREER
```

Ranking	Metro Area
1	Raleigh-Durham, NC
2	Middlesex-Somerset-Hunterdon, NJ
3	Minneapolis-St. Paul, MN-WI
4	Rochester, NY
5	Denver, CO
6	Boston, MA
7	Pittsburgh, PA
8	Salt Lake City-Ogden, UT
9	Dallas, TX
10	San Jose, CA
11	Washington, DC-MD-VA
12	Atlanta, GA
13	Richmond-Petersburg, VA
14	Seattle, WA
15	Nassau-Suffolk, NY
16	Chicago, IL
17	Philadelphia, PA-NJ
18	Honolulu, HI
19	San Francisco, CA
20	St. Louis, MO-IL

At the same time, you should consider communities that are experiencing the greatest job growth. During the period 1978-82, for example, the U.S. Department of Labor found the following metropolitan areas generated the greatest and the least number of jobs:

```
┌──────── GREATEST AND LEAST JOB GROWTH ─────────┐
│                    IN METRO AREAS               │
```

Greatest growth	Percent increase	Least growth	Percent decrease
1. Portsmouth-Dover-Rochester, NH-ME	63	1. Beaver County, PA	-23
2. Fort Pierce, FL	54	2. Syracuse, NY	-22
3. Bryan-College Station, TX	53	3. Anderson, IN	-20
4. Lafayette, LA	48	4. Kokomo, IN	-18
5. Midland, TX	48	5. Peoria, IL	-16
6. Atlantic City, NJ	47	6. Benton Harbor, MI	-16
7. Ocala, FL	39	7. Lorain-Elyria, OH	-15
8. Orlando, FL	39	8. Flint, MI	-15
9. Colorado Springs, CO	38	9. Muskegon, MI	-15
10. West Palm Beach-Boca Raton-Delray Beach, FL	38	10. Battle Creek, MI	-15

LOOK FOR THE MOST
SOLID METRO AREAS

Metropolitan areas exhibiting strong performance in several sectors — climate, arts, transportation, health care, education, safety, recreation, housing, and economics — should prove to be very attractive areas in the long-term. *Places Rated* found nine metropolitan areas it considers to be super-solid metropolitan areas:

```
┌──────────SUPER-SOLID METROPOLITAN AREAS──────────┐
```

Metro Area (by rank)	Highest Rank	Lowest Rank
1. Asheville, NC	Climate	Arts
2. Cincinnati, OH-KY-IN	Arts	Housing
3. Greensboro-Winston-Salem-High Point,NC	Climate	Economics
4. Harrisburg-Lebanon-Carlisle, PA	Transportation	Recreation
5. Knoxville, TN	Climate	Education
6. Louisville, KY	Health Care	Economics
7. Nashville, TN	Health Care	Crime
8. Pittsburgh, PA	Education	Housing
9. Raleigh-Durham, NC	Health Care	Housing

Other high ranking solid metropolitan areas include Albany-Schenectady-Troy, NY; Alton-Granite City, IL; Binghamton, NY; Buffalo, NY; Charlottesville, VA; Evansville, IN; Middlesex-Somerset-Hunterdon, NJ; New Haven-Meriden, CT; Oklahoma City, OK; Omaha, NE; Portland, ME; Roanoke, VA; St. Louis, MO; Springfield IL; Syracuse, NY; and Wilmington, DE. But keep in mind that many of these communities are statistically good places to live. They may or may not be the best places for you to find a job and re-career.

LOCATE THE RIGHT SIZE COMMUNITY

What size community do you prefer working and living in during the next 10 years? Many people prefer large metropolitan areas because of the wider range of amenities and opportunities found in such areas as compared to smaller communities. Others prefer the atmosphere of a medium to small-sized community. Using the same indicators of livability, *Places Rated Almanac* identifies the 20 best metropolitan areas according to size:

———— BEST METRO AREAS BY SIZE ————

Best Large Metro Areas (population 1,000,000 or more)	
Rank	Metro Area
1	Pittsburgh, PA
2	Boston, MA
3	San Francisco, CA
4	Philadelphia PA-NJ
5	Nassau-Suffolk, NY
6	St. Louis, MO-IL
7	Seattle, MO-IL
8	Atlanta, GA
9	Dallas, TX
10	Buffalo, NY
11	Baltimore, MD
12	Washington, DC-MD-VA
13	Cincinnati, OH-KY-IN
14	New York, NY
15	Chicago, IL

16	San Jose, CA
17	San Diego, CA
18	Denver, CO
19	Cleveland, OH
20	Tampa-St. Petersburg-Clearwater, FL

Best Medium-Sized Metro Areas
(population 250,000 to 1,000,000)

1	Raleigh-Durham, NC
2	Louisville, KY-IN
3	Knoxville, TN
4	Albany-Schnectady-Troy, NY
5	Syracuse, NY
6	Albuquerque, NM
7	Harrisburg-Lebanon-Carlisle, PA
8	Richmond-Petersburg, VA
9	Providence, RI
10	Middlesex-Somerset-Hunterdon, NJ
11	Rochester, NY
12	Wilmington, DE-NJ-MD
13	Omaha, NE-IA
14	Bridgeport-Milford, CT
15	Greensboro-Winston-Salem-High Point, NC
16	New Haven-Meriden, CT
17	Nashville, TN
18	Johnson City-Kingsport-Bristol, TN-VA
19	Oklahoma City, OK
20	Monmouth-Ocean, NJ

Best Small Metro Areas
(population less than 250,000)

1	Norwalk, CT
2	Burlington, VT
3	Charlottesville, VA
4	Asheville, NC
5	Stamford, CT
6	Portland, ME
7	Danbury, CT
8	Galveston-Texas City, TX
9	South Bend-Mishawaka, IN
10	Middletown, CT
11	Bangor, ME

12	Roanoke, VA
13	Springfield, IL
14	Lynchburg, VA
15	Boulder-Longmont, CO
16	Cumberland, MD-WV
17	Kenosha, WI
18	Champaign-Urbana-Rantoul, IL
19	Muncie, IN
20	La Crosse, WI

FIND THE BEST PLACE TO LIVE

Community growth and decline trends should be considered as part of your job and career options. If you live in a declining community with few opportunities for your skills and interests, seriously consider relocating to a growth community. Depressed communities simply do not generate enough jobs for their populations. Many communities with populations of 100,000 to 500,000 offer a variety of employment and life style opportunities.

Except for a few people, one's work should not become one's life. Economic development and job generation are only two of many important community choice concerns. Using 11 indicators of "living", *Places Rated Almanac* in the mid-1980s identified what it considers to be the 50 best communities in America in terms of their mix of climate, topography, housing, health care, environment, safety, transportation, education, arts, recreation, and economics:

50 BEST METROPOLITAN AREAS

Rank	Metro Area	Highest Rank	Lowest Rank
1	Pittsburgh,PA	Education	Housing
2	Boston, MA	Health Care	Housing
3	Raleigh-Durham, NC	Health Care	Housing
4	San Francisco, CA	Climate	Housing
5	Philadelphia, PA-NJ	Education	Housing
6	Nassau-Suffolk, NY	Health Care	Transportation
7	St. Louis, MO-IL	Education	Crime
8	Louisville, KY-IN	Health Care	Economics
9	Norwalk, CT	Climate	Housing

10	Seattle, WA	Recreation	Housing
11	Atlanta, GA	Transportation	Recreation
12	Dallas, TX	Arts	Crime
13	Buffalo, NY	Arts	Economics
14	Knoxville, TN	Climate	Education
15	Baltimore, MD	Transportation	Housing
16	Washington, DC-MD-VA	Trans/Educ.	Housing
17	Cincinnati, OH-KY-IN	Arts	Housing
18	Burlington, VT	Transportation	Climate
19	Albany-Schenectady-Troy, NY	Transportation	Climate
20	Syracuse, NY	Transportation	Economics
21	Albuquerque, NM	Transportation	Crime
22	Harrisburg-Lebanon-Carlisle, PA	Transportation	Recreation
23	Richmond-Petersburg, VA	Transportation	Crime
24	Providence, RI	Education	Housing
25	New York, NY	Health Care, Transportation, Arts	Crime
26	Chicago, IL	Health Care, Arts	Housing
27	San Jose, CA	Climate	Housing
28	San Diego, CA	Climate	Housing
29	Middlesex-Somerset-Hunterdon, NJ	Education	Housing
30	Denver, CO	Transportation	Housing
31	Cleveland, OH	Transportation, Arts	Housing
32	Rochester, NY	Education	Climate
33	Charlottesville, VA	Education	Housing
34	Wilmington, DE-NJ-MD	Education	Crime
35	Tampa-St. Petersburg-Clearwater, FL	Economics	Climate
36	Asheville, NC	Climate	Arts
37	Omaha, NE-IA	Health Care	Climate
38	Los Angeles-Long Beach, CA	Arts	Crime
39	Bridgeport-Milford, CT	Arts	Housing
40	Norfolk-Virginia Beach--Newport News, VA	Arts, Recreation	Transportation
41	Greensboro-Winston-Salem-High Point, NC	Climate	Economics
42	New Haven-Meriden, CT	Education	Housing

43	Bergen-Passaic, NJ	Education	Housing
44	Nashville, TN	Health Care	Crime
45	Johnson City-Kingsport- Bristol, TN-VA	Crime	Transportation
46	Oklahoma City, OH	Economics	Crime
47	Monmouth-Ocean, NJ	Recreation	Housing
48	Anaheim-Santa Ana, CA	Climate	Housing
49	Jacksonville, FL	Recreation	Crime
50	Stamford, CT	Health Care	Housing

These rankings will undoubtedly change for the 1990s. It is best to consult the latest edition of *Places Rated Almanac* to see how particular communities rank according to each and every indicator. This book is available in most libraries and major bookstores.

SELECT A LOCATION PROPERLY

You and your family must take into consideration several factors and questions when deciding on which communities to target your job search:

- Where would you like to live for the next 5, 10, or 20 years?

- What is the relative cost of living?

- How attractive are the educational, social, and cultural activities?

- What are the economic and psychological costs of making a move?

- What job and career opportunities are there for us?

- How can we best conduct a job search in another community?

Many people answer these questions by remaining in their community or by targeting growth communities. The exodus from the declining industrial cities in the Northeast and North Central regions to the Sunbelt began in the 1960s, expanded in the 1970s, and continued into the 1980s with the inclusion of the energy rich Rocky Mountain states. Several metropolitan areas in all regions will have abundant job opportunities for *skilled* workers during the 1990s.

Targeting a job search in metropolitan Los Angeles, San Diego, San Antonio, Atlanta, Boston, and Washington, DC may be a wise move. While these areas will experience numerous urban problems over the next decade, their problems are ones of growth — traffic congestion, pollution, city planning, crime, and housing shortages — not ones of decline. We believe it is better to experience the problems of growth than of decline. In a situation of decline, your livelihood becomes threatened. In a situation of growth, your major problem may be fighting the traffic congestion in order to get to a job which offers a promising career.

New frontiers for renewed job and career prosperity abound throughout America if you are willing to pack your bags and move. But remember, most of these frontiers require skilled individuals. If you don't possess the necessary skills for industries in other communities, consider getting retraining before making a move. Unfortunately, many people making moves today do not have the necessary skills to succeed in new communities.

Making a community move on your own involves taking risks. Many people, for example, are locked into financial obligations, such as a mortgaged house which doesn't sell well in what may be a depressed housing market. If you find yourself locked in financially, you may want to consider taking an immediate financial loss in anticipation of renewed prosperity in a community which is experiencing promising growth and prosperity. You may recoup your immediate losses within a year or two. However, you will have to pass through a transition period which can be difficult if you don't approach it in a positive, up-beat manner. The old saying, *"There is no gain without pain"* is appropriate in many situations involving community moves.

CONSIDER THE FINANCIAL COSTS

The financial costs of relocating will vary depending on your situation. They can be major, especially if you move to a community with high housing costs. Studies conducted by Runzheimer International, for example, found the average costs of relocating in 1987 to be $36,253 for homeowners and $10,503 for non-homeowners. The major costs of relocating include:

1. Search for housing — travel, child care, and associated expenses.

2. Closing costs on both the old and new homes.

3. Increases in mortgage payments or apartment rent.

4. Temporary living expenses.

5. Cost of a bridge, equity, or swing loan.

6. Costs of maintaining two residents during the relocation period — very high if old home does not sell immediately.

7. Shipment of household goods.

8. Final moving expenses.

9. Possible increase in cost of living — property and sales taxes, food, utilities.

10. Travel and job search costs for working spouse.

11. Expenses for marketing a home or subletting an apartment.

12. Miscellaneous costs — deposit monies, decorating costs, fees, dues.

Housing can be a major cost if you move to a community with expensive housing. The National Association of Realtors reported the median home price for the top 25 metropolitan areas in 1988 to be as follows:

MEDIAN HOME PRICES FOR THE TOP 25 METROPOLITAN AREAS	
1 Honolulu	$198,400
2 New York/New Jersey/Long Island	186,600
3 Orange County, CA	183,800
4. San Francisco Bay Area	178,800
5 Boston	176,900
6 Hartford	166,400
7 Los Angeles	159,900
8 San Diego	134,400
9 Washington D.C.	132,400
10 Providence	123,300
11 Riverside/San Bernadino	95,500
12 West Palm Beach/Boca Raton/Delray Beach, FL	94,500

13	Chicago	92,800
14	Dallas/Ft. Worth	85,900
15	Seattle/Tacoma	85,100
16	Minneapolis/St. Paul	84,400
17	Denver	83,700
18	Baltimore	83,600
19	Albany/Schenectady/Troy, NY	82,800
20	Philadelphia	81,400
21	Albuquerque	79,700
22	Phoenix	79,000
23	Orlando	78,700
24	Ft. Lauderdale/Hollywood/Pompano Beach	78,600
25	Miami/Hialeah	78,000

On the other hand, once you buy into these communities, your housing investment should appreciate significantly. In the long-term, you will probably realize a handsome return on your investment. The basic problem is initially buying into the higher priced housing, and especially if comparable housing was much less expensive in your last community.

CONDUCT A LONG-DISTANCE JOB SEARCH

How do you target your job search on a particular community? If you decide to remain in your present community, your job search is relatively manageable on a day-to-day basis. If you target another community, you will need to conduct a long-distance job search which requires more extensive use of the mail and telephone as well as carefully planned visits to the community. In fact, you will probably use your job search time more efficiently with a long-distance campaign. In both situations, you need to conduct community research prior to initiating the major communication steps in your job search.

Most of your community research can be conducted in the library. You need names, addresses, and phone numbers of potential employers. Use the major directories, as we identified in Chapter Nine, such as the ***Dun & Bradstreet's Middle Market Directory*** and ***Who's Who in Commerce and Industry***. The Yellow Pages of telephone directories are especially useful sources for identifying the business and commercial structure of communities as well as for addresses and telephone numbers. The larger the community, the more specialized the businesses. For example, New York City has several businesses specializing in manufacturing manhole covers! At the same time, write to chambers of commerce for information on the community and to companies for annual reports and other organizational literature. Homequity provides relocation counseling services. If you call their toll-free number (800/243-1033), you can receive free information on housing and schools in any community as well as spouse career counseling. You can also write to them for information: Homequity Destination Services, 107 Newtown Road, Danbury, CT 06813. United Van Lines' Betty Malone Relocation Services (800/325-3870) will send you free information on 7,000 cities, and many banks will supply you with relocation information. Another good source for conducting a job search is Fran Bastress' comprehensive job search guide for spouses: *The Relocating Spouse's Guide to Employment* (Woodley Publications). This book is available directly through Impact Publications by completing the order form at the end of this book.

Part of your research may involve narrowing the number of communities you are considering. If you identify 10 alternative communities, outline the criteria by which to evaluate the 10 communities. For example, you may be particularly interested in moving to a community which has a good climate, excellent cultural facilities, unique recreational opportunities, and a sound educational infrastructure in addition to numerous job and career opportunities in your area of interest and skill. Select three communities and initiate a writing campaign for more information. If at all possible, schedule a trip to the cities to get an on-site view or feel for the relative environments. Further try to narrow your choices by rank-ordering your preferences among the three communities. Concentrate most of your job search efforts on your top priority community.

Your next step is to develop a strategy for penetrating both the advertised and hidden job markets. If you are conducting a job search outside your present community, the advertised job market will be most accessible to you. However, you need to link into the hidden job market, where most of the good jobs are located. Doing this from a distance is somewhat difficult, but nonetheless it can be managed.

PENETRATE THE LOCAL JOB MARKET

The advertised job market is always the easiest to access. Buy a newspaper and read the classified ads. Contact an employment firm and they will eagerly assist you. Walk into a personnel office and they may permit you to fill out an application form.

If you target a community from a distance, begin by subscribing to a local newspaper; the Sunday edition will most likely meet your needs. This newspaper also will give you other important information on the community — housing market, economics, politics, society, culture, entertainment, and recreation. Survey the help wanted ads to get a feel for the structure of the advertised job market. Remember, these are not necessarily indicative of the true employment picture in a community — only 20 to 30 percent of the job market. Write letters to various companies and ask about job opportunities. You also may want to contact one or more professional employment agencies or job search firms — preferably fee-paid ones — for job leads. But remember our warnings in Chapter Five about possible frauds and hucksters!

Efforts to penetrate the advertised job market should be geared toward uncovering the hidden job market. For example, in reading the Sunday newspaper, watch for names of important people in the society or "Living" section. You may want to contact some of these people by using an approach letter as we outlined in Chapters Nine and Ten. The employment agencies may give some indication of the general employment situation in the community — both advertised and hidden job markets. The chamber of commerce might be able to give you some job leads other than those advertised.

If you are conducting a long-distance job search, we recommend following the same procedures we outlined in Chapter Ten on networking. *Preparation* is the key to success. Do your research on potential employers, write letters, make phone calls, and schedule informational and referral interviews. The major difference in this situation is your timing. In addition, you need to give more information to your contacts. In your letter mention that you are planning to move to their community and would appreciate their advice on job opportunities for someone with your qualifications. Mention that you plan to visit the community on such and such a date and would appreciate an opportunity to discuss your job search plan at that time. In this case, enclose your resume with the letter and request a reply to your inquiry. Most people will reply and schedule an interview or refer you to someone else.

You should set aside one or two weeks — preferably more — to literally blitz the community with informational and referral interviews. This requires doing a considerable amount of advance work. For example, use your present community to practice informational and referral interviewing. Contact employers in your area who are in similar positions. Many of them may give you referrals to friends and colleagues in your targeted community.

With limited contacts, you will probably need to use the "cold turkey" approach more frequently from a distance. You should make most of your key contacts at least four weeks before you plan to visit your targeted community. Within two weeks of your visit, you should have scheduled most of your interviews.

Try to schedule at least three interviews each day. You will probably do more because each interview will yield one or two referrals to others. Five interviews a day are manageable if you don't need to spend a lot of time traveling from one site to another. Plan to keep the sites near each other for each day. Within a two week period, you should be able to conduct 40 to 60 interviews. Use the weekends to research the community further. Contact a realtor who will be happy to show you around the community and inform you of different housing alternatives, neighborhoods, schools, taxes, public services, shopping centers, and a wealth of other community information. You should reserve the last two days for following up on referrals. Scheduling interviews with referrals will have to be made by telephone because of the time factor.

After concluding your one to two week visit, follow up your interviews with thank-you letters, telephone calls, and letters indicating continuing interest and requesting referrals.

If you receive an invitation to a formal job interview, be sure to clarify the financial question of who pays for the interview. Normally if the employer has requested the interview, the company pays the expense to and from the out of town interview. However, if you have invited yourself to an interview by stating that you will be "in town," expect to pay your own expenses. If you are unclear about who initiated the interview, simply ask the employer *"How should we handle the travel expense?"* You'll get a clarification, and there will be no misunderstanding.

IDENTIFY OPPORTUNITY STRUCTURES

Each community has its own social, economic, political, and job market structure. Your job is to understand and use the particular job market structure in your targeted community. Therefore, we outline the case of Washington, D.C. for illustrative purposes. The principles for identifying and using the institutional and personal networks will remain the same for most communities even though the individuals, groups, and institutions differ.

The degree of structure differs for every community. However, one thing is relatively predictable: most communities lack a coherent structure for processing job information efficiently and effectively.

Each community is made up of numerous individuals, groups, organizations, and institutions that are involved in pursuing their own interests in cooperation and competition with one another. The Yellow Pages of your telephone book best outline the major actors. Banks, mortgage companies, advertising firms, car dealers, schools, churches, small businesses, industries, hospitals, law firms, governments, and civic and voluntary groups do their "own thing" and have their own internal power structure. No one dominates except in small communities which also are company towns – paper mills, mining companies, universities, or steel mills. At the same time, the groups overlap with each other because of economic, political, and social needs. The bank, for example, needs to loan money to the businesses and churches. The businesses, in turn, need the educational institutions. And the educational institutions need the businesses to absorb their graduates. Therefore, individuals tend to cooperate in seeing that people playing the other games also succeed. Members of school boards, medical boards, and the boardrooms of banks and corporations will overlap and give the appearance of a "power structure" even though power is structured in the loosest sense of the term. The game players compete and cooperate with each other as well as co-op one another. The structures they create are your *opportunity structures* for penetrating the hidden job market.

Take the example of Washington, D.C. The opportunity structures for your job search networks are relatively well defined in this city. While government is the major institution, other institutions are well defined in relation to the government. Within government, both the political and administrative institutions function as alternative opportunity structures in the Washington networks: congressional staffs, congressional committees, congressional subcommittees, congressional bureaucracy, executive staff, departments, independent executive agencies, and independent regulatory agencies. Outside, but clinging to, government are a variety of other groups and networks: interest groups, the media, professional associations, contractors, consultants, law firms, banks, and universities and colleges. As illustrated on page 267, these groups are linked to one another for survival and advancement. Charles Peters (*How Washington Really Works*) calls them "survival networks" which function in the "make believe world" of Washington, D.C. Ripley and Franklin (*Congress, Bureaucracy*, and *Public Policy*) identify the key-political dynamics as "subgovernments," the interaction of interest groups, agencies, and congressional committees.

For years Washington insiders have learned how to use these "survival networks" and "subgovernments" to advance their careers.

WASHINGTON NETWORKS

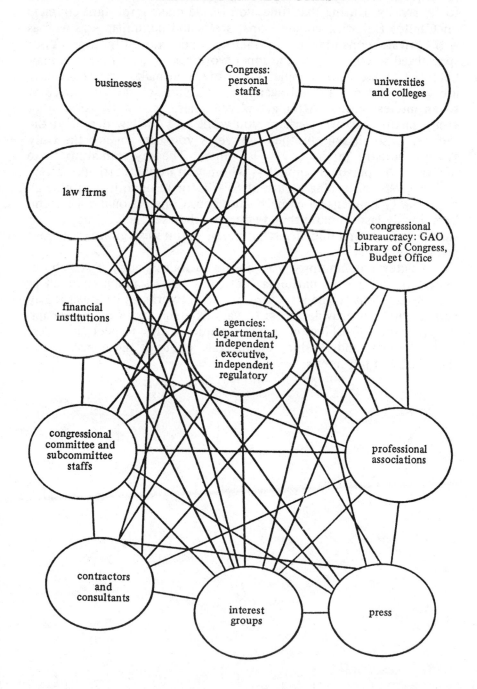

A frequent career pattern would be to work in an agency for three to four years. During that time, you would make important contacts on Capitol Hill with congressional staffs and committees as well as with private consultants, contractors, and interest groups. Your specialized knowledge on the inner workings of government is marketable to these other people. Therefore, you make a relatively easy job change from a federal agency to a congressional committee or to an interest group. After a few years here, you move to another group in the network. Perhaps you work on your law degree at the same time so that in another five years you can go into the truly growth industry in the city — law firms. The key to making these moves is the personal contact — whom you know. Particular attention is given to keeping a current SF-171 or resume, just in case an opportunity happens to come by for you. Congressional staff members usually last no more than two years; they set their sights on consulting and contracting firms, agencies, or interest groups for their next job move.

Whatever community you decide to focus your job search on, expect it to have its particular networks. Do as much research as possible to identify the structure of the networks as well as the key people who can provide access to various elements in the opportunity structures. Washington is not unique in this respect; it is just better known, and Washingtonians talk about it more because of their frequent job moves.

Chapter Fifteen

START YOUR OWN BUSINESS

We expect the 1990s to be another strong decade for entrepreneurship in America. Millions of small businesses will develop in response to new opportunities in high-tech and service industries. Self-employment and start-up businesses will remain great frontiers for careering and re-careering in the 1990s.

CONSIDER THE ALTERNATIVES AND RISKS

The largest number of job and career opportunities in America are found among small businesses — not large Fortune 500 corporations. Indeed, we expect large corporations in the 1990s to continue emphasizing productivity by introducing new technology and mangement systems to improve the efficiency and effectiveness of the workplace. In other words, they will continue to cut back on the fastest growing corporate expense — personnel. The advancement hierarchies of large companies will shorten and career opportunities narrow as these companies further automate as well as reduce the number of middle management personnel. Many of these displaced personnel will become entrepreneurs, starting both small and medium-sized businesses.

Since nearly 90 percent of all new jobs will be created by small businesses, you may wish to target your job search toward opportunities with small businesses. Finding a job with a small business will require a great deal of research because most such businesses are not well known among job seekers.

One other alternative is to start your own business. Indeed, nearly 600,000 new businesses are started each year. During the 1990s millions of individuals will be "pushed" or "pulled" from what were once seen as promising jobs and careers with companies to form their own businesses. As work becomes more centralized, advancement opportunities become more limited, and starting a business becomes easier, millions of individuals will opt for starting their own businesses in the 1990s.

While nearly 600,000 new businesses are started each year, grim business statistics also discourage would-be entrepreneurs: another 400,000 to 500,000 businesses fail each year; 50 percent fail within the first 38 months; and nearly 90 percent fail within 10 years. Unfortunately, starting your own business is a risky business; the statistical odds are against anyone becoming a successful entrepreneur.

Nonetheless, owning your business is a viable careering and re-careering alternative to working for someone else — if you approach business intelligently. Many people fail because they lack the necessary ingredients for success. In this chapter we outline the basics for getting started in owning your business and employing yourself.

LEARN TO TAKE RISKS

You will find few challenges riskier than starting your own business. At the same time, you may experience your greatest professional satisfaction in running your own business.

Starting a business means taking risks. First, you will probably go into debt and realize little income during the first two years you are building your business even though you had grandiose visions of becoming an overnight success. You may be under-capitalized or have overhead costs higher than anticipated. It takes time to develop a regular clientele. What profits you do realize are normally plowed back into the business in order to expand operations and guarantee larger future profits. Second, business is often a trial and error process in which it is difficult to predict or ensure outcomes. Due to unforeseen circumstances beyond your control, you may fail even though you work hard and make intelligent investment decisions. Third, you could go bankrupt and lose more than just your investments of time and money.

At the same time, owning your own business can be tremendously satisfying. It is the ultimate of independence. Being your own boss means you are in control, and no one can fire you. You are rewarded in direct proportion to your productivity. Your salary is not limited by a boss, nor are your accomplishments credited to others. Unless you decide otherwise, you are not wedded to an 8 to 5 work routine or a two week vacation. Depending on how successful your business becomes, you may be able to retire young and pursue other interests. You can turn what you truly enjoy doing, such as hobbies, into a profitable, rewarding, and fun career.

But such self-indulgence and gratification has costs. You will probably need at least $20,000 to $40,000 of start-up capital, or perhaps as much as $350,000, depending on the type of business you enter. No one will be sending you a paycheck every two weeks so you can regularly pay your bills. You may work 12 and 14 hour days, seven days a week, and have no vacation during the first few years. And you may become heavily indebted, experience frequent cash flow problems, and eventually have creditors descend on you.

Why, then, start your own business? If you talk to people who have worked for others and then started their own businesses, they will tell you similar stories. They got tired of drawing a salary while making someone else rich. They got bored with their work and hated the 8 to 5 routine. Some were victims of organizational politics. On a more positive note, many started businesses because they had a great idea they wanted to pursue or they wanted the challenge of independently accomplishing their own goals.

If you decide to go into business for yourself, be sure you know what you want to do and be willing to take risks. Don't expect to get rich overnight or sit back and watch your business grow on its own. Be prepared to work long and hard hours, experience disappointments, and challenge yourself to the limits.

There are few things that are more self-actualizing than running your own business. But you must have realistic expectations as well as a motivational pattern which is conducive to taking risks and being an entrepreneur. In Chapter Six you identified your motivational patterns and skills. If you like security, predictability, and stability, you probably are a candidate for a position where someone hands you a paycheck each week. If you read and believe in a get-rich-quick book which tries to minimize your risks and uncertainty, you probably have been ripped-off by an enterprising author who is getting rich writing books for naive people!

POSSESS THE RIGHT
STRENGTHS FOR SUCCESS

How can you become self-employed and successful at the same time? No one has a magical success formula for the budding entrepreneur — only advice. We do know why many businesses fail, and we can identify some basic characteristics for success. Poor management and decision-making lie at the heart of business failures. Many people go into business without doing sufficient market research; they under-capitalize; they select a poor location; they incur extremely high and debilitating overhead costs; they lack commitment; they are unwilling to sacrifice; they can't read or count; and they lack interpersonal and salesmanship skills.

On the positive side, studies continue to identify something called "drive," or the need to achieve, as a key characteristic of successful entrepreneurs. As Kellogg (*Fast Track*, McGraw-Hill) and others have found, young achievers and successful entrepreneurs possess similar characteristics: *"A high energy level, restless, a willingness to work hard and take risks, a desire to escape from insecurity"*.

Successful business people combine certain motivations, skills, and circumstances. Contrary to popular myths, you don't need to be rich or have an MBA or business experience to get started. If you are willing to gamble and are a self-starter, self-confident, an organizer, and you like people, you should consider this entrepreneurial alternative in your careering and re-careering decisions. These characteristics along with drive, thinking ability, human relations, communication, technical knowledge, hard work, persistence, and good luck are essential ingredients for business success. If these are among your strengths, as identified in Chapter Six, you may be a good candidate for starting your own business with a high probability of success. If you feel you have recurring weaknesses in certain areas, you may want to consider finding a business partner who has particular complementary strengths for running a business.

KNOW YOURSELF

There are many different ways to get started in business. You can buy into a franchise which can initially cost you $20,000 to $500,000. Advertisements in the *Wall Street Journal* are a good source for hundreds of franchise opportunities from flipping hamburgers to selling animals. You can join someone else's business on a full-time or part-time basis as a partner or employee in order to get some direct business experience. You can try your hand at a direct-sales business such as Amway, Shaklee, or Avon. Hundreds of new direct-sales businesses modeled after Amway's business methods are now marketing every conceivable product — soap, typewriters, canoes, motor oil, and milk. You can buy someone else's business or you can start your own business from scratch.

Your decision on how to get started in business should be based upon the data you generated on your skills and goals in Chapters Six and Seven. Do not go into business for negative reasons — get fired, hate your job, can't find work. Unfortunately, many people go into business with totally unrealistic expectations as well as with little understanding of their own goals, skills, and motivations. For example, while it is nice to work around pretty clothes, owning a dress shop requires handling inventory and personnel as well as paying the rent and doing bookkeeping. Getting all those pretty dresses on the rack is hard work! Many people also don't understand how the business world works. It requires a great deal of interpersonal skill to develop and expand personal networks of creditors, clients, colleagues, and competitors.

Therefore, you should do two things before you decide to go into business. First, thoroughly explore your goals and motivations. The questions are familiar:

- What do you want to do?
- What do you do well?
- What do you enjoy doing?

Second, research different types of businesses in order to better understand advantages, disadvantages, procedures, processes, and possible problems. Talk to business persons about their work. Try to learn as much as possible about the reality before you invest your time and money. Surprisingly, few people do this. Many people leap into a business that they think will be great and then later learn it was neither right for them nor did they have realistic expectations of what was involved. This is precisely why so many businesses fail each year.

You should approach business opportunities the same way you approach the job market: do research, develop networks, and conduct informational and referral interviews. Most business people, including your competition, will be happy to share their experiences with you and assist you with advice and referrals. Such research is absolutely invaluable. If you fail to do it initially, you will pay later on by making the same mistakes that millions of others have made in starting their own businesses in isolation of others. *Don't be high on motivation but low on knowledge and skills, for "thinking big" is no substitute for doing the work!*

LOOK FOR NEW OPPORTUNITIES

Most business people will tell you similar stories of the reality of running your own business. Do your market research, spend long hours, plan, and be persistent. They also will give you advice on what businesses to avoid and what business routines you should be prepared to handle.

Many service and high-tech businesses will be growing in the 1990s. Given the changing demographic structure — fewer young people, more elderly, the two career family — numerous opportunities are arising for small personal service businesses to meet the needs of the elderly and career-oriented families. Businesses relating to restaurants, home maintenance, health care, housing for the elderly, and mortuaries and cemeteries should expand considerably during the next two decades.

Opportunities are also available for inventive business persons who can make more productive use of busy peoples' time — fast foods, financial planning, and mail-order shopping. The information and high-tech revolutions are taking place at the same time two career families do not have time to waste standing in lines at banks, grocery stores, and department stores. Mail-order or computer assisted home and office-based shopping should increase dramatically during the next decade.

A service business is particularly attractive. It is easy to establish, it requires a small initial investment, and the bookkeeping is relatively simple. You can operate from your home and thus keep your overhead down.

Knowing these trends and opportunities is important, but they should not be the only determining factors in choosing a business. You should start with *yourself* by again trying to identify a business that is fit for you rather than one you think you might fit into.

PREPARE THE BASICS

You also need to consider several other factors before starting a business. Since a business requires financing, locating, planning, developing customer relationships, and meeting legal requirements, be prepared to address these questions:

┌─── **BASIC BUSINESS PREPARATION QUESTIONS** ───┐

1. **How can I best finance the business?** Take out a personal or business loan with a bank? Go into a partnership in order to share the risks and costs? Get a loan from the Small Business Administration?

2. **How much financing do I need?** Many businesses fail because they are under-capitalized. Others fail because of over spending on rent, furnishings, inventory, personnel, and advertising.

3. **Where is my market?** Just in this community, region, or nationwide? Mail-order businesses enable you to expand your market nationwide whereas retail and service businesses tend to be confined to particular neighborhoods or communities.

4. **Who are my suppliers?** How many must I work with? What about credit arrangements?

5. **Where is the best location for the business?** Do you need to open a store or operate out of your home? If you need a store or office, is it conveniently located for your clientele? "Location is everything" still best summarizes the success of many businesses, especially McDonalds.

6. **How should the business be legally structured?** Sole proprietorship, partnership, or corporation? Each has advantages and disadvantages. A corporation has the best tax advantages.

7. **What licenses and permits do I need?** These consist of local business licenses and permits, federal employee identification numbers, state sales tax number, state occupational licenses, federal licenses and permits, and special state and local regulations which vary from state to state and from community to community. What type of insurance do I need? Fire, theft, liability, workers' compensation, and auto?

8. **How many employees do I need?** Can I do without personnel initially until the business expands? Should

I use part-time and temporary help?

9. **What business name should I use?** If incorporated, is anyone else using the name? If a trade name, is it registered?

10. **What accounting system should I use?** Cash or accrual? Can I handle the books or do I need a part-time or full-time accountant?

11. **Do I need a lawyer?** What type of lawyer? What legal work can I do myself?

12. **How do I develop a business plan?** A business plan should include a definition of the business, a marketing strategy, operational policies, purchasing plans, financial statements, and capital raising plans.

GET USEFUL ADVICE

If you decide to go into business, make sure you choose the right business for your particular skills, abilities, motivation, and interests. A good starting point is Douglas Gray's *The Entrepreneur's Complete Self-Assessment Guide* (TAB Books). This book provides you with useful exercises for assessing your suitability for becoming an entrepreneur. For a good overview of the many decisions you must make in establishing a small business, see Bernard Kamaroff's *Small-Time Operators* (Bell Springs Publishing). This book provides you with all the basic information you need for starting your own business, including ledger sheets for setting up your books. Albert Lowry's *How to Become Financially Successful By Owning Your Own Business* (Simon and Schuster) also outlines the basics for both small-time and big-time operators. Several other books provide similar how-to advice for the neophyte entrepreneur:

Jeffrey P. Davidson, *Avoiding the Pitfalls of Starting Your Own Business* (Walker and Co.)

James W. Halloran, *The Entrepreneur's Guide to Starting a Successful Business* (TAB Books)

Arnold S. Goldstein, *Starting on a Shoestring: Building*

A Business Without a Bankroll (Wiley and Sons)

R. W. Bly and G. Blake, *Out On Your Own: From Corporate to Self-Employment* (Wiley and Sons)

Patricia A. Way, *Small Businesses That Grow and Grow and Grow* (Betterway Publications)

The J. K. Lasser Tax Institute, *How to Run a Small Business* (St. Martin's Press)

C.D. Peterson, *How to Leave Your Job and Buy a Business of Your Own* (St. Martin's Press)

Ina Lee Selden, *Going Into Business For Yourself: New Beginnings After 50* (American Association of Retired Persons)

C. Revel, *184 Businesses Anyone Can Start* (Bantam Books)

The federal government will help you with several publications available through the Small Business Administration: 1441 L Street, NW, Washington, D.C. 20416, Tel. 800/368-5855. SBA field offices are located in 85 cities. The Consumer Information Center publishes a free booklet entitled *More Than a Dream: Running Your Own Business:* Dept. 616J, Pueblo, Colorado 81009. The Internal Revenue Service sponsors several one-day tax workshops for small businesses. Your local chamber of commerce also can give you useful information.

If you are interested in how to get started in a particular small business, write for information from the American Entrepreneurs Association, 2392 Morse Avenue, Irving, CA 92714-6234 or use their toll-free numbers: 800/421-2300 or 800/421-2345. This organization offers a comprehensive set of services for starting small businesses. These include a free catalog of products and services, the magazine *Entrepreneur*, and the Entrepreneur Institute (talk to Dennis Landry for advice). To help you get off in the right direction, this organization also publishes over 300 helpful small business start-up and operation manuals which include businesses such as energy stores, video stores, seminars, pet cemeteries, health clubs, pizza parlors, travel agencies, dating services, rent-a-hot tub, furniture stripping, pipe shop, discos, and maid services. For a six-month free subscription to *Money Making Opportunities* magazine, which lists hundreds of mail order ads, write to Money Making Opportunities, 11071 Ventura Blvd., Studio City, California 91604. These publications will give you a sampling of alternative businesses you can establish. However, beware of hucksters who may advertise in business magazines. Many want your money for "proven success" and "get-rich-quick" formulas that don't even work for the advertisers!

CONTINUE SUCCESS

The factors for operating a successful business are similar to the 20 principles we outlined in Chapter Five for conducting a successful job search. Once your initial start-up problems are solved, you must organize, plan, implement, and manage in relation to your goals. Many people lack these abilities. Some people are good at initially starting a business, but they are unable to follow through in managing day-to-day routines once the business is established. And others have the ability to start, manage, and expand businesses successfully.

Be careful about business success. Many business people become obsessed with their work, put in 12 and 14 hour days continuously, and spend seven day weeks to make the business successful. Unwilling to delegate, they try to do too much and thus become a prisoner to the business. The proverbial *"tail wagging the dog"* is a common phenomenon in small businesses. For some people, this life style feeds their ego and makes them happy. For others, the 8 to 5 routine of working for someone else on salary may look very attractive. Therefore, you must be prepared to change your life style when embarking on your own business. Your major limitation will be yourself. So think it over carefully, do your research, and plan, organize, implement, and manage for success. The thrill of independence and success is hard to beat!

Chapter Sixteen

TAKE ACTION TO IMPLEMENT YOUR FUTURE

Understanding without action is a waste of time. And buying a how-to book without implementing it is certainly a waste of money. Many people read how-to books, attend how-to seminars, and do nothing other than read more books and attend more seminars. While these activities become forms of therapy for some individuals, they should lead to positive actions for you.

YOU MUST UNDERSTAND
AND IMPLEMENT

From the very beginning of this book we stressed the importance of both understanding the job market and developing appropriate job search strategies for getting the job you want. We make no assumptions nor claim any magic is contained in this book. Rather, we have attempted to assemble useful information to help you analyze the present, project yourself into the future, and develop careering and re-careering strategies that will work for you. Individual chapters examined the present and future job markets as well as outlined in how-to terms specific careering and re-careering skills for making your own future. We have done our part in getting you to the implementation stage. What happens next is your responsibility.

The methods we outlined in previous chapters have worked for thousands of individuals who have paid $2,000 to $12,000 to get similar information from the high-paid professionals. While you may want to see a professional for assistance at certain steps in your job search, if you are self-motivated you can do everything on your own with a minimum expenditure of money. The major cost will be your time and effort.

But you must make the effort and take the *risk of implementing* this book. Careering and re-careering take work and are risky businesses. You try something new and place your ego on the line. You subject yourself to the possibility of being rejected several times. And this is precisely the major barrier you will encounter to effective implementation. For many people are unwilling to take more than a few rejections.

WELCOME REJECTIONS

Planning is the easy part of any task. You can set goals and outline a course of action divorced from the reality of actually doing it. But if you don't take action, you will not get your expected results. You must implement if you want desired results.

Once you take action, be prepared for rejections. Employers will tell you *"Thank you — we'll call you,"* but they never do. Other employers will tell you *"We have no positions available at this time for someone with your qualifications"* or *"You don't have the qualifications necessary for this position."*

Rejections are a normal part of the process of finding employment. More important, you must be rejected before you will be accepted. Expect 10 rejections or "nos" for every acceptance or "yes" you receive. If you quit after five or eight rejections, you prematurely end your job search. If you persist in collecting two to five more "nos," you will likely receive a "yes." Most people quit prematurely because their ego is not prepared for more rejections. Therefore, you should welcome rejections as you seek more and more acceptances.

GET MOTIVATED AND WORK HARD

Assuming you have a firm understanding of each job search skill and how to relate them to your job search, what do you do next? The next steps involve *motivation and hard work*. Our experience is that individuals need to be sufficiently *motivated* to make the first move and do it properly. If you go about your job search half-heartedly — you just want to "test the waters" to see what's out there for you — don't expect to be successful. You must be *committed* to achieving specific goals. Make the decision to properly develop and implement your job search and be prepared to work hard in achieving your goals.

FIND TIME

Once you've convinced yourself to take the necessary steps to finding a job or changing and advancing your career, you need to find the *time* to properly implement your job search. This requires setting aside specific blocks of time for identifying your motivated skills, developing your resume, writing letters, making telephone calls, and conducting the necessary research and networking required for success. This takes time. If you are a busy person, like most people, you simply must make the time.

Practice your own versions of time management and productivity. Get better organized, give some things up, or cut back on all your activities. If, for example, you can set aside one hour each day to devote to your job search, you will spend seven hours a week or 28 hours a month on your search. However, you should and can find more time than this for these activities. Time and again we find successful job hunters are ones who *routinize* a job search schedule and keep at it. They make contact after contact, conduct numerous informational interviews, submit many applications and resumes, and keep repeating these activities in spite of encountering rejections. They learn that success if just a few more "nos" and informational interviews away!

COMMIT YOURSELF IN WRITING

You may find it useful to commit yourself in writing to achieving job search success. This is a very useful way to get both motivated and directed for action. Complete the following job search contract and keep it near you — put it in your briefcase or on your desk.

YOUR JOB SEARCH CONTRACT

1. I will begin my job search on _____.

(date)

2. I will involve _____ with my
    job search.   (individuals/groups)

3. I will complete my skills identification
    step by _____.

(date)

4. I will complete my objective statement
    by _____.

(date)

5. I will complete my resume by _____ .

(date)

6. Each week I will:

    - make _____ new job contacts.

(#)
    - conduct _____ informational interviews.

(#)
    - follow-up on _____ referrals.

(#)

7. My first job interview will take place during the week
    of _____ .

(date)

8. I will begin my new job or carrer on _____ .

(date)

9. I will manage my time so that I can successfully com-
    plete my job search and find a high quality job.

    Signature: _____

    Date: _____

COMPLETE WEEKLY PERFORMANCE REPORTS

You should also complete weekly performance reports on your activities. These reports identify what you actually *accomplished* rather than what your good intentions tell you to do. Make copies of the following performance and planning report form and use one each week to track your actual progress and plan your activities for the next week.

YOUR WEEKLY JOB SEARCH PERFORMANCE

1. The week of: _____
   (date)

2. This week I:
   A. Wrote _____ job search letters.
      (#)
   B. Sent _____ resumes and _____ letters to potential employers.
   C. Completed _____ applications.
   D. Made _____ job search telephone calls.
   E. Completed _____ hours of job research.
   F. Set up _____ appointments for informational interviews.
   G. Conducted _____ informational interviews.
   H. Received _____ invitations to a job interview.
   I. Followed up on _____ contacts and _____ referrals.

3. Next week I will:
   A. Write _____ job search letters.
   B. Send _____ resumes and _____ letters to potential employers.
   C. Complete _____ applications.
   D. Make _____ job search telephone calls.
   E. Complete _____ hours of job research.
   F. Set up _____ appointments for informational interviews.
   G. Conduct _____ informational interviews.

4. Summary of progress this week in relation to my Job Search Contract:

   _____

   _____

   _____

   _____

If you fail to meet these written commitments, issue yourself a revised and updated contract. But if you must do this three or more times, we strongly suggest you quit kidding yourself about your motivation and commitment to find a job. Start over again, but this time consult a professional who can provide you with the necessary *structure* to better enable you to make progress in finding a job.

A professional may not be cheap, but if paying for help gets you on the right track and results in the job you want, it's money well spent. Do not be *"penny-wise but pound foolish"* with your future. If you must seek professional advice, be sure you are an informed consumer according to our "shopping" advice in Chapter Five.

CAREER AND RE-CAREER IN YOUR FUTURE

The continuing transformation of American society will require millions of individuals to re-career in the years ahead. The nature of jobs and careers are changing as the workplace becomes transformed due to the impact of new technology. Many career fields in demand today may well be glutted tomorrow.

Throughout this book we have emphasized the importance of *being prepared* for turbulent times. The age of the generalist armed with job search skills alone is passing. The emerging society requires a new type of *generalist-specialist* who is trained for today's technology, *flexible* enough to be retrained in tomorrow's technology, and *adaptive* to new jobs and careers that will arise today and tomorrow. In other words, the society needs more and more generalist-specialists who welcome change by being willing and able to re-career. Knowing and practicing the job search skills outlined in this book, these people also are continuously learning new work-content skills in order to better position themselves in tomorrow's job market. *They transform their careering skills into re-careering competencies*.

You should be prepared to develop and practice re-careering competencies for the decades ahead. We recommend one final re-careering action on your part. Make an effort *to learn one new skill each year*; the skill can be related to work, family, community, or a hobby such as building bookcases, operating different computer software packages, repairing appliances, or remodeling your home. If you do this, you will be better prepared for making the career transitions necessary for functioning effectively in turbulent times!

Appendix A
RESUMES

 ·

The following resume examples represent the five most common types of resumes: traditional chronological, improved chronological, combination, functional, and resume letter. The same fictitious individual is used in order to demonstrate how one person's qualifications can be presented in these different formats.

The *traditional chronological resume* includes a hodge-podge of information on the individual's history. Chronology is the guiding organizational principle for this resume. It tends to display the individual's weaknesses rather than strengths. For example, it lacks a job objective, includes such negatives as "divorced," "terminated," and "bartender." The usual statistics on height, weight, birth, and health do not enhance this resume. Hobbies are irrelevant, and references may be in for a surprise when the employer calls them unexpectedly.

Subsequent resume examples follow key organizational principles discussed in Chapter Eight: focus on an objective; state most important information first; include only information strengthening the objective: and layout is attractive and eye pleasing.

The *improved chronological resume* stresses skills and accomplishments but organizes them chronologically. A functional skills vocabulary is used for summarizing each position. Inclusive dates are placed at the end of each position summary, because they are the least important consideration but employers expect dates nonetheless.

The ***combination resume*** stresses skills and accomplishments ("Areas of Effectiveness") in relation to an objective as well as includes a chronological work history section. A personal statement appears in order to give the resume a distinctive personal quality. A second page, "Supplemental Information," is attached to further strengthen the major thrust of the resume as well as provide more specific content for the functional skills and work history categories.

Functional resumes stress the job objective, education, skills, and accomplishments. Work history is purposefully absent because in most cases the person using this type of resume has little job-related experience. Education is normally placed immediately after the objective for similar reasons — educational experience is more relevant to the objective than work-related experience.

The ***resume letter*** targets a particular position by stressing one's skills and accomplishments in direct relation to an employer's position. This is a good device to use if your general resume does not specifically address an employer's needs. It is a good way to create flexibility in your job search campaign. However, if an employer requests a resume, you should send one accompanied by a cover letter.

Traditional Chronological Resume

RESUME

James C. Astor	Weight:	190 lbs.
4921 Tyler Drive	Height:	6'0"
Washington, D.C. 20011	Born:	June 2, 1954
	Health:	Good
	Marital Status:	Divorced

EDUCATION

1983-1984: M.A., Vocational Counseling, Virginia Commonwealth University, Richmond, Virginia.

1972-1976: B.A., Psychology, Roanoke College, Salem, Virginia.

1968-1972: High School Diploma, Richmond Community High School, Richmond, Virginia.

WORK EXPERIENCE

6/13/84 to 2/22/88: Supervisory Trainer, GS-12, U.S. Department of Labor, Washington, D.C. Responsible for all aspects of training. Terminated because of budget cuts.

9/10/82 to 11/21/83: Bartender, Johnnie's Disco, Richmond, Virginia. Part-time while attending college.

4/3/80 to 6/2/82: Counselor, Virginia Employment Commission, Richmond, Virginia. Responsible for interviewing unemployed for jobs. Resigned to work full-time on Master's degree.

8/15/77 to 6/15/79: Guidance counselor and teacher, Petersburg Junior High School, Petersburg, Virginia.

2/11/75 to 10/6/75: Cook and Waiter, Big Mama's Pizza Parlor, Roanoke, Virginia. Part-time while attending college.

PROFESSIONAL AFFILIATIONS

American Personnel and Guidance Association
American Society for Training and Development
Personnel Management Association
Phi Delta Pi

HOBBIES

I like to play tennis, bicycle, and hike.

REFERENCES

David Ryan, Chief, Training Division, U.S. Department of Labor, Washington, D.C. 20012, (212) 735-0121.

Dr. Sara Thomas, Professor, Department of Psychology, George Washington University, Washington, D.C. 20030 (201) 621-4545.

Thomas V. Grant, Area Manager, Virginia Employment Commission, Richmond, Virginia 26412, (804) 261-4089.

Improved Chronological Resume

JAMES C. ASTOR
4921 Tyler Drive
Washington, D.C. 20011   212/422-8764

OBJECTIVE: A training and counseling position with a computer
              firm, where strong administrative, communication, and
              planning abilities will be used for improving the work
              performance and job satisfaction of employees.

EXPERIENCE: U.S. Department of Labor, Washington, D.C.
              Planned and organized counseling programs for 5,000
              employees. Developed training manuals and conducted
              workshops on interpersonal skills, stress management,
              and career planning; resulted in a 50 percent decrease
              in absenteeism. Supervised team of five instructors and
              counselors. Conducted individual counseling and
              referrals to community organizations. Advised govern-
              ment agencies and private firms on establishing in-
              house employee counseling and career development
              programs. Consistently evaluated as outstanding by
              supervisors and workshop participants. 1984 to
              present.

              Virginia Employment Commission, Richmond,
              Virginia.
              Conducted all aspects of employment counseling.
              Interviewed, screened, and counseled 2,500 jobseekers.
              Referred clients to employers and other agencies.
              Coordinated job vacancy and training information
              for businesses, industries, and schools. Reorganized
              interviewing and screening processes which improved
              the efficiency of operations by 50 percent. Cited in
              annual evaluation for "outstanding contributions to
              improving relations with employers and clients."
              1980-1982.

              Petersburg Junior High School, Petersburg, Virginia.
              Guidance counselor for 800 students. Developed
              program of individualized and group counseling.
              Taught special social science classes for socially mal-
              adjusted and slow learners. 1977-1979.

EDUCATION: M.A., Vocational Counseling, Virginia Commonwealth
              University, Richmond, Virginia, 1984.

              B.A., Psychology, Roanoke College, Salem, Virginia,
              1976.

REFERENCES: Available upon request.

Combination Resume

-------JAMES C. ASTOR -------
4921 Tyler Drive
Washington, D.C. 20011   212/422-8764

OBJECTIVE: A training and counseling position with a computer firm, where strong administrative, communication, and planning abilities will be used for improving the work performance and job satisfaction of employees.

AREAS OF EFFECTIVENESS

ADMINISTRATION: Supervised instructors and counselors. Co-ordinated job vacancy and training information for businesses, industries, and schools.

COMMUNICATION: Conducted over 100 workshops on inter-personal skills, stress management, and career planning. Frequent guest speaker to various agencies and private firms. Experienced writer of training manuals and public relations materials.

PLANNING: Planned and developed counseling programs for 5,000 employees. Reorganized inter-viewing and screening processes for public employment agency. Developed program of individualized and group counseling for community school.

WORK HISTORY: Supervisory Trainer, U.S. Department of Labor, Washington, D.C., 1984 to present.

Counselor, Virginia Employment Commission, Richmond, Virginia, 1980-1982.

Guidance counselor and teacher, Petersburg Junior High School, Petersburg, Virginia 1977-1979.

EDUCATION: M.A., Vocational Counseling, Virginia Commonwealth University, Richmond, Virginia, 1984.

B.A., Psychology, Roanoke College, Salem, Virginia, 1969.

PERSONAL: Enjoy challenges and working with people. . . interested in productivity. . . willing to relocate and travel.

Combination Resume – continued

SUPPLEMENTAL INFORMATION   JAMES C. ASTOR

Continuing Education and Training

- Completed 12 semester hours of computer science courses.
- Attended several workshops during past three years on employee counseling and administrative methods:

    "Career Development for Technical Personnel," Professional Management Association, 3 days, 1987.

    "Effective Supervisory Methods for Training Directors," National Training Associates, 3 days, 1988.

    "Training the Trainer," American Society for Training and Development, 3 days, 1988.

    "Time Management," U.S. Department of Labor, 3 days, 1987.

    "Career Development for Technical Personnel," Professional Management Associates, 3 days, 1987.

    "Counseling the Absentee Employee," American Management Association, 3 days, 1986.

Training Manuals Developed

- "Managing Employee Stress," U.S. Department of Labor, 1985.
- "Effective Interpersonal Communication in the Workplace," U.S. Department of Labor, 1981.
- "Planning Careers Within the Organization," U.S. Department of Labor, 1987.

Research Projects Completed

- "Employee Counseling Programs for Technical Personnel," U.S. Department of Labor, 1988. Incorporated into agency report on "New Directions in Employee Counseling."
- "Developing Training Programs for Problem Employees," M.A. thesis, Virginia Commonwealth University, 1984.

Professional Affiliations

- American Personnel and Guidance Association
- American Society for Training and Development
- Personnel Management Association

Educational Highlights

- Completing Ph.D. in Industrial Psychology, George Washington University, Washington, D.C., 1991.
- Earned 4.0/4.0 grade point average as graduate student.

Functional Resume

JAMES C. ASTOR

4921 Tyler Drive	Washington, D.C. 20011	212/422-8764

OBJECTIVE: A training and counseling position with a computer firm, where strong administrative, communication, and planning abilities will be used for improving the work performance and job satisfaction of employees.

EDUCATION: Ph.D. in process, Industrial Psychology, George Washington University, Washington, D.C.

M.A., Vocational Counseling, Virginia Commonwealth University, Richmond, Virginia, 1984.

B.A., Psychology, Roanoke College, Salem, Virginia, 1976.

AREAS OF EFFECTIVENESS:

Administration

Supervised instructors and counselors. Coordinated job vacancy and training information for businesses, industries, and schools.

Communication

Conducted over 100 workshops on interpersonal skills, stress management, and career planning. Frequent guest speaker to various agencies and private firms. Experienced writer of training manuals and public relations materials.

Planning

Planned and developed counseling programs for 5,000 employees. Reorganized interviewing and screening processes for public employment agency. Developed program of individualized and group counseling for community school.

PERSONAL: Enjoy challenges and working with people. . . interested in productivity. . . willing to relocate and travel.

REFERENCES: Available upon request.

Resume Letter

4921 Tyler Drive
Washington, D.C. 20011
March 15, 19___

Doris Stevens
STR Corporation
179 South Trail
Rockville, Maryland 21101

Dear Ms. Stevens:

STR Corporation is one of the most dynamic computer companies in the nation. In addition to being a leader in the field of small business computers, STR has a progressive employee training and development program which could very well become a model for other organizations. This is the type of organization I am interested in joining.

I am seeking a training position with a computer firm which would utilize my administrative, communication, and planning abilities to develop effective training and counseling programs. My experience includes:

Administraton: Supervised instructors and counselors. Coordinated job vacancy and training information for businesses, industries, and schools.

Communication: Conducted over 100 workshops on interpersonal skills, stress management, and career planning. Frequent guest speaker to various agencies and private firms. Experienced writer of training manuals and public relations materials.

Planning: Planned and developed counseling programs for 5,000 employees. Reorganized interviewing and screening processes for public employment agency. Developed program of individualized and group counseling for community school.

In addition, I am completing my Ph.D. in industrial psychology with emphasis on developing training and counseling programs for technical personnel.

Could we meet to discuss your program as well as how my experience might relate to your needs? I will call your office on Tuesday morning, March 23, to arrange a convenient time to meet with you.

I especially want to show you a model employee counseling and career development program I recently developed. Perhaps you may find it useful for your work with STR.

Sincerely yours,

James C. Astor

Appendix B
LETTERS

The following examples cover the major types of letters you will write during your job search campaign. An example of a resume letter is not included because it is a subject of Appendix A.

The *cover letter* is in response to a classified ad. Following the principle of providing "cover" for advertising the resume, this letter mainly highlights interest. The writer takes the initiative to contact the employer by requesting an interview.

The *approach letters* represent two different situations. In the first letter the writer uses a referral to introduce herself. In the second example the writer introduces herself without prior contacts — the "cold turkey" approach. The writers in both examples are careful not to suggest that they are looking for a job through this individual. Instead, they want information and advice.

The *thank-you letters* are written for several occasions. The four examples include post-job interview, post-informational interview, job rejection, and job offer acceptance situations. In each case, the thank-you letter should communicate enthusiasm and thoughtfulness. When you write such letters, avoid the standard thank-you language. Make your letter express *you* rather than a model of a good letter.

You will find other occasions for writing letters which are not included with our examples. These might include sending a thank-you letter in response to information received over the telephone or through the mail or when declining a job offer or terminating employment for another job. The principles of good letter writing also pertain to these situations.

Cover Letter

2842 South Plaza
Chicago, Illinois 60228
March 12, 19__

David C. Johnson
Director of Personnel
Bank of Chicago
490 Michigan Avenue
Chicago, Illinois 60222

Dear Mr. Johnson:

The accompanying resume is in response to your listing in the Chicago Tribune for a loan officer.

I am especially interested in this position because my experience with the Small Business Administration has prepared me for understanding the financial needs and problems of the business community from the perspectives of both lenders and borrowers. I wish to use this experience with a growing and community-conscious bank such as yours.

I would appreciate an opportunity to meet with you to discuss how my experience will best meet your needs. My ideas on how to improve small business financing may be of particular interest to you. Therefore, I will call your office on the morning of March 17 to inquire if a meeting can be scheduled at a convenient time.

I look forward to meeting you.

Sincerely yours,

Joyce Pitman

Approach Letter: Referral

821 Stevens Points
Boston, MA 01990
April 14, 19___

Terri Fulton
Director of Personnel
TRS Corporation
6311 W. Dover
Boston, MA 01991

Dear Ms. Fulton:

Alice O'Brien suggested that I contact you about my interest in personnel management. She said you are one of the best people to talk to in regard to careers in personnel.

I am leaving government after seven years of increasingly responsible experience in personnel. I am especially interested in working with a large private firm. However, before I venture further into the job market, I want to benefit from the experience and knowledge of others in the field who might advise me on opportunities for someone with my qualifications.

Perhaps we could meet briefly sometime during the next two weeks to discuss my career plans. I have several questions which I believe you could help clarify. I will call your office on Tuesday, April 22, to schedule a meeting time.

I look forward to discussing my plans with you.

Sincerely yours,

Katherine Kelly

Approach Letter: Cold Turkey

2189 West Church Street
New York, NY 10011
May 3, 19__

Patricia Dotson, Director
Northeast Association for
    the Elderly
9930 Jefferson Street
New York, NY 10013

Dear Ms. Dotson:

    I have been impressed with your work with the elderly. Your organization takes a community perspective in trying to integrate the concerns of the elderly with those of other community groups. Perhaps other organizations will soon follow your lead.

    I am anxious to meet you and learn more about your work. My background with the city Volunteer Services Program involved frequent contact with elderly volunteers. From this experience I decided I preferred working primarily with the elderly.

    However, before I pursue my interest further, I need to talk to people with experience in gerontology. In particular, I would like to know more about careers with the elderly as well as how my background might best be used in the field of gerontology.

    I am hoping you can assist me in this matter. I would like to meet with you briefly to discuss several of my concerns. I will call next week to see if your schedule permits such a meeting.

    I look forward to meeting you.

Sincerely,

Carol Timms

Thank-You Letter: Post-Informational Interview

9910 Thompson Drive
Cleveland, Ohio 43382
June 21, 19___

Jane Evans, Director
Evans Finance Corporation
2122 Forman Street
Cleveland, Ohio 43380

Dear Ms. Evans:

Your advice was most helpful in clarifying my questions on careers in finance. I am now reworking my resume and have included many of your thoughtful suggestions. I will send you a copy next week.

Thanks so much for taking time from your busy schedule to see me. I will keep in contact and follow through on your suggestion to see Sarah Cook about opportunities with the Cleveland-Akron Finance Company.

Sincerely,

Daryl Haines

Thank-You Letter: Post-Job Interview

2962 Forrest Drive
Denver, Colorado 82171
May 28, 19___

Thomas F. Harris
Director, Personnel Department
Coastal Products Incorporated
7229 Lakewood Drive
Denver, Colorado 82170

Dear Mr. Harris:

Thank you again for the opportunity to interview for the marketing position. I appreciated your hospitality and enjoyed meeting you and members of your staff.

The interview convinced me of how compatible my background, interest, and skills are with the goals of Coastal Products Incorporated. My prior marketing experience with the Department of Commerce has prepared me to take a major role in developing both domestic and international marketing strategies. I am confident my work for you will result in increased profits within the first two years.

For more information on the new product promotion program I mentioned, call David Garrett at the Department of Commerce; his number is 202/726-0132. I talked to Dave this morning and mentioned your interest in this program.

I look forward to meeting you again.

Sincerely,

Tim Potter

Thank-You Letter: Job Rejection

564 Court Street
St. Louis, MO 53167
April 29, 19__

Ralph Ullman, President
S. T. Ayer Corporation
6921 Southern Blvd.
St. Louis, MO 53163

Dear Mr. Ullman:

I appreciated your consideration for the Research Associate position. While I am disappointed in not being selected, I learned a great deal about your corporation, and I enjoyed meeting with you and your staff. I felt particularly good about the professional manner in which you conducted the interview.

Please keep me in mind for future consideration. I have a strong interest in your company. I believe we would work well together. I will be closely following the progress of your company over the coming months. Perhaps we will be in touch with each other at some later date.

Best wishes.

Sincerely,

Martin Tollins

Thank-You Letter: Job Offer Acceptance

7694 James Court
San Francisco, CA 94826
June 7, 19___

Judith Greene
Vice President
West Coast Airlines
2400 Van Ness
San Francisco, CA 94829

Dear Ms. Greene:

I am pleased to accept your offer, and I am looking forward to joining you and your staff next month.

The customer relations position is ideally suited to my background and interests. I assure you I will give you my best effort in making this an effective position within your company.

I understand I will begin work on July 1. If, in the meantime, I need to complete any paper work or take care of any other matters, please contact me.

I enjoyed meeting with you and your staff and appreciated the professional manner in which the hiring was conducted.

Sincerely,

Joan Kitner

Appendix C

BIBLIOGRAPHY FOR CAREERING AND RE-CAREERING

Hundreds of career planning and job search books of varying quality are published each year. Finding the right book for your particular needs and interests can be a bewildering experience.

The following bibliography of career resources represents some of the best literature written on a variety of career and job search subjects. You may wish to consult some of these books for further information in developing your own careering and re-careering plans.

Most career and job search books address their subjects from three different approaches:

- **Process and strategy skills:** Books designed to teach individuals key job search process and strategy skills. These books emphasize "how" questions. They are strong on generalities but weak on specifics.

- **Employment fields:** Books designed to outline various employment fields. These books emphasize "what" and "where" questions. They are strong on specifics but often lack a strong process framework from which to relate the details of each field to job search strategies and tactics.

- **Special groups**: Books designed to address key career issues for special groups, such as minorities, artists, public employees, military personnel, youth, and women. These books emphasize "what" and "how" questions. Their strengths and weaknesses vary.

The best literature will incorporate process and strategy skills while addressing the specifics of employment fields and the needs of special groups.

1. JOB SEARCH STRATEGIES AND TACTICS

Figler, Howard E., *The Complete Job Search Handbook* (New York: Holt, Rinehart, and Winston, 1988).

Hecklinger, Fred J. and Bernadette M. Curtin, *Training for Life: A Practical Guide to Career and Life Planning* (Dubuque, IA: Kendell/Hunt Publishing, 1984).

Irish, Richard K., *Go Hire Yourself An Employer* (New York: Doubleday, 1987).

Kennedy, Joyce Lain and Darryl Laramore, *The Career Book* (Lincolnwood, IL: National Textbook, 1988).

Lathrop, Richard, *Who's Hiring Who* (Berkeley, CA: Ten Speed Press, 1977).

Leape, Martha P., *The Harvard Guide to Careers* (Cambridge, MA: Harvard University Press, 1987).

Rogers, Edward J., *Getting Hired* (Englewood, NJ: Prentice-Hall, 1982).

Sher, Barbara, *Wishcraft: How To Get What You Really Want* (New York: Ballantine, 1983).

Snelling, Sr., Robert O., *The Right Job* (New York: Viking Penguin, 1987).

Stanat, Kirby W., *Job Hunting Secrets & Tactics* (Piscataway, NJ: New Century Publishers, 1977).

Studner, Peter K., *Super Job Search* (Los Angeles, CA: Jamenair Ltd., 1987).

2. SKILLS IDENTIFICATION, TESTING, AND SELF-ASSESSMENT

Bolles, Richard N., *The New Quick Job Hunting Map* (Berkeley, CA: Ten Speed Press, 1985).

Bolles, Richard N., *The Three Boxes of Life* (Berkeley, CA: Ten Speed Press, 1981).

Bolles, Richard N., *What Color Is Your Parachute?* (Berkeley, CA: Ten Speed Press, 1989).

Branden, Nathaniel, *How to Raise Your Self-Esteem* (New York: Bantam, 1986).

Crystal, John C. and Richard N. Bolles, *Where Do I Go From Here With My Life?* (Berkeley, CA: Ten Speed Press, 1979).

Gale, Barry and Linda Gale, *Discover What You're Best At* (New York: Simon & Schuster, 1983).

Holland, John L., *Making Vocational Choices: A Theory of Vocational Personalities and Work Environments* (Palo Alto, CA: Counseling Psychologists Press, 1984).

Miller, Arthur F. and Ralph T. Mattson, *The Truth About You: Discover What You Should Be Doing With Your Life* (Tappan, NJ: Fleming H. Revell Co., 1977).

Moskowitz, Robert, *How to Organize Your Work and Your Life* (New York: Doubleday, 1981).

Rosen, Marcia, *Test Your Own I.Q.* (New York: Putnam, 1986).

3. RESEARCH ON CITIES, FIELDS, AND ORGANIZATIONS

Adams Inc., Bob (ed.), *The Job Bank Series: Atlanta, Boston, Chicago, Dallas, Denver, Detroit, Florida, Houston, Los Angeles, Minneapolis, New York, Ohio, Philadelphia, San Francisco, St. Louis, Washington, DC* (Boston, MA: Bob Adams, Inc., 1988).

Adams Inc., Bob (ed.)., *The National Job Bank* (Boston, MA: Bob Adams, Inc., 1988).

Camden, Bishop, Schwartz, Greene, Fleming-Holland, *"How to Get a Job in. . ." Insider's City Guides: Chicago, Dallas/Ft. Worth, Los Angeles, New York* (Chicago, IL: Surrey, 1985-1987).

Career Associates, *Career Choices Series: Art, Business, Communications and Journalism, Computer Science, Economics, English, History, Law, Mathematics, MBA, Political Science and Government, Psychology* (New York: Walker and Co., 1983)

Career Associates, *Career Choices Encyclopedia* (New York: Walker and Co., 1985).

Career Press, *The Career Directory Series: Advertising, Book Publishing, Magazine Publishing, Marketing, Newspaper Publishing, Public Relations* (Hawthorne, NJ: The Career Press, 1989).

Hopke, William (ed.), *Encyclopedia of Careers and Vocational Guidance* (Chicago, IL: J. G. Ferguson, 1987).

Krantz, Les, *The Jobs Rated Almanac* (New York: Pharos Books, 1988).

Levering, Robert, Milton Moskowitz, and Michael Katz, *The 100 Best Companies To Work For In America* (Chicago, IL: NAL, 1985).

Norback, Craig T., *Careers Encyclopedia* (Lincolnwood, IL: National Textbook, 1988).

Plunkett, Jack W., *The Almanac of American Employers* (Chicago, IL: Contemporary Books, 1985).

Schwartz, Lester and Irv Brechner, *The Career Finder* (New York: Ballantine, 1982).

U.S. Department of Labor, *The Occupational Outlook Handbook* (Washington, DC: U.S. Department of Labor, 1988).

Wright, John W., *The American Almanac of Jobs and Salaries* (New York: Avon, 1987).

4. RESUMES, LETTERS, AND NETWORKING

Fry, Ronald W., *Your First Resume* (Hawthorne, NJ: Career Press, 1988).

Jackson, Tom, *The Perfect Resume* (New York: Doubleday, 1981).

Krannich, Ronald L. and William Banis, *High Impact Resumes and Letters* (Manassas, VA: Impact Publications, 1988).

Krannich, Ronald L. and Caryl Rae Krannich, *Networking Your Way to Job and Career Success* (Manassas, VA: Impact Publications, 1989).

Parker, Yana, *The Damn Good Resume Guide* (Berkeley, CA: Ten Speed Press, 1986).

Schuman, Nancy and William Lewis, *Revising Your Resume* (New York: Wiley, 1987).

5. DRESS, APPEARANCE, AND IMAGE

Bixler, Susan, *The Professional Image* (New York: Putnam, 1984).

Jackson, Carole, *Color Me Beautiful* (Washington, DC: Acropolis, 1986).

Molcho, Samy, *Body Speech* (New York: St. Martin's Press, 1984).

Molloy, John T., *Dress For Success* (New York: Warner, 1975).

Molloy, John T., *The Woman's Dress For Success Book* (New York: Warner, 1988).

Nicholson, JoAnne and Judy Lewis-Crum *Color Wonderful* (New York, Bantam, 1986).

Wallach, Janet, *Working Wardrobe* (New York: Warner, 1981).

6. INTERVIEWS AND SALARY NEGOTIATIONS

Beatty, R. H., *The Five Minute Interview* (New York: Wiley, 1986).

Chapman, Jack, *How to Make $1000 a Minute: Negotiating Salaries and Raises* (Berkeley, CA: Ten Speed Press, 1988).

Chastain, Sherry, *Winning the Salary Game* (New York: Wiley, 1980).

Kennedy, Marilyn Moats, *Salary Strategies* (New York: Scribners, 1982).

Krannich, Caryl and Ronald, *Interview for Success* (Manassas, VA: Impact Publications, 1988).

Medley, H. Anthony, *Sweaty Palms* (Berkeley, CA: Ten Speed Press, 1984)

Vlk, Suzee, *Interviews That Get Results* (New York: Simon & Schuster, 1984).

Yate, Martin, John, *Knock 'Em Dead With Great Answers to Tough Interview Questions* (Boston, MA: Bob Adams, Inc., 1986).

7. EDUCATORS

Bastress, Fran, *Teachers in New Careers* (Cranston, RI: Carroll Press, 1984).

Edelfelt, Roy, *Careers in Education* (Lincolnwood, IL: National Textbook, 1988).

Krannich, Ronald L. and William Banis, *Moving Out of Education: The Educator's Guide to Career Management and Change* (Manassas, VA: Impact Publications, 1981).

Levin, Joel, *How to Get a Job in Education* (Boston: Bob Adams, 1988).

Pollack, · Sandy, *Alternative Careers for Teachers* (Boston, MA: Harvard Common Press, 1986).

8. PUBLIC-ORIENTED CAREERS

Krannich, Ronald L. and Caryl Rae Krannich, *The Complete Guide to Public Employment* (Manassas, VA: Impact Publications, 1986).

Lauber, Daniel, *The Compleat Guide to Jobs in Planning and Public Administration* (Evanston, IL: Planning/Communications, 1986).

McAdams, Terry W., *Careers in the Nonprofit Sector* (Washington, DC: The Taft Group, 1986).

Phillips, David Atlee, *Careers in Secret Operations* (Bethesda, MD: Stone Trail Press, 1984).

Waelde, David E., *How to Get a Federal Job* (Washington, DC: FEDHELP, 1987).

Wood, Patricia B., *The 171 Reference Book* (Washington, DC: Workbooks, Inc., 1986).

9. INTERNATIONAL AND OVERSEAS JOBS

Beckmann, David M., Timothy J. Mitchell, and Linda L. Powers, *The Overseas List* (Minneapolis, MN: Augsburg Publishing, 1986).

Cantrell, Will and Terry Marshall, *101 Ways to Find an Overseas Job* (McLean, VA: Cantrell Corporation, 1987).

Foreign Policy Association (ed.), *Guide to Careers in World Affairs* (New York: Foreign Policy Association, 1987).

Powers, Linda (ed.), *Careers in International Affairs* (Washington, DC: Georgetown University School of Foreign Service, 1986).

Win, David, *International Careers: An Insider's Guide* (Charlotte, VT: Williamson Publishing, 1987)

10. MILITARY

Bradley, Jeff, *A Young Person's Guide to the Military* (Boston, MA: Harvard Common Press, 1987).

Garlock, Michael, *From Soldier to Civilian* (New York: Arco-Prentice Hall, 1988).

Marrs, Texe and Karen Read, *The Woman's Guide to Military Service* (Cockeysville, MD: Liberty Publishing, 1986).

Nyman, Keith O., *Re-Entry: Turning Military Experience Into Civilian Success* (Harrisburg, PA: Stackpole Books, 1983).

Petit, Ron, *From the Military to a Civilian Career* (Harrisonburg, VA: Maron Publications, 1984).

11. WOMEN AND SPOUSES

Bastress, Fran, *The Relocating Spouse's Guide to Employment* (Chevy Chase, MD: Woodley Publications, 1987).

Catalyst, *What to Do With the Rest of Your Life* (New York: Simon & Schuster, 1980).

Lesis, William and Nancy Schuman, *Back to Work: A Career Guide For the Returnee* (Woodbury, NY: Barron's, 1985).

Machlowitz, Marilyn, *Advanced Career Strategies For Women* (Boulder, CO: CareerTrack Publications, 1986).

Zeitz, Baila and Lorraine Dusky, *The Best Companies for Women* (New York: Simon and Schuster, 1988).

12. COLLEGE STUDENTS

Falvey, Jack, *After College: The Business of Getting Jobs* (Charlotte, VT: Williamson Publishing, 1986).

Fry, Ronald W., *Internships in Advertising, Marketing, Public Relations, and Sales* (Hawthorne, NJ: Career Press, 1988).

Fry, Ronald W., *Internships in Newspaper, Magazine, and Book Publishing* (Hawthorne, NJ: Career Press, 1988).

Jobst, Katherine (ed.), *Internships: 30,000 On-the-Job Training Opportunities for College Students and Adults* (Cincinnati, OH: Writer's Digest, 1989).

Lento-McGovern, Diane, *Life After College: Which Direction is Best For You?* (White Hall, VA: Betterway Publications, 1986).

Munschauer, John L., *Jobs For English Majors and Other Smart People* (Princeton, NJ: Peterson's Guides, 1986).

Nadler, Burton Jay, *Liberal Arts Jobs* (Princeton, NJ: Peterson's Guides, 1985).

Phifer, Paul, *College Majors and Careers* (Garrett Park, MD: Garrett Park Press, 1987).

Reyes-Guerra, David R. and Allan M. Fischer, *The Engineering/High-Tech Student's Handbook* (Princeton, NJ: Peterson's Guides, 1988).

Salzman, Marian and Nancy Marx, *MBA Jobs!* (New York: AMACOM, 1986).

Salzman, Marian and Nancy Marx Better, *Wanted: Liberal Arts Graduates* (New York: Doubleday, 1987).

13. CHILDREN, YOUTH, AND SUMMER JOBS

Billy, Christopher (ed.), *Summer Opportunities For Kids and Teenagers* (Princeton, NJ: Peterson's Guides, 1988).

Catalyst, *It's Your Future: Catalyst's Career Guide For High School Girls* (Princeton, NJ: Peterson's Guides, 1982).

Children's Dictionary of Occupations (Bloomington, IL: Meridian Educational Corp., 1985).

Greenberg, Jan W., *The Teenager's Guide to the Best Summer Opportunities* (Boston, MA: Harvard Common Press.

Lee, Rose P., *A Real Job For You: An Employment Guide For Teens* (White Hall, VA: Betterway Publications, 1984).

14. MINORITIES, IMMIGRANTS, AND DISABLED

Friedenberg, Joan E. and Curtis H. Bradley, *Finding a Job in the United States* (Lincolnwood, IL: National Textbook, 1986).

Johnson, Willis L. (ed.), *Directory of Special Programs for Minority Group Members* (Garrett Park, MD: Garrett Park Press, 1986).

Lewis, Adele and Edith Marks, *Job Hunting for the Disabled* (Woodbury, NY: Barron's, 1983).

Nivens, Beatryce, *The Black Woman's Career Guide* (New York: Doubleday, 1987).

15. EXPERIENCED AND ELDERLY

Allen, Jeffrey G. and Jess Gorkin, *Finding the Right Job in Midlife* (New York: Simon & Schuster, 1985).

Birsner, E. Patricia, *The 40+ Job Hunting Guide* (New York: Prentice-Hall, 1986).

Birsner, E. Patricia, *Job Hunting For the 40+ Executive* (New York: Facts On File, 1984).

Falvey, Jack, *What's Next? Career Strategies After 35* (Charlotte, VT: Williamson Publishing, 1986).

Morgan, John S., *Getting a Job After 50* (Blue Ridge Summit, PA: TAB Books, 1987).

Myers, Albert and Christopher Anderson, *Success Over Sixty* (New York: Simon & Schuster, 1986).

16. ALTERNATIVE CAREER FIELDS

Billy, Christopher (ed.), *Business and Management Jobs* (Princeton, NJ: Peterson's Guides, 1988).

Billy, Christopher (ed.), *Engineering, Science, and Computer Jobs* (Princeton, NJ: Peterson's Guides, 1988).

Cordoza, Anne and Suzee J. Vlk, *The Aerospace Career Handbook* (New York: Arco, 1984).

Cordoza, Anne and Suzee J. Vlk, *The Robotics Careers Handbook* (New York: Arco, 1984).

Field, Shelly, *Career Opportunities in the Music Industry* (New York: Facts on File, 1986).

Hawes, Gene R. and Douglas L. Brownstone, *The Outdoor Careers Guide* (New York: Facts on File, 1986).

Leonard, Mark, *Careers in Engineering* (Lincolnwood, IL: National Textbook, 1988).

Marrs, Texe W., *Careers With Robots* (New York: Facts on File, 1988).

Mogal, Leonard, *Making It in the Media Professions* (Chester, CT: Globe Pequot, 1988).

"Opportunities in. . ." Career Series (113 titles), (Lincolnwood, IL: National Textbook, 1984-1989).

Rubin, K. *Flying High in Travel: A Complete Guide to Careers in the Travel Industry* (New York: Wiley, 1986).

Rucker, T. Donald D. Keller, *Planning Your Medical Career* (Garrett Park, MD: Garrett Park Press, 1987).

INDEX

AUTHOR

Ronald L. Krannich is President of Development Concepts Incorporated, a training, publishing, and consulting firm specializing in the career and travel fields. A former university professor, he is a noted lecturer, consultant, and writer. He has conducted numerous workshops and seminars on career development, job search, and outplacement as well as directed several research projects in the United States and abroad. Widely published in major journals and national publications, his most recent books include *Networking Your Way to Job and Career Success, Successful Salary Negotiations, High Impact Resumes and Letters, Interview for Success, Re-Careering in Turbulent Times, Moving Out of Education, Moving Out of Government, Shopping in Exotic Places, Shopping in Exotic Thailand*, and *Shopping in Exotic Hong Kong*. He can be contacted through the publisher.

CAREER RESOURCES/ ORDER INFORMATION

Call or write Impact Publications to receive a free copy of their latest comprehensive, illustrated, and annotated catalog of over 500 career resources.

The following careering and re-careering resources, many of which are mentioned in Appendix C, are available directly from Impact Publications. Complete the following form or list the titles, enclose payment, and send your order to:

> **IMPACT PUBLICATIONS**
> Careers Department
> 10655 Big Oak Circle
> Manassas, VA 22111-3040
> Tel. 703/361-7300

Orders from individuals must be prepaid by check, moneyorder, Visa or MasterCard number. We accept telephone orders with a Visa or MasterCard number. All prices include postage and handling.

Qty	Code	TITLES	Price	TOTAL
		JOB SEARCH STRATEGIES AND TACTICS		
____	182NT	Career Book	$32.95	____
____	13IM	Careering and Re-Careering for the 1990s	$13.95	____
____	3PH	Getting Hired	$9.95	____
____	10DD	Go Hire Yourself an Employer	$9.95	____
____	1HU	Harvard Guide to Careers	$9.95	____
____	1JR	Super Job Search	$24.95	____
____	10BF	Wishcraft	$7.95	____
		SKILLS IDENTIFICATION, TESTING, AND SELF-ASSESSMENT		
____	43SS	Discover What You're Best At	$11.95	____
____	21BA	How to Raise Your Self-Esteem	$16.95	____
____	17TS	New Quick Job Hunting Map	$3.95	____
____	16PT	Test Your Own I.Q.	$7.95	____

____	7TS	Three Boxes of Life	$10.95	_____
____	5TS	What Color Is Your Parachute	$18.95	_____
____	9TS	Where Do I Go From Here With My Life?	$11.95	_____

RESEARCH ON CITIES, OCCUPATIONS, JOBS, AND ORGANIZATIONS

____	1NL	100 Best Companies to Work For in America	$10.95	_____
____	1CT	Almanac of American Employers	$17.95	_____
____	1AV	American Almanac of Jobs and Salaries	$14.95	_____
____	3WK	**Career Choices Series**: Art, Business, Communications and Journalism, Computer Science, Economics, English, History, Law, Mathematics, MBA, Political Science and Government, Psychology ($7.95 each or $89.95 for 12 volumes)	$89.95	_____
____	17WK	Career Choices Encyclopedia	$72.95	_____
____	1CP	**Career Directory Series**: Advertising, Book Publishing, Magazine Publishing, Marketing, Newspaper Publishing, Public Relations ($37.95 each or $224.95 for all 6 volumes)	$224.95	_____
____	8BF	Career Finder	$10.95	_____
____	179NT	Careers Encyclopedia	$32.95	_____
____	1FG	Encyclopedia of Careers and Vocational Guidance (3 volumes)	$94.95	_____
____	3AD	**Job Bank Series**: Atlanta, Boston, Chicago, Dallas, Denver, Detroit, Florida, Houston, Los Angeles, Minneapolis, New York, Ohio, Philadelphia, San Francisco, St. Louis, Washington, DC ($14.95 each or $199.95 for set of 16)	$199.95	_____
____	31SM	Jobs Rated Almanac	$16.95	_____
____	4AD	National Job Bank	$199.95	_____
____	173NT	Occupational Outlook Handbook	$24.95	_____

RESUMES, LETTERS, AND NETWORKING

____	7TS	Damn Good Resume Guide	$7.95	_____
____	2IM	High Impact Resumes and Letters	$13.95	_____
____	11IM	Networking Your Way to Job and Career Success	$13.95	_____

____	15DD	Perfect Resume	$10.95	____
____	62WI	Revising Your Resume	$14.95	____
____	9CP	Your First Resume	$11.95	____

DRESS, APPEARANCE, AND IMAGE

____	3SM	Body Speech	$16.95	____
____	3AC	Color Me Beautiful	$17.95	____
____	10BA	Color Wonderful	$11.95	____
____	2WN	Dress For Success (Men)	$11.95	____
____	6PT	Professional Image	$10.95	____
____	13WN	Woman's Dress For Success Book	$9.95	____
____	14WN	Working Wardrobe	$12.95	____

INTERVIEW AND SALARY NEGOTIATIONS

____	55WI	Five Minute Interview	$12.95	____
____	22TS	How to Make $1,000 a Minute	$8.95	____
____	3IM	Interview For Success	$11.95	____
____	20SS	Interviews That Get Results	$10.95	____
____	8AD	Knock 'Em Dead	$18.95	____
____	21TS	Sweaty Palms	$10.95	____

EDUCATORS

____	3HC	Alternative Careers For Teachers	$17.95	____
____	183NT	Careers in Education	$11.95	____
____	29AD	How to Get a Job in Education	$21.95	____
____	6IM	Moving Out of Education	$29.95	____
____	1BT	Teachers in New Careers	$13.95	____

PUBLIC-ORIENTED CAREERS

____	1WB	171 Reference Book	$18.95	____
____	1TG	Careers in the Nonprofit Sector	$26.95	____
____	1ST	Careers in Secret Operations	$10.95	____
____	1PC	Compleat Guide to Jobs in Planning and Public Administration	$11.95	____
____	4IM	Complete Guide to Public Employment	$15.95	____
____	1FH	How to Get a Federal Job	$16.95	____

INTERNATIONAL AND OVERSEAS JOBS

____	1EH	101 Ways to Find an Overseas Job	$34.95	____
____	1GT	Careers in International Affairs	$12.95	____
____	1FP	Guide to Careers in World Affairs	$12.95	____
____	4WL	International Careers	$12.95	____

_____ 1AU The Overseas List $13.95 _____

MILITARY

_____ 2MA From the Military to a Civilian Career $10.95 _____
_____ 133PH From Soldier to Civilian $13.95 _____
_____ 1SP   Re-Entry $12.95 _____
_____ 1LI   Woman's Guide to Military Service $10.95 _____
_____ 2HC   Your Person's Guide to the Military $18.95 _____

WOMEN AND SPOUSES

_____ 24CR Advanced Career Strategies For Women $17.95 _____
_____ 13BR Back to Work $8.95 _____
_____ 80SS Best Companies For Women $21.95 _____
_____ 2BT   Relocating Spouse's Guide to Employment $14.95 _____

COLLEGE STUDENTS

_____ 1WL   After College $11.95 _____
_____ 19CP College Majors and Careers $16.95 _____
_____ 38PE Engineering/High-Tech Student's Handbook $10.95 _____
_____ 6WD   Internships: 30,000 On-the-Job Training
            Opportunities $24.95 _____
_____ 11CP Internships in Advertising. . . $13.95 _____
_____ 12CP Internships in Newspaper. . . $13.95 _____
_____ 49PE Liberal Arts Jobs $11.95 _____
_____ 7BW   Life After College $9.95 _____
_____ 25DD Wanted — Liberal Arts Graduates $11.95 _____

CHILDREN, YOUTH, AND SUMMER JOBS

_____ 3MD   Children's Dictionary of Occupations $11.95 _____
_____ 3PE   It's Your Future (young women) $11.95 _____
_____ 1BW   A Real Job For You $9.95 _____
_____ 3HC   Teenager's Guide to the Best
            Summer Opportunities $18.95 _____

MINORITIES, IMMIGRANTS, AND DISABLED

_____ 13DD Black Woman's Career Guide $26.95 _____
_____ 4GP   Directory of Special Programs For
            Minority Group Members $26.95 _____
_____ 167NT Finding a Job in the United States $8.95 _____
_____ 6BR   Job Hunting For the Disabled $10.95 _____

EXPERIENCED AND ELDERLY

___ 112PH	40+ Job Hunting Guide	$10.95	___
___ 38SS	Finding the Right Job in Midlife	$8.95	___
___ 26TB	Getting a Job After 40	$29.95	___
___ 13FF	Job Hunting For the 40+ Executive	$19.95	___
___ 36SS	Success Over Sixty	$10.95	___
___ 3WL	What's Next	$11.95	___

ALTERNATIVE CAREER FIELDS

___ 60AR	Aerospace Career Handbook	$9.95	___
___ 7PE	Business and Management Jobs	$21.95	___
___ 17FF	Career Opportunities in the Music Industry	$14.95	___
___ 184NT	Careers in Engineering	$11.95	___
___ 21FF	Careers With Robots	$24.95	___
___ 8PE	Engineering, Science, and Computer Jobs	$23.95	___
___ 56WI	Flying High in Travel	$14.95	___
___ 1PQ	Making It in the Media Professions	$16.95	___
___ 24NT	**"Opportunities in. . ." Series** (113 titles; $11.95 each or $1099.95 for set; contact publisher for titles)	$1099.95	___
___ 20FF	Outdoor Career Guide	$20.95	___
___ 15GP	Planning Your Medical Career	$17.95	___
___ 61AR	Robotics Career Handbook	$9.95	___

SUBTOTAL ___

Virginia residents add 4.5% sales tax ___

TOTAL ENCLOSED ___